On Modern British Fiction

On Modern British Fiction

EDITED BY

Zachary Leader

OXFORD

UNIVERSITY PRESS

OXFORD

UNIVERSITY PRESS

Great Clarendon Street, Oxford OX2 6DP

Oxford University Press is a department of the University of Oxford.
It furthers the University's objective of excellence in research, scholarship,
and education by publishing worldwide in

Oxford New York

Auckland Bangkok Buenos Aires Cape Town Chennai
Dar es Salaam Delhi Hong Kong Istanbul Karachi Kolkata
Kuala Lumpur Madrid Melbourne Mexico City Mumbai Nairobi
São Paulo Shanghai Taipei Tokyo Toronto

Oxford is a registered trade mark of Oxford University Press
in the UK and in certain other countries

Published in the United States
by Oxford University Press Inc., New York

© The various contributors 2002

The moral rights of the authors have been asserted
Database right Oxford University Press (maker)

First published 2002

British Library Cataloguing in Publication Data
Data available

Library of Congress Cataloging in Publication Data
On modern British fiction / edited by Zachary Leader.
p. cm.
Includes index.
1. English fiction—20th century—History and criticism.   I. Leader, Zachary.
PR883.O5 2002   823'.91 409—dc21   2002072743

ISBN 0-19-924932-6

10 9 8 7 6 5 4 3 2

Typeset in Sabon
by Kolam Information Services Pvt Ltd, Pondicherry, India
Printed in Great Britain on acid-free paper by
Biddles Ltd, Guildford and King's Lynn

Acknowledgements

I am grateful to Robert C. Ritchie of the Huntington Library, San Marino, California, for hosting the conference out of which this book grew. I also thank Sophie Goldsworthy and Frances Whistler of Oxford University Press and Philip Bassett, Alan Bell, Selina Hastings, Rhoda Koenig, Douglas Matthews, and Tamsin Todd.

The original version of one essay, Martin Amis's 'Against Dryness', appeared in *Talk Magazine* (28 November 2001) and the *Guardian* (21 December 2001). Two other essays, both commissioned for the book, have appeared previously: James Wood's 'V.S. Pritchett and English Comedy', in an altered and abridged version in the *Times Literary Supplement* (4 January 2002), and Ian McEwan's 'Mother Tongue: A Memoir', in the *Guardian* (13 October 2001).

Contents

Introduction

This collection of essays grew out of a conference entitled 'The Novel in Britain, 1950–2000', held in April 2000 at the Huntington Library in San Marino, California. Half the book's contributors attended the conference, though not all delivered papers at the time, or the papers included here. In commissioning papers (for both conference and book) I mostly specified broad topics—tradition, nationality, genre, the market—and asked potential contributors to produce what they considered important or suggestive instances and examples rather than to survey the field. The book mixes novelists, academics, reviewers, a publisher, and an editor. Contributors were chosen in part because of their willingness to discriminate or judge as well as interpret, but the essays are otherwise very different in character—in tone, register, methodology, length. Some contributors tie their observations about the fiction they discuss closely to the period; others sees such observations as circular ('the work is evidence for the way things were in Britain or the world, and it is because they were that way that the work is as it is'). The book does not aspire to comprehensiveness nor does it offer any single approach or overarching theory, though one contributor has bravely declared its unsystematic or non-totalizing character 'British'. That some writers are discussed at length and others not (or not discussed at all) is largely a matter of contingency: these were the writers or writings the contributors wished to discuss.

A word about the book's title. By 'modern' is mostly meant post-1950, as in the conference title, rather than post-1945, the year the war ended, or post-1947, the year of Indian independence (one of those moments, according to the playwright David Edgar, 'when an age ends'[1]), or post-1954, the date of the publication of the first novels of Kingsley Amis, William Golding, and Iris Murdoch (the novels in question were *Lucky Jim, Lord of the Flies,* and *Under the Net),* or even post-1878 (the date Malcolm Bradbury calls 'as good a place as any for observing the great turn of the novel . . . out of Victorianism and into the spirit of the modern'[2]). 'Post-war' was rejected for the title on several grounds. The year 1945 not only saw the war's end but Clement Attlee's landslide Labour victory after the dissolution of Churchill's wartime cabinet. But the new dawn it promised was short-lived, blackened by an economy in ruins. For one critic of the period, Bernard Bergonzi, 'the immediate postwar years, which coincided with the period in office of the Labour government from 1945 to 1951, in many ways continued the wartime atmosphere. The enemy may have been defeated but the weary public was enjoined to Work or Want. . . . Physical reconstruction was slow to get under way, rationing was in some respects more severe than in wartime.'[3] Though the immediate post-war period saw the publication of important British fiction, its authors were for the most part already established, and looked back, in several ways, to the war and the world the war unravelled.

'Modern', then, refers to fiction written after 1950 and means to signal a new dispensation: new writers, new issues, new forms, a new world—the world, among other things, of the hydrogen bomb, developed in the 1950s, of the Cold War, of the dissolution of empire (though India gained its freedom in 1947, most colonies were granted independence during the 1950s and 1960s), of the weakening, if hardly the dissolution, of class ties

---

[1] From Act 1, Scene 1 of Edgar's *Destiny* (1976), in David Edgar, *Plays: 1* (London: Methuen Drama, 1987), 317.

[2] Malcolm Bradbury, *The Modern British Novel 1878–2001,* 2nd edn. (Harmondsworth: Penguin, 2001), 20.

[3] Bernard Bergonzi, *Wartime and Aftermath: English Literature and its Background 1939–1950* (Oxford: Oxford University Press, 1993), 83.

and loyalties, and with it the proliferation of regional or vernacular voices.

Whether it makes sense to group today's British novelists, including those who have come to prominence only very recently (and thus barely figure in the chapters that follow) with their predecessors from the 1950s is a question raised by several contributors. The intervening decades have transformed Britain and the world, bringing, among other turbulences, the sexual revolution, the women's movement, gay liberation, the demise of communism, multiculturalism, environmentalism, devolution, globalization, the rise of Europe. 'The project is to become an American novelist,' Martin Amis jokingly informed the conference in California. How jokingly? A. S. Byatt thinks there is a gender component involved in the question of American influence. 'The thesis that modern British fiction is peculiarly invigorated by and derives from recent American writing seems to me to have a limited truth,' she has pronounced. 'It applies to men, like Boyd and Amis, but not to almost any women I can think of.'[4] She may be right, but women novelists from Britain also look abroad; Hilary Mantel has no wish to become an American novelist, but she, too, has a project: to become a European novelist.

As several contributors make clear, the term 'British' is as problematic as 'modern', probably more so. This book takes a relaxed or roomy view of the term, including, for example, Katherine Bucknell's essay about the later fiction of Christopher Isherwood. Isherwood left Britain for America in 1939 and lived for almost fifty years in Southern California, for the last forty of them as a United States citizen. Yet the complex story of his decision to abandon fiction completely (twenty or so years before his death and while still productive in other genres) sheds light on a number of aspects of modern British fiction, regardless of whether his post-1950s novels can fairly be called

---

[4] Quoted in a panel discussion entitled 'The Man in the Back Row Has a Question', *Paris Review*, 146 (Spring 1998), 171.

British. Had contributors wished to discuss authors born and raised outside the United Kingdom—the Dublin-born Elizabeth Bowen, for example, or the American-born Paul Theroux, both long-time residents of Britain—I would not have objected; just as I did not object to Michael Wood's wish to compare Rushdie and Naipaul. As for the political implications of the term 'British' (as opposed to 'English', 'Scottish', 'Welsh') these are examined in several chapters. To Mantel, who grew up in a village in the north of England but does not feel English ('Englishness was white, male, southern, Protestant and middle class'), '"Britain" can be used as a geographical term, but it has no definable cultural meaning.' To Lindsay Duguid, in contrast, being or becoming British, in the context of the history of the modern novel, is a sign of cultural maturity. 'Above all,' she writes of fictional change in the last fifty years, 'the English novel grew up, forgot its bourgeois origins, took in foreign influences—from Ireland, Scotland, India, the Caribbean—became the British novel. And lived happily ever after.'

This book opens with a series of chapters on a deep-rooted 'English' strain of modern British fiction, that of comic satire. James Wood grounds his generalizations about English comedy in V. S. Pritchett's stories, which he sees as both modern and Dickensian (Dickens being 'the decisive influence on post-war English comedy'), English and anti-English (that is, constricted or frustrated by Englishness). Something of this sense of constriction or frustration is picked up in P. N. Furbank's piece on Angus Wilson, which anatomizes Wilson's penchant for 'sending up', focusing on its dangers and cruelties. Ian McEwan's memoir, among other things, delicately personalizes the anxieties these cruelties prompt and are prompted by, while also evoking something of the Pritchett world. Two more general chapters follow, by Christopher Hitchens and Elaine Showalter, looking, respectively, at the political conservatism of English comic fiction, and at 'Ladlit', as sure a sign as any that not all branches of English fiction have grown up or matured.

Problems of nationality figure more directly, though also more abstractly, in the chapters that follow, beginning with Michael Wood's comparison of Salman Rushdie and V. S. Naipaul, which meditates the theme of homelands, real and imaginary. The note of 'liberation, even in the midst of sadness' Wood detects in the Naipaul of *The Enigma of Arrival* (1987) is sounded also in the chapter that follows, by Hilary Mantel, subtitled 'At Home in Europe', which closes with an invocation of 'Janus, the double-faced god, the guardian of gates and doors'. The magical ability of at least one British novelist to imagine her way through gates and doors and into other homelands—German, Russian, Italian —is then celebrated by Wendy Lesser's chapter on Penelope Fitzgerald.

Questions of nationality dovetail into those of form in the chapters that follow. Katherine Bucknell's biographical account of 'Why Christopher Isherwood Stopped Writing Fiction' relates Isherwood's gathering dissatisfaction with 'invention' to subsequent fictional experiments by other writers, in particular writers of 'documentary and biographical fiction'. That Isherwood's difficulties with fictional realism were hardly unique is amply illustrated in Valentine Cunningham's chapter, which inspects a range of modern fictional forms, focusing in particular on the clash in Iris Murdoch's novels between ethical realism, which she intensely theorised and sought to practise, and her leanings to myth, transcendence, the miraculous, her very own version of 'magical realism'. As for the political implications of formal innovation, these lie at the heart of Liam McIlvanney's chapter on post-war Scottish fiction, in which Muriel Spark's tightly controlled narratives are contrasted with those of James Kelman and Alasdair Gray. In Gray's *Lanark* (1981), the title character interrupts the narrator to ask: 'How do you know this? Who are you anyway? . . . What bits will you leave out?'—questions McIlvanney links with Kelman's claim that 'getting rid of that standard third-party narrative voice is getting rid of a whole value-system'.

The note of defiance sounded in Kelman and Gray (as in earlier authors of regional or vernacular fiction) is heard also in the extravagant claims sometimes made for popular or genre fiction. Patrick Parrinder's 'The Ruined Futures of British Science Fiction' treats these claims seriously when voiced by J. G. Ballard, for whom 'science fiction is the apocalyptic literature of the twentieth century, the authentic language of Auschwitz, Eniwetok, and Aldermaston'. He also briskly dismisses Anthony Burgess's pronouncement that there is 'not one SF writer whom we would read for his style' (by citing Burgess himself, as well as Ballard). Martin Priestman, in contrast, raises doubts about the literary status of crime fiction, or at least that of its most acclaimed British practitioner. Taking P. D. James as an example of an author said to combine the virtues of the novel proper with those of popular detective fiction, he argues that the formal requirements of her preferred mode, the classic whodunit, inevitably limit or inhibit thematic and psychological development. The result, even in the hands of this most high-minded of practitioners, is 'a finally frustrating experience, not sufficiently alleviated by the sense that it was fun while it lasted'.

From popular or genre fiction, the book moves to more general topics: to fiction's relation to television and film; to publishing and the shaping power of the market; to reviewing. When asked the question 'What is meant by success for a writer in Britain?' Julian Barnes responded: 'Receiving a large enough advance to fund the next book; having all your books still in print; being in airport bookstalls and bestseller lists. Decreasingly, it means having the respect of your peers; increasingly, the respect—or fleeting attention—of people without the slightest interest in literature.' Malcolm Bradbury concurs: 'Today, commercial—as opposed to critical—success is the dominant factor.'[5] One way such success is achieved is through screen adaptation. Elizabeth Jane Howard has both adapted her novels for the screen and had

---

[5] Both comments from the 1998 *Paris Review* panel, 172–3.

them adapted by others, most recently in the BBC series *The Cazalets* (2001). Though alert to the dangers of screen translation, she approves of dramatizing novels because, among other reasons, 'they might expose some elements of the human condition that reach beyond the dreary spectacle of people killing one another, bonking, and wanting more money'. Martin Amis, too, approves of adaptation, or some adaptation (though in *Money* (1984), as Elaine Showalter reminds us, he writes hilariously about the sort of people who do the adapting). Amis's account of Richard Eyre's *Iris* (2002), a film version of John Bayley's books about Iris Murdoch, is alert both to the virtues and accuracies of Eyre's film and to what Amis sees as a crucial generic difference between film and fiction. Along the way it also comments suggestively on the Englishness of the Bayleys ('if you're an American, you *don't* know the type') and on the watery, oceanic feel of the Murdoch world, both real-life and fictional.

In the penultimate chapter in the volume, Dan Franklin, publishing director of Jonathan Cape, offers an insider's view of commissioning and editing 'at the "sharp" end of the literary business, where the stakes in the roulette game of contemporary literary publishing get alarmingly high'. One striking feature of Franklin's chapter is the international character of the market he negotiates. Another is his optimism: 'good fiction—whether "literary" or "commercial"—is selling faster and more expensively than ever before'. This optimism is echoed in the last chapter, 'Before It Becomes Literature: How Fiction Reviewers Have Dealt with the English Novel', Lindsay Duguid's history of changing styles both of novel reviewing and of the novel itself. Duguid is fiction editor of the *TLS* and writes wryly about the posturing and positioning of reviewers; yet her piece ends with praise both for those who take the job seriously (almost always for risible fees) and for the richness and variety of the books she is able to send them to review. To publisher and editor, at least, far from being dead or in decline, fiction in Britain is in rude good health.

I

V. S. Pritchett and English Comedy

JAMES WOOD

A friend once told me a true story, about a provincial dentist, a man called Miller, who kept a copy of *Who's Who* open on the waiting-room table. The book was always agape at the letter 'M', indeed at the pages of notable Millers, as if the dentist wanted his patrons to notice something. But the dentist was not one of those Millers; he was nowhere to be found in *Who's Who*. He kept the book open at the place where he *would* be, if he *were* in it.

This little tale seems comic, universally and in a local English application. It might be Russian, or French, or even German (one might recall the dentist in *Buddenbrooks*, that surprisingly comic novel, who keeps a parrot in his office pretentiously named Josephus). The universal element is the comedy of desire, our sense of the provincial dentist as the possessor of a busy soul, congested by aspiration. He is a man in some ways free in spirit, free to expand and enlarge himself on private gusts of want. But he is also a figure of comic pathos because in fact he is tied to the train of his destiny by the modesty of his ticket; he won't, as it were, ever get to Moscow. Bergson, in his essay on comedy, says that comedy begins when the individual solipsistically defies society and goes his own way. Bergson adds that comedy's task is then corrective: society, via laughter, must rebuke this waywardness, expose it. But Bergson's idea of comedy seems too saturated in Molière, too infected by the idea of satirical reprimand. It leaves no room for sympathy. Surely, we both laugh at, and feel for, the English dentist, as we move in and out of sympathy with Bottom the weaver, or Don Quixote and Sancho Panza, or Uncle Toby, or Zeno, or Pnin. And, surely, we feel this paradoxical estrangement and identification, this shuffle of affiliation and distance, because the dentist is himself so paradoxical: he is defying society in one sense, but also yearning to belong to it in another. He is absurd, not wrong. He lives in two societies, ours and his own; he is a solipsistic universalist.

The particular English inflection has to do with the nature of the dentist's aspiration, the snobbery of his desires, their pettiness. Smollett, Sterne, or Dickens might easily have invented such a man; Austen's Sir Walter Elliot is a dislikable, upper-class version. Schopenhauer argues that comedy frequently arises from the incongruity between our concepts and objective reality, which seems a fair definition of the dentist's plight. He mentions a drawing by Tischbein, of a room entirely empty of furniture and illuminated by a blazing fire in a grate. In front of the fire stands a man whose shadow starts from his feet and stretches across the whole room. Tischbein has this comment beneath his drawing: 'This is a man who did not want to succeed in anything in the world, and made nothing of life; now he is glad that he can cast such a large shadow.'

Schopenhauer asserts that the seriousness expressed by this drawing and this kind of humour is of the kind encapsulated in the advice: 'get beyond the world, for it is nought'[1]—which Schopenhauer would say. But the seriousness of Tischbein's drawing surely also resides in the comic and forlorn prospect

---

[1] Arthur Schopenhauer, *The World as Will and Representation*, vol. ii, trans. E. F. J. Payne (New York: Dover Publications, 1969), ch. 8, 'On the Theory of the Ludicrous'.

of a man consoling himself with the fantasy that even if he cannot be a success in the world, he can be a success in his own home and right now with his own shadow! In other words, we are brought back again to the dentist and the comic pathos involved in modest aspirations that do not know their own modesty.

This universal comedy of aspiration, and of the incongruity between the real and the perceived, is richly found in the comic world of V. S. Pritchett, a writer both very English and in revolt against Englishness. Pritchett has disappeared into a vague posterity; indeed, even while alive he became somewhat cloudily venerable. He may not be very much read now, and even to his admirers may seem only a fine minor writer. But he may also be exemplary, because his gentle literary struggle—that of broadening, Russianizing, internationalizing English comedy—is still significant even as his stories fade a little from the canon.

Pritchett was born in 1900, in Ipswich, into a lower-middle-class family, and died in 1998, in London. His mother was illiterate but a natural storyteller; his father, a Micawber-like figure who became a Christian Scientist, saw himself as the hero of a story, his own. Pritchett once said that his father 'must have been very shy, for in public he had somehow to make himself into a person visible to all. In restaurants he was a mixture of the obsequious and the bumptious; he would speak to the manager in a very pretentious way.'[2] In his autobiography, he beautifully fixes his father in a moment of small desire: 'I loved seeing the sad voluptuous pout of his lips as he carved a joint and the modest look on his face when, at my house, he passed his plate up and said, as his own mother had before, "Just a little more". It should have been his epitaph.'[3]

Pritchett's world, like Larkin's or Orwell's, is distinct, in a modern-antique way: velvet-lined pubs, cocky salesmen with poor teeth, tired municipal grasses, inflamed women, and

---

[2] V. S. Pritchett, interviewed in John Haffenden, *Novelists in Interview* (London: Methuen, 1985), 212.
[3] V. S. Pritchett, *A Cab at the Door* (London: Chatto and Windus, 1968), 143.

sherry-fed courage. He sees the managed restlessness of ordinary life in such communities, he sees that such societies organize themselves like morbid conspiracies, and that the surest way of escaping such a world may be internal—by living out some kind of theatrical expansion of the self, by turning life into performance and spectacle. He got much of this from Dickens, and indeed Dickens has been the decisive influence on post-war English comedy: in Muriel Spark, in early Naipaul, overwhelmingly and detrimentally in Angus Wilson, also in Salman Rushdie (again detrimentally), in Angela Carter and Martin Amis, one finds Dickens's impress, in particular the interest in the self as a public performer, an interest in grotesque portraiture and loud names, and in character as caricature, a vivid blot of essence.

Pritchett was perhaps the most subtle Dickensian of these post-war writers: he represents, if it were possible, an attempt to blend Dickens and Chekhov. He wrote very well about Dickens, and the way his characters 'take on the dramatic role of solitary pronouncers. All Dickens's characters, comic or not, issue personal pronouncements that magnify their inner life . . . what we find in this comedy is people's projection of their self-esteem . . . all are actors . . . . They live by some private idea or fiction . . . . Our comedy, Dickens seems to say, is not in our relations with each other but in our relations with ourselves.'[4] They are people, he wrote, whose inner lives hang out of them on their tongues. Likewise, many of Pritchett's characters, in the stories he wrote between the late 1930s and the late 1980s, are internal expansionists. The theatrical, expansive tendency is the closest we get to a definition of human nature in Pritchett's work.

Often, as in the true story about the dentist, these little billowings of pride and greed are social, and have to do with stolen calibrations of prestige. In his story 'Sense of Humour', published in 1938, a young couple are having to drive a corpse, in a

---

[4] V. S. Pritchett, *George Meredith and English Comedy* (London: Chatto and Windus, 1970), 20.

hearse, to the mother of the deceased. The circumstances are both grim and banal. They have the use of the hearse because the father of the driver is an undertaker. As they proceed through small English towns, some bystanders take off their hats, and others salute. The man driving the car thinks that it is like being at a wedding; the woman by his side laughs that 'it's like being the King and Queen'.[5] A characteristic principle of English comic inversion is taking place here: what should be sad is actually funny, and it is hard not to think that Pritchett had in mind Mrs Gargery's funeral in *Great Expectations*, which is comic when it should be solemn, and grotesquely ritualized when it should be spontaneous; the reader perhaps drifts from Pritchett's scene back to Dickens and on to 'The Whitsun Weddings', and how Larkin describes the women at those weddings as sharing the secret 'like a happy funeral'.[6]

There is an English dialectic, in Pritchett's comedy, of shyness and public performance. The shyer his characters are, the more they are likely to perform and expand in public; but the more they expand and perform, the lonelier, more secretive they actually are. This is the case in one of his most celebrated stories, 'The Fall'. A group of accountants are having their annual dinner in a drab, large Midlands city that 'smelled of coal'.[7] One of their number, the inappropriately named Mr Peacock, is dressing for dinner. He is a shy fantasist, a man who has to gather his selves for public events, and then display them in a series of performances. His social origins, about which he is touchy, are humble: his parents had a fish-and-chip shop. At the dinner, we see him falling into comic routines which he has rehearsed, and doing different voices—American South, Scots, Cockney.

But Mr Peacock has a secret pride as well as a secret vulnerability: his brother is a famous movie star, and he is quite pleased

[5] V. S. Pritchett, *The Complete Short Stories* (London: Chatto and Windus, 1990), 16.

[6] Philip Larkin, *The Whitsun Weddings* (London: Faber and Faber, 1964), 22.

[7] *Complete Short Stories*, 444.

to let people know it. His brother has a well-known stage fall; a big man, he can collapse with impunity, and then get up. Peacock starts showing his colleagues how this is done. At first, they are admiring, but Peacock, who has had too much to drink, doesn't know when to stop: '"My brother weighs two hundred and twenty pounds," he said with condescension to the man opposite. "The ordinary person falls and breaks an arm or a foot, because he doesn't know. It's an art." His eyes conveyed that if the Peacocks had kept a fried-fish shop years ago, they had an art.'[8] He accosts strangers, and offers to show them the famous stage fall. Soon, he is alone in the large dining room, falling and rising, falling and rising, the only audience of his performance. The story has an immense comic pathos, because of the power of its irony. We see things through Peacock's eyes, yet we can see what he cannot: that he has become a boring drunk who falls to the floor, heavily and without his brother's grace. The story, one of great delicacy, ends with Peacock standing in an empty lounge in the hotel, not unlike the man in Tischbein's drawing, before a portrait of Queen Victoria, preparing to fall to the ground.

What is especially English, apart from the settings, about Pritchett's comedy? After all, these winds of fantasy and dream are everywhere in comic literature. How is Peacock different, really, from Gogol's Akakay Akakievich, an internal expansionist who, once he gets his fine new coat, is described thus: 'From that time onwards his whole life seemed to have become richer, as though he had married and another human being was by his side.'[9] As I have suggested, Pritchett's comedy, grounded in the Quixotic battle between internal fantasy and objective reality, certainly has a universal dimension. But distinct English lineaments emerge, too. One of those is the class saturation of the comedy. Another is the subtle way in which Pritchett implies

    [8] Ibid. 442.
    [9] Nikolai Gogol, 'The Overcoat', in *The Diary of a Madman and Other Stories*, trans. Ronald Wilks (Harmondsworth: Penguin, 1972), 86.

that these characters' expansions are cheap domestic versions of their country's enlargements: as their country once expanded, so they now expand. Each is a pocket imperialist, in a colony of one. Pritchett liked the way Dickens's characters drew on their sense of themselves as what he called 'walking legends', and he liked to quote this outburst by Pecksniff, in which Pecksniff historicizes his feelings by comparing them to the princes who were murdered in the tower of London: 'My feelings, Mrs Todgers, will not consent to be entirely smothered like the young children in the Tower. They are grown up and the more I press the bolster on them, the more they look round the corner of it.'[10]

In his own work, many of his characters link themselves, with clinging grandiosity, to British history and expansion. There is Peacock, anachronistically offering himself, as it were, to Queen Victoria; or the couple in 'Sense of Humour', riding in the hearse and imagining themselves royalty. And there is a wonderful moment in a story called 'The Wheelbarrow', in which a Welsh taxi-driver, Evans, has offered to help a lady clear out her late aunt's house. Evans has been truculent and obscure, but suddenly bursts into evil foliage when he picks up a volume of verse from an old box in the house, glances at it, and then throws it down: ' "Everyone knows", he said scornfully, "that the Welsh are the founders of all the poetry in Europe".'[11]

Or consider 'When My Girl Comes Home'. In this long story, written shortly after the Second World War, a young woman, Hilda, returns from a Japanese prison camp to London—or so her family thinks, a tight-knit, mean little court of judges. Initially, all of them want to bathe in the reflected glory of Hilda's return. Mr Fulmino, a relative by marriage, has been responsible for the logistics of this homecoming: 'Mr Fulmino . . . expanded in his chair with the contentment of one who had personally operated a deeply British miracle. It was he who had got Hilda

[10] Quoted in *George Meredith and English Comedy*, 21.
[11] *Complete Short Stories*, 418.

home.'[12] She arrives by train, and her mother announces with
what Pritchett calls 'acquisitive pride' that Hilda was 'in the first
class'.[13]

In fact, Hilda was not really in a prison camp. She had been
living in India with an Indian husband, who died, and then
married a Japanese man, who also died, and is now waiting for
the arrival of a wealthy American, Mr Gloster. Her family, at
first dazzled by her celebrity and her expensive clothes, becomes
jealous, decides that she is a whore, and closes ranks against her.
(Surely Pinter read this story, and worked a variation on it in his
play *The Homecoming*.) Mr Fulmino is tremendously proud
that he has brought Hilda home: '"I wrote to Bombay", said
Mr Fulmino. "He wrote to Singapore", said Mrs Fulmino. Mr
Fulmino drank some tea, wiped his lips, and became geog-
raphy.'[14] Recall Pinter, who learned so much from Pritchett
about comic speech: in *The Homecoming*, Lenny, as it were,
colonizes Venice. For no apparent reason, and with splendid
illogicality, he says: 'Not dear old Venice? ... You know, I've
always had a feeling that if I'd been a soldier in the last war—
say in the Italian campaign—I'd probably have found myself in
Venice.'[15] Lenny speaks of Venice as if he were speaking of dear
old London, or dear old Blighty.

There is an obvious paradox, however: Pritchett's characters
colonize at a time when their country was withdrawing from
empire. They are children of diminishment. One might call them
fat ambassadors of their country in a lean age. In this sense, they
are not really linked to English history, and are not the retro-
active thief of history that Dickens presents in Pecksniff. They
are trying to escape from history, they are travelling in the
opposite direction to the little grey determinism of their times.
But to no avail. Pritchett's stories overflow with failure. And one
notices something very English, that unlike the comic fantasists
in Proust or Gogol or Tolstoy, or even sometimes in Chekhov,

[12] Ibid. 444.   [13] Ibid. 442.   [14] Ibid. 445.
[15] Harold Pinter, *The Homecoming*, Act 1 (New York: Grove Press, 1965), p.30.

16 · *James Wood* ·

comic expansion is simultaneously the measure of failure. Indeed, one notices that Pritchett's descriptions of the way his characters' bodies change when they are expanding themselves tend to convert those moments into areas of shame: 'One Sunday Argo looked at his feet sticking out boastfully from the bottom of the bed.'[16] Or this marvellous phrase: 'He had also the look of a man who had decided not to buy another suit in his life, to let cloth go on gleaming with its private malice.'[17] Or this: 'By nature Dr Ray was a man of disguises, and a new one with every sentence. Two whiskies stabilised him. A heavy, guilty blush came down from the middle of his head, enlarged his ears, and went below his collar.'[18] Elsewhere, Pritchett writes of a woman who became 'swollen with shame'.[19] There is a sense in which all of his characters blush to have aspirations at all; they blush to colonize.

So much for Pritchett's Englishness. As with his characters, what is interesting about Pritchett is both his deep Englishness and his deep flight from Englishness. He was a great traveller, was fluent in French and Spanish, and he had read deeply the entire European canon of the novel. Like one of his characters, he was in disguise: he played the role of English mildness and softened ambition. But English comedy clearly frustrated him. Unfairly (and uncharacteristically unfairly), he lumped together Fielding, Scott, Jane Austen, Trollope, George Eliot, Kipling, Wells, Waugh, and Powell into a so-called 'masculine' tradition, which he characterized, in his book *George Meredith and English Comedy*, as 'sanguine, sociable, positive, morally tough, believes in good sense...suspects sensibility'. His own comic tendency inclined towards what he called 'the feminine, the affectable'. 'Suppose you value your privacy,' he wrote, 'value imagination and sensibility more than common sense. Suppose you live not by clock time, but by the uncertain hours of your feeling...Then you will be with Sterne in the disorderly, talka-

[16] *Complete Short Stories*, 680.
[17] Ibid. 872.   [18] Ibid. 332.   [19] Ibid. 367.

tive, fantasticating tradition.'[20] This tradition, he wrote, included Peacock, Dickens, Meredith, Joyce, and Beckett.

Of course, Pritchett's chosen 'feminine' tradition actually represents a good description of Jane Austen, a supposedly 'masculine' writer: sensibility finally triumphing over sense, as it always does in her novels. But I think that Pritchett invented this unfair division because he was really defining himself against the dominant English comedy of his day—that of Waugh and the early Powell, in which characters are clicked like draughts across metropolitan boards; a comedy of apparent heartlessness, in which the novelist is always a knowing adjective ahead of his characters.

The kind of English comedy Pritchett opposed can be found throughout Waugh's early novels. The famous passage in *Decline and Fall*, for instance, about the Welsh brass band, is still praised as a characteristic piece of English literary fun:

Ten men of revolting appearance were approaching from the drive. They were low of brow, crafty of eye and crooked of limb. They advanced huddled together with the loping tread of wolves, peering about them furtively as they came, as though in constant terror of ambush; they slavered at their mouths, which hung loosely over their receding chins, while each clutched under his ape-like arm a burden of curious and unaccountable shape.[21]

Pritchett never wrote about this passage, but seen from his eyes, it must only have seemed the crudest comedy. First that adjective, 'revolting', is clumsy because it so brutally reveals the author's cards, and sets up the passage in such undergraduate terms. And then there is the way Waugh lumpily insists on the men's animality, telling us first that they were 'wolves', and then reminding us that they 'slavered' and were 'ape-like'. And then there is the foundation of the comedy itself—the idea that humour is skin deep, for one thing; and that the Welsh are

---

[20] *George Meredith and English Comedy*, 17.
[21] Evelyn Waugh, *Decline and Fall* (London: Chapman and Hall, 1928), 80.

inherently funny, for another. One naturally thinks by contrast of Pritchett's Welshman, Evans, who is so subtly mocked and yet so subtly comprehended when he attempts to make his claim for the Welsh as the greatest poets of Europe.

Faithful to Dickens, but eager to expand English comedy, Pritchett Russianized it, finding above all in Chekhov an inwardness and hospitality to fantasy which he could make use of. His phrase about not living by 'clock time but by the uncertain hours of your feeling' (as well as exemplary of the gently metaphorical style of Pritchett's criticism) is acute, for in Chekhov we feel that his characters' inner lives have a limitless quality, that they are laxly calendared. And like the Chekhovian Henry Green, Pritchett found a way of speaking from within his community—precisely what shocked Waugh, when he read *Loving*. (Waugh wrote to Green that he found the book 'obscene': 'You are debasing the language vilely'.[22]) The English novelists, after all, are remarkably intrusive, always breaking in to speak over their characters and tell us what to think, mummifying them somewhat in strips of essayism: this is true of Fielding, Eliot, Forster, and on to Angus Wilson and A. S. Byatt. In Chekhov however, the prose has the texture of its content: it doesn't seek to illuminate its perfection but lightens a path for its own developing cognition. When similes, metaphors, and images are used, they are poetic, but also the kinds of observations the characters themselves might have used.

Pritchett's detail has this quality. Sometimes by the use of free indirect speech, at other times by handing over his stories to narrators, he produces a strange, rich prose, full of travelling hesitancies, which might nevertheless have been alighted upon by his characters. In 'Sense of Humour', the man who narrates the story is sitting in the hearse next to a woman who says, in Chekhovian manner, 'I want to get away... I've had enough.' And the narrator adds, superbly: 'She had a way of getting angry

---

[22] Quoted in Jeremy Treglown, *Romancing: The Life and Work of Henry Green* (London: Faber and Faber, 2000), 161.

with the air, like that.'[23] Or take the moment in 'When My Girl
Comes Home' when Hilda describes her mother's death. Hilda is
in the kitchen, and hears a shout from the bedroom—'like a man
selling papers'.[24] That really is as good as Chekhov. Or this from
'The Necklace', in which a man who does not understand his
wife—he is an uneducated window-cleaner—watches her put
on a necklace, and comments: 'When women put on something
new, they look high and mighty, as if you had got to get to know
them all over again.'[25] Even when Pritchett uses what Barthes
called the reference code—in which appeal is made to something
we all know, a consensual or universal truism—it is from within,
not without: 'We were in the middle of one of those brassy
fortnights of the London summer when English life, as we
usually know it, is at a standstill, and everyone changes.'[26]

Pritchett said that it is very hard for an English writer to write
like Chekhov, with the Russian's open-endedness, 'since some
sort of practical or responsible instinct works against it',[27] but,
along with Green, Pritchett brought, in moments like these,
something new to English comic narrative—a curious mysterious delicacy, not unlike a softer and more ironic Lawrence, so
that Pritchett stories creep up on the reader, not frontally but
sideways or from behind, as a ship is boarded. Like Shakespeare
and Dickens, he saw that the metaphorical is central to writing,
and central to character; that characters expand via metaphor—
they are, as the word suggests, carried over, changed into something else in the process of using metaphor—and that readers
expand metaphorically when they encounter metaphor. It can
and should be said of Pritchett that he secures the Englishness of
metaphor while carrying it over into something forever un-
English, forever changed.

[23] *Complete Short Stories*, 16.
[24] Ibid. 474.   [25] Ibid. 500.   [26] Ibid. 470.
[27] John Haffenden, *Novelists in Interview*, 219.

2

No Laughing Matter:
A Word on Angus Wilson

P. N. FURBANK

This chapter has to begin autobiographically. During the 1970s I had a flat in the same house, near Regent's Park, as Angus Wilson and his friend Tony Garrett. They also had a house in Suffolk, where they spent more of their time. Nevertheless I saw a fair amount of Angus, whom indeed I had known earlier, and can report his conversation as marvellously, and almost invariably, funny. It was the thing that first struck one about him.

Of course the funniness was far from summing him up as a person. Still, it was enchanting. I remember meeting him and Tony in the street, in Camden Town, and his greeting me with: 'I said to Tony, "Who is that great beauty coming this way? Can it be Lady Diana?"'[1] Again in the street, he exclaimed, apropos of nothing: 'I've been thinking about something that you haven't: Why did Keats say "I stood tiptoe on a little hill". Why did he have to stand tiptoe? Quite unnecessary, I should have thought.' On another occasion I came upon him standing rigid at the bottom of the stairs, in the pose of a lost child. So I asked him if the 'Birmingham' school of novelists meant anything to him.

---

[1] Lady Diana Cooper, who was indeed a famous beauty.

'Nothing whatever,' he replied. 'They didn't write about *any-body* I knew.' I: 'What about Walter Allen?' Angus: 'He's very *small*, isn't he?' I: 'Still....' Angus: 'Yes, you got out of him as much as you could.'

He liked to sing on the stairs in a loud cracked voice, no doubt expecting to be heard. It might be 'The red red rawbin | Goes bob-bob-bobbin' | Alawng'; or 'You're not too young, you're not too old | If it's strictly on the Q.T. | Tara-ra-ra-boomteay'; or '... girl and a feller | Under that umbrella | Moon'. Equally, he would soliloquize on the stairs. I heard him exclaim, to nobody in particular, 'The whole civilization is retreating, so far as I can see.' I lent him some cufflinks, when he was going to a party at the zoo to meet the Queen Mother, and he reported later that the Queen Mother had said, for some reason in pidgin-English: 'Writer Man, he have nicey links.' Meeting me in the British Museum, with Tony, he said severely: 'You shouldn't be here. This is a place for old *fogeys*. Anyway, I can tell you that a lot of the books are fakes. I have consulted the same books in libraries at Oxford and Cambridge: completely different texts.'

Angus was also an excellent mimic, better than most indeed in that he was able to invent convincing dialogue; though it was always an added funniness that they were 'Angus' imitations, retaining an element of Angus himself.

The funniness fed into his short stories and novels. The joke at the heart of his first collection of stories, *The Wrong Set* (1949), is exceedingly funny as well as full of significance. The Labour Britain of the immediate post-war period, as Wilson presents it, is a scene of chaos, 'class' concepts having fallen into confusion, a process aided by the cross-'class' homosexual chase, and below everything a panic fear of an atomic holocaust. In the title story, Vi's confused reminiscence of Edwardian social canons— cabling her sister that her nephew Norman is 'in the wrong set' —most beautifully and hilariously epitomizes the chaos.

'Taking off' and 'sending up' are not synonomous, and it is his passion for sending up that I am most concerned with here

—the ruthless eye for cliché, the habit of mind that made him, for his own pleasure, impersonate the pompous pundit who would pronounce 'the whole civilization' to be 'retreating'. Significantly, there is already a hint of it in a piece, 'In the Park', which he published as a young schoolboy, in the *Adelphi* magazine.[2] 'Then a soldier laughed quite near at hand; he and his girl were having a devil of a good time with an umbrella that had been blown completely inside out.'

In his novels and stories this 'sending up' is his basic manner of presenting characters. He depicts people by reducing them to a bundle of favourite clichés and daydreams, and it is not until he has done so that his pity and sympathy can come into play.

One does not find, indeed, very much pity and sympathy in *The Wrong Set*, though this first book is as good as anything he ever wrote—one finds them mostly, perhaps, for Lois in 'A Story of Historical Interest'.[3] But the sending-up system is already the staple of the writing. And what one notices, even here, is that it is sometimes applied without artistic logic.

No problem with the story 'Saturnalia', since it is a complete welter of clichés: of verbal clichés, or clichés of thought and daydreams, quotations from cheap fiction, fake Irish accents and Irish charm, Kensington trying to sound 'Knightsbridge' and self-conscious Cockney 'saltiness'. The proclaimed purpose of this staff dance in a private hotel is to break down class barriers, and this is finally achieved, by a universal determination to get laid. (Even the scholarly retired colonial governor, learning that the pageboy is an expert swimmer, examines his life-saving medal 'with keen interest'.)

But indeed, in *The Wrong Set*, there is almost always an artistic justification for this emphasis on clichés. In 'Mother's

---

[2] *Adelphi* (Feb. 1925), in 'The Contributors' Club' section.

[3] Her widowed father, an erstwhile Edwardian man-about-town, has had a stroke, and Lois, who has made such an effort, against her real nature, to be the sort of loving sporty 'pal' she imagines he would like, finds he is much more interested in his sexy Irish nurse and the 'odiously eupeptic' nursing-home matron.

Sense of Fun' it is her 'sense of fun', and the repertoire of cliché-formulas that goes with it, which have become Donald's special torment.

He had often thought that to find his mother's phrases one would have to go to English translations of opera or the French and German prose books that he had used at school. It always 'rained cats and dogs', that is if the rain did not 'look like holding off'; Alice Stockfield 'was a bit down in the mouth' but then she 'let things get on top of her'.[4]

'A Crazy Crowd' is subtle in the way it exposes, little by little, the self-applause and egotism reflected in the cliché of belonging to a 'crazy crowd'. Again, in 'A Visit in Bad Taste', the sending up of Margaret's daydreams ('She put the tiny liqueur glass of light emerald—how Malcolm always laughed at her feminine taste for crème de menthe—upon the mantlepiece between the Chelsea group of Silenus and a country girl and the plain grey bowl filled with coppery and red-gold chrysanthemums') admirably reinforces the irony in the word 'taste'. The point of the story, of course, is to expose the use of 'taste'—visual taste and intellectual *chic*—as an excuse for vicious egoism, a moral taste which is very bad indeed. One notices a faint problem—who is actually having the cliché thought in ' "That's where we differ" said Malcolm and for a moment his handsome, high-cheekbone face with its Roman nose showed all his Covenanting ancestry'? But the point is not really important. Though there is also a tiny slip in logic in the narration. One reads: '. . . it was not for nothing one felt that the progressive weeklies were so neatly piled on the table beside him [Malcolm]'; but the narrative has created no place for a 'one', a detached observer.

This passion for sending up seems to me central to Wilson's work as a novelist, and moreover it led to brilliant achievements. On the other hand, as I shall want to argue, he was not entirely in control of it. In his first novel, *Hemlock and After* (1952), it is more or less out of hand.

---

[4] *The Wrong Set* (London: Secker and Warburg, 1949), 187–8.

The trouble arises, at least partly, from the fact that the hero, Bernard Sands, is too much like Angus Wilson himself, so that one does not know whose irony it is that one is getting.[5] At the opening of the novel Bernard, a highly esteemed novelist, has just—by great efforts of diplomacy—obtained Treasury approval for a home for young writers, at a country mansion called Vardon Hall. Bernard is a declared humanist but prone to irony and a sending-up outlook, with the saving grace that, when necessary, he can send himself up too. His reflections on his success over Vardon Hall are typical of this.

For a Grand Old Man of Letters it had become fairly plain sailing: even, he reflected with satisfaction, for a Grand Enfant Terrible, though he instantly reminded himself of the histrionic dangers—the knickerbockered, bearded, self-satisfied quizzing air—of the position he had won in English life.[6]

His wife, Ella, is suffering from a crippling nervous breakdown. However, in the first chapter, he has persuaded her to come with him to a morning drinks party, thrown by his atrociously snobbish daughter-in-law, Sonia. The guests are mostly extremely right-wing, prompting much sending up on Bernard's part. '"Oh God", said Bernard, "Sonia's busy broom seems always to have swept up the dregs of our dear local gentry". He spoke the last word in inverted commas.'

The party is the sort of thing that Wilson does extremely well. His spokesman Bernard relishes silently sending up 'season-ticket country gentlemen', affecters of 'pastiche Edwardian' speech, and 'the new middle-class rebels', who have belatedly discovered foreign travel. Matters are complicated, moreover, by his own self-criticism. 'He hastily convicted himself of that worst of snobberies—chic snobbery.'

---

[5] He said himself that he did not think he had quite brought Bernard off as a character.

[6] *Hemlock and After* (London: Secker and Warburg, 1952), 11.

But the sending up goes on, in just the same tone, where Bernard is not present. Ella struggles to make conversation with a lady who (going one better than the 'middle-class rebels') has been to Lascaux, and she succeeds in interesting her. Ella's interlocutor, we learn, 'was a great reader of Virgina Woolf, and she saw the conversation as an important interchange by two women on a significant level'.

The point as regards Bernard is neatly encapsulated in a passage later on in the novel. Bernard by now is in a state of distress; the opening of Vardon Hall, and his defeatist speech at it, have been a disaster; and to relieve the conflicts in his mind he resorts to long and depressing country walks, 'in stout brogues and heavy high-necked sweater', climbing field-gates and stiles with 'a cumbrous, unconvincing jauntiness'. We are told about this 'jauntiness' as if it were something a spectator could have observed, and not been convinced by, though a moment's reflection tells us this must simply be Bernard's own gloomy self-mockery. But we have the feeling that the difference would hardly have been noticed by Angus Wilson.

Equally, Ella's private reflections when, still drowned in deep depression, she is talking with her brother, Bill, seem too sharp, too poised.

While Bill rambled on, Ella remembered their father prosing in the same manner at the rectory table. Bill had been the rebel of the family and inevitably had ended by assuming his father's mantle. It was the kind of situation, she reflected, that was the core of the old 'psychological novel'.

'I can always get you turkey eggs when you want 'em', she heard Bill say.

It was difficult to imagine when she *would* want them, . . .[7]

The jokes are nice but not in character, or at least not dramatically appropriate.

---

[7] Ibid. 116.

Not impossibly, Wilson intended this novel to be a comprehensive conspectus of sending-up styles. Bernard is bisexual, and, during Ella's long illness, he has acquired a young boyfriend, Eric. Eric lives with his widowed mother, the 'life-loving' but possessive Celia Craddock, and the narrator gives us Celia's fantasies in a familiar 'style indirect libre' manner—i.e. pretending to report objectively, but in fact catching and parodying the subject's accents.

Celia Craddock preserved most of her old evening dresses of brocade, of real lace or of the sort of velvet you don't see now.... Alan [Eric's elder brother] had always been too manly a child to concern himself with her clothes, nor would she have wished it otherwise. Like his father, he had that masculine blindness to what she wore, that made the ocasional gruff compliment so strangely important to a woman when it came.[8]

Then there is the, quite different, malicious sending-up practised by Bernard's homosexual acquaintances—serving, in those pre-Wolfenden days, as a sort of homosexual lingua franca. (Wilson captures it very expertly.) Bernard takes Eric to the theatre, and in the bar during the interval they meet the venomous Sherman Winter, a theatrical designer, and Bernard's ex-boyfriend Terence. Sherman, we learn, 'had fallen into a conventional, caricatured pansy manner when he was quite young and, finding it convenient, had never bothered to get out of it.'

'Terence', he said, 'is battling at the bar. It suits him to the ground. Pure Barker's sales. Bless his little Kensington heart. Bernard, my dear, you look tired'. And as Bernard was about to speak, 'Oh, I know, bitching me! Tired equals old. You must make him rest, dear', he said to Eric: 'you know, feet up and forty winks. Not that I should think you'd be much good at making people rest', he stared Eric up and down; 'you look a proper little fidget to me.'[9]

[8] *Hemlock and After* (London: Secker and Warburg, 1952), 126.
[9] Ibid. 88.

Eric shares with Bernard the faculty of sending himself up. He indulges, quite deliberately, in narcissistic daydreams, for instance one in which he figures as 'the youngest of Lorenzo's pages ... loved not only for his beauty, but for his talents ... His treble voice in madrigal was judged the loveliest in Tuscany. But it was a certain gentle grace ... that distinguished him from the other pages—a grace that spoke of nobler birth than that union between a passing *condottiere* and lady of the court which common gossip gave to him.' At this point in his reveries Eric begins to giggle. 'The nobler birth, he decided, was a little too much, and the treble voice.'

One of the things that Bernard loves about Eric is his way of switching from 'nonsense' to 'youthful seriousness' (though he can imagine Terence telling him 'Of course you would like it, dear, it's just the sort of warm whimsy that you probably used in your own little North Oxford nursery'). But the reader notices that, for Bernard, 'seriousness' has to imply boyishness, which is itself to send seriousness up. One sometimes gets the impression from this novel that anything in the human world can be 'sent up', ironized and put in inverted commas.

One of the chapters in *Hemlock and After* is headed 'Life-loving Ladies'. The ladies in question are the self-dramatizing Celia Craddock and the appalling procuress and blackmailer Mrs Curry, who loves everything round her to be 'all cosy and warm'. I need to make a digression here, for in 1953 Wilson published *For Whom the Cloche Tolls*, a comic evocation of the 'Twenties', with 'high-camp' illustrations, wittily satirizing 'Twenties' dress-styles, by Philippe Jullian. One somehow expects the book to be brittle and malicious, but in fact it is much the most benign of Wilson's writings. It consists of obituary memories by friends and relations of (to use some words by Cecil Beaton) the 'fun-mad, man-mad Maisie', frequenter of Mayfair, Montmartre, and the Riviera, victim of passing passions for professional dancers and pugilists, a hopeless mother who was yet cherished by her children. Of the children, Bridget is conventional and the son, 'Tata', is an aesthete and 'queer'. 'Tata' once briefly found employment as a cinema pianist but gave the job up and 'made lampshades at home for friends', before becoming a monk in Chile. The impoverished Maisie dies in 1951, and 'Tata's' letter to her sister-in-law Alice is really the heart of the book. 'Tata' writes that, 'With all her faults and follies, Maisie had a "natural" understanding of life's joys.' She had 'an infinite capacity for what we all worshipped in the twenties, but only a few like her understood'; she was 'the rare person who accepted and used life in whatever sphere she was compelled to live'; and what went along with this was that she did not understand humour and satire.

If people were being witty, she would sit bolt upright, her cigarette holder held a little before her face to disguise her shyness, and, when she thought that something humorous had been said, she would burst out into a polite but entirely artificial laugh. Bridget and I used to be terribly embarrassed by this—in our own different ways, we were brimming over with sense of humour—but I realize now that Maisie didn't need the self-protection from life that humour provides.[10]

What this last remark shows—for 'Tata' is not being ironical —is that Wilson, though so obsessed by humour, is also distrustful of it, seeing it as an expression or fear or bad faith. His novel *Hemlock and After* could be said to be a critical investigation of this whole subject of humour and sending up. Bernard and Ella's daughter, Elizabeth, has a 'special bright slang' (beautifully rendered by Wilson), and her parents diagnose it as 'brightly disguised boredom'. She works for a women's magazine and, having to purvey clichés in its pages, she overacts her contempt for what she writes. 'She ended her dictation and, turning to the secretary, added, "And that, dear, should be practised over the sink. It should be done preferably in black velvet off the shoulders and a train. They tell me they've had some startling results

---

[10] Angus Wilson and Philippe Jullian, *For Whom the Cloche Tolls* (London: Secker and Warburg, 1973 edn.), 74–5.

in Potter's Bar."' Her secretary, who lives in Finchley, wonders if she thought she was the only member of the editorial staff 'who apologized for her copy by making jokes about the suburbs'.

Elizabeth and Terence begin an affair, and both find it at first a relief not to have to talk in inverted-commas style—'bright' in her case and 'camp' in his. Nevertheless when, on their long aimless bus-rides through London, they amuse themselves with 'nonsense' dialogues, Terence cannot help thinking that she tends to prolong her parodies to a point where he becomes embarrassed. (Nor can he altogether suppress the thought of how his 'camp' friends would mock their relationship.) It is for such reasons that, before long, the affair breaks down. Terence tells Elizabeth:

'I know I oughtn't to have let it happen, but I also know that I can't stand it much now and soon I shan't be able to stand it at all. The same cosiness every evening, the same little warm jokes and happy matinées.
  I feel I could almost scream.'

In the novels that follow *Hemlock* we frequently experience the same trouble as in that novel, of not knowing where the ironies come from, or who owns them. It is not so pressing, however, in its immediate successor, *Anglo-Saxon Attitudes*, partly because it has a stronger and more convincing plot. From other points of view, moreover, the wit, malice, and comic fantasy are as fresh here as in the short stories. 'Sending up' is most naturally suited to the short-story form, where characters enjoy only a brief existence. In short stories, it is quite sufficient for the awful to be funny. One thinks of the bedroom scene in *The Wrong Set* between Vi, the nightclub pianist, and her lover, Trevor, the bogus ex-public school boy, whose manners in public—helped by his monocle and 'soldier's moustache'—are so gallant, at least in Vi's eyes.

Trevor put his trousers to press under the mattress, gave himself a whisky in the toothglass, refilled it with Milton and water and put in his dentures. Then he sat in his pants, suspenders and socks squeezing blackheads from his nose in front of a mirror. All this time they kept on rowing. At last Vi cried out 'Alright, alright, Trevor Cawston, but I'm still going'. 'O.K.' said Trevor 'how's about a little loving?' So then they broke into the old routine.[11]

Nevertheless, there are passages in *Anglo-Saxon Attitudes* where the funniness of the awful is exploited just as brilliantly. The hero Gerald Middleton's estranged wife, Ingeborg, with her elephantine playfulness, love of the simple and elemental, and total blindness to anyone else's feelings, is actually a frightening character, as we discover later, yet Wilson is able to be funny at her expense and, in some curious way, his blithe comic ruthlessness helps to humanize her. She makes a fetish of Christmas and organizes a children's carol singing, at which she leads them in a simple Jutland peasant song.

At the end of the song, Mrs. Middleton called up a very angel-pretty little boy of six from the audience—there was nothing she liked more than angelic faces in children—'And now little Maurice Gardner will sing a verse of *Holy Night* and we shall sing the choruses. Little Maurice is a very shy, special little boy', she said to the audience, 'so we must all help him'.

When no sound came from his terror-struck mouth, she bent down from the heavens above and placing her huge doll's face close to his, she asked, 'What is the matter, Maurice? Have the trolls bewitched your tongue?' so creating a deep psychic trauma that was to cause him to be court-martialled for cowardice many years later in World War III.[12]

Nevertheless, in these middle-period novels, one also finds miscalculations of tone: for instance, in a way very relevant to my theme, in the opening section of *The Old Men at the Zoo* (1961). The 'I' character, Simon Carter, is a youngish erstwhile Treasury official, recently given the post of Secretary to the London Zoo. In him Wilson is evidently meaning to examine

---

[11] *The Wrong Set*, 99–100.
[12] *Anglo-Saxon Attitudes* (London: Secker and Warburg, 1956), 94.

the bureaucratic mind. Carter is an expert administrative tactician, impatient with muddle, and rather a bully. He is also a passionate animal lover, greatly preferring animals to human beings. He dislikes almost all of his colleagues and underlings, mentally lampooning them for their cliché behaviour ('The little dainty touches Mrs. Purrett had added of artcraft and home from home seemed more revolting than usual to me'), and for their (to him) hideous bodies. It is a favourite habit of his to identify his older colleagues with animal species ('The Director, round toucan's eye fixed stolidly ahead, long tapir's nose pointing us ever on, stood full square on his magnanimity').

The day on which the novel opens has been a stressful one, a young keeper having been horribly mangled and killed by a giraffe. Carter suspects criminal negligence somewhere in the organization. At last, in the evening of this day, he finds relief in mimicking the old men at the zoo, for the entertainment of his rich wife, Martha, and her guests. 'But as I really let myself go and gave them Leacock and Sanderson, Beard and Englander all in full mimicry, but hobbling with sciatica, deaf as posts, peering blindly with the vain, failing eyesight of old age, Jane and Martha began to feel relief in laughter until Martha cried.'

It is as though Carter's expert mimicry was meant to seem a saving grace, but it does not strike us that way. He appears to us throughout as truly odious, to a degree that I think that Wilson did not quite intend. The novel is set in the (then) near future; and amidst the havoc of a non-nuclear war between Britain and a united Europe, Simon Carter, a lover of badgers, will be forced to roast and eat a badger. The full force of this horrific irony seems to depend on a sympathy for Carter which we have never felt.

One gets the impression that, though always at the centre of Wilson's thoughts, mimicry and lampoon and sending up (of oneself as much as of others) are gradually changing their character for him, beginning to seem more like an affliction, and to some degree inspiring guilt feelings. 'Tata's' remark in *For Whom the Cloche Tolls*—'Maisie did not need the self-protection from life that humour provides'—was, after all, a serious one, and *No Laughing Matter* (1967) is almost entirely devoted to its implications.

The novel is a family saga, involving three generations, and no doubt vaguely intended to parody Galsworthy. The family in question comprises William Matthews ('Billy Pop'), a would-be novelist and essayist of the 'gentle humour' school—a dressy, idle, and impecunious caricature of the stylish 'Man about town'; his wife, Clara ('The Countess'), a histrionic and promiscuous egotist, who insists on the admiration due to a Lady of Quality; and their six children, whose careers the reader will be following. The Matthews live in shabby-genteel style in cheap lodgings near Victoria. The 'Countess' despises and bullies 'Billy Pop' as a literary and a sexual failure and flirts with, or is vicious towards, her children as the mood takes her.

The novel opens, rather effectively, with a visit by the Matthews to the Wild West show at the Earl's Court exhibition, just before the First World War. With their minds full of cowboy and waggon-trail fantasies, the children and their parents parade through the crowds singing, proudly advertising themselves as a united 'happy family'. Even this day ends in bickering, however; and indeed the family is very far from being a happy one. Billy Pop and the Countess are, in fact, impossible parents. It is a fact that the children are well aware of: and as a relief to their desperation (several of them being excellent mimics) they institute the 'Game', in which they ritually impersonate and travesty their parents. (There is here perhaps a suggestion of the Areopagus of children in the novels of Ivy Compton-Burnett, a writer Wilson greatly admired.)

It is an ambitious novel. Wilson risks various mildly 'experimental' procedures, like running together, without a clear transition, literal narration and daydream, or the voices of different characters—or again, as a Brechtian *Verfremdungseffekt*, converting certain scenes into a playlet (in which the characters can wink at, or exchange confidences with, the audience). It is also, one must certainly say, a very serious novel, attempting to grapple with a subject rarely dealt with before: humour as a form of self-protection and expression of impotence.

However, this novel seems to suffer from an absolutely basic and fatal flaw. For Wilson's method entails that Billy Pop and the Countess are sent up from the beginning. They are never for a moment allowed their ordinary flesh-and-blood humanity. Hence the children's 'Game' is only a travesty of what is already a travesty. There seems no way of distinguishing their sending up of their parents from the author's own. It is, moreover, impossible to regard the near-tragic effort of the children to find their parents funny, as funny in itself. The effect on the reader of so much continuous and unrelieved sending up is debilitating, even excruciating. Wilson's writing has here lost that impenitent, inspiriting funniness which was its secret.

3

Mother Tongue: A Memoir

IAN MCEWAN

I don't write like my mother, but for many years I spoke like her, and her particular, timorous relationship with language has shaped my own. There are people who move confidently within their own horizons of speech; whether it is Cockney, Estuary, RP, or Valley Girl, they stride with the unselfconscious ease of a landowner on his own turf. My mother was never like that. She never owned the language she spoke. Her displacement within the intricacies of English class, and the uncertainty that went with it, taught her to regard language as something that might go off in her face, like a letter bomb. A word bomb. I've inherited her wariness, or more accurately, I learned it as a child. I used to think I would have to spend a lifetime shaking it off. Now I know that's impossible, and unnecessary, and that you have to work with what you've got.

'It's a lot of cars today, id'n it?'

I am driving Rose into the Chilterns to a nature reserve where we will stroll about and share our sandwiches and a flask of tea. It is 1994, still many years to go before the first signs of the vascular dementia that is currently emptying her mind. Her little remarks, both timid and intimate, do not necessarily require a response.

'Look at all them cows.' And then later, 'Look at them cows and that black one. He looks daft, dud'n he?'

'Yes, he does.'

When I was 18, on one of my infrequent visits home, resolving yet again to be less surly, less distant, repeated conversations of this kind would edge me towards silent despair, or irritation, and eventually to a state of such intense mental suffocation, that I would sometimes make excuses and cut my visit short.

'See them sheep up there. It's funny that they don't just fall off the hill, dud'n it?'

Perhaps it's a lack in me, a dwindling of the youthful fire, or perhaps it's a genuine spread of tolerance, but now I understand her to be saying simply that she is very happy for us to be out together seeing the same things. The content is irrelevant. The business is sharing.

I remember other journeys in the Home Counties we took together by train in the mid-1950s. Typically, they would end on the station platform of our destination with my mother taking from her handbag a scented embroidered handkerchief, dabbing it on her tongue, and screwing a wet corner into some portion of my face. The idea was to rid me of 'smuts', entities in which I had no faith at all. I was to be made fresh-faced for whichever aunt or friend of hers we were visiting.

The trains were of the old-fashioned sort, with corridors, and leather straps to hold the windows open, and dusty compartments in which it was common to hold polite conversations with strangers. On one occasion a lady got in who must have appeared to Rose to have considerable social standing. They began to talk and I remember being surprised by the change in my mother's voice. She measured out her sentences as she strained for her correct version of speech.

I was to hear the same transformation many years later, when my father was commissioned from the ranks. There were two tribes of officers: those who were drawn from the middle classes and had been to Sandhurst, and those who had risen from being ordinary soldiers and who never got much beyond the rank of major. All my parents' friends belonged in the second group.

Whenever some gathering in the officers' mess obliged my mother to hold a conversation with the colonel's wife, the posh voice would creep in, with its distorted vowels—yais, naice—and aitches distributed generously to make up for the ones that were dropped elsewhere. But most significantly, Rose spoke very slowly on these occasions, almost lugubriously, aware of all the little language traps that lay ahead.

When I was 11, I was sent from North Africa, where my father was stationed, to attend school in England. By any standards, Woolverstone Hall was a curious place, a rather successful experiment by a left-wing local authority in old-fashioned embourgoisement. It had the trappings of a public school—Adam style country house, huge grounds, rugby pitches, a genially Philistine headmaster—and so on. But this ethos was rather stylishly undermined by the intake of mostly grammar-school level working-class lads from central London. There were some Army brats like me (their fathers all commissioned from the ranks) as well as a tiny smattering of boys from bohemian middle-class backgrounds.

During my early teens, as my education progressed, I was purged of my mother's more obvious traits, usually by a kind of literary osmosis—when I was 14 I was an entranced reader of the handful of novels Iris Murdoch had published. I was also reading Graham Greene. Slowly, nothink, somethink, cestificate, skelington, chimley all went, as well as the double negatives and mismatched plurals.

Sometimes I took myself in hand. I was in the first year of my sixth form when I arranged for my best friend, Mark Wing-Davey, a rare and genuine middle-class type, to say 'did' out loud every time I said 'done' in error. Very kindly, he done this for me. But he got into serious trouble one afternoon in a history lesson. I was earnestly delivering a prepared piece about the bold reforms of Pope Gregory the Seventh (how I loved to intone 'the extirpation of simony') when Mark loyally murmured a 'did'. The history master, a kind Welshman, Mr Watts, whom we called Charlie because of his striking non-resemblance to the drummer, became incensed by what he considered to be a display of rudeness and snobbery. To prevent Mark being ordered from the room, I had to intervene and explain our agreement.

But these adjustments of speech and writing were superficial, and relatively easy. They formed part of that story, familiar in English biography, in which children who received the education their parents did not, were set on a path of cultural dislocation. What tends to get said is that the process is alienating and painful. But it seems to me now that there is more to it. There are gains as well as losses, at least for a writer. Exile from a homeland, though obviously a distressing experience, can bring a writer into a fruitful, or at least a usefully problematic, relationship with an adopted language. A weaker version of this, but still a version, is the internal exile of social mobility, particularly when it is through the layered linguistic density of English class.

When I started writing seriously, in 1970, I may have dropped all or most of my mother's ways with words, but I still had her attitudes, her wariness, her unsureness of touch. Many writers let their sentences unfold experimentally on the page in order to find out what they are, where they are going, and how they can be shaped. I would sit without a pen in my hand, framing a sentence in my mind, often losing the beginning as I reached the end, and only when the thing was secure and complete would I set it down. I would stare at it suspiciously. Did it really say what I meant? Did it contain an error or an ambiguity that I could not see? Was it making a fool of me? Hours of effort produced very little, and very little satisfaction. From the outside, this slowness and hesitancy may have looked like artistic scrupulousness, and I was happy to present it that way, or let others do it for me. I was pleased when people spoke approvingly of the 'hard surface' of my prose; that was something I could hide behind. In fact, my method represented an uncertainty that was partly social. I was joining the great conversation of literature which generally was not conducted in the language of Rose or my not-so-distant younger self. The voices of giants were rumbling over my head as I piped up to begin, as it were, my own conversation on the train.

Of course, those remarks copied into a 1994 notebook after our visit to the nature reserve give no sense of Rose's warmth in conversation, her particular emotional tone. In the summer of 1970 I went with my father to collect her from the military hospital in Millbank, London, where she was recovering from a stomach operation. It was customary for officers and their wives to occupy different wards from the other ranks and their wives. There was a noisy, tearful scene in the corridor outside Rose's ward as we were coming away. A dozen patients, the young wives of privates and corporals, gathered to say goodbye and give presents to the woman who—so they said—had listened to their problems and given them her wise advice. In convalescene, Rose must have deserted her ward. She had been the wife of a sergeant, and before that, in her first marriage, of a private soldier. She would have felt comfortable among the younger women in the other ranks' ward. And she was also in her element in a heart-to-heart. No language perils there.

When I was six and we were living in Army quarters in Singapore, I remember how I liked to loll unobtrusively on the floor behind the sofa when my mother had a friend round. I would listen in to these roaming, intimate heart-to-hearts. Broadly, they fell into two groups—operations, and bad behaviour. How compelling and gory they were, these accounts of flesh under knife, and the aftermath. I'm sure they exerted their subliminal pull on my first short stories. And with so many bad people in the world, what a lucky six-year-old I thought I was, when my mother and her friends were always on the side of the good.

In my second term at Woolverstone I was sent on an errand to the headmaster's secretary. The office was empty, and while I waited I saw on a desk a confidential report card with my name on it. 'Hopelessly shy', 'Can't get a word out of him', and worryingly, 'An intimate boy'. I half knew what the word meant. But surely you had to be intimate *with* someone. I looked the word up and saw in a secondary meaning the mention of secrets. I had none, but it was true that I only spoke freely on a one-to-one basis. I never acted in plays, I never spoke in class, I rarely spoke up when I was in a group of boys. Intimacy was what loosened my tongue, and I was always on the lookout for the one true best friend.

My father loved to take control in a group of friends, especially if he could make them laugh, so I was far closer to my mother in conversational style. In my first stories I wanted to get as close as possible, put my lips to the reader's inner ear. These were almost parodies of artificial intimacy. Entering a public arena for the first time, I strove—too desperately, some said—to provide lurid secrets for a set of deranged narrators. Like men who had been alone too long, they had much to tell. Forcing them to confess at a couple of hundred words a day, and within a literary tradition, I thought I was freeing myself from my past. Writers who fictionalize their childhoods, I declared in my first interviews, bored me. The business is to invent. So I invented— intimately, with the embarrassed hesitancy of the inarticulate— in my mother tongue.

Rose Moore was born in 1915 in the village of Ash, near the military town of Aldershot. Her father was a painter-decorator. One of my first memories is of visiting him in the larger of two upstairs bedrooms where he lay dying of TB. The house then, in the early 1950s, was as it had been during my mother's childhood. A steep, unlit central stairway, gas lighting, a gloomy kitchen smelling of damp and gas, the brighter unused front parlour, the scullery with a copper under which a fire was lit every Monday for the weekly wash. In the garden, a plum tree and the wooden privy perched over its horrible pit. Beyond, Farmer Mayhew's meadows stretching away to a low ridge of hills known as the Hog's Back.

Rose was the eldest of five. Her mother was a reluctant housewife, a chain smoker who liked to walk to Aldershot to window shop, leaving her first-born to mind the younger ones. Granny

Moore had come over from Ireland at the age of 16 with a college education, according to my mother, who left school at 14. The age at which people went to college or left it meant little to her. She did not know where her mother grew up, or what her background was. My father, who grew up in Govan, Glasgow, also knew little about his family line. His parents were both tram drivers for the City Corporation, and their parents were agricultural labourers from the Stirling area. That was all he was told. This uncurious rootlessness characterizes our family. I feel it myself, a complete lack of interest in family trees, or poking around in parish registers. Two or three generations back is the land, and most certainly a hard life. But whose land, and precisely what kind of life are forgotten. Not even that—they were never known.

Rose developed rickets from malnutrition. In a photograph taken in 1918 with her parents—her father was just back from the war—she is wearing calipers on her legs. Poverty went for the bone. Like many of her generation and class, Rose lost all her teeth in her twenties. During my childhood her false sets—top and bottom, lurking at night like bear traps in a glass tumbler by her bedside—were always giving her trouble. Another impediment to easy speech.

In the mid-1930s Rose married Ernest Wort, also a house painter, and my half-brother, Roy, and my half-sister, Margy, were born. Rose often told this story to illustrate the 'ignorance of them times': when she was going into labour with her first child she believed and feared that 'it was going to come out of my bottom'. The astonished midwife set her straight. Ern was no great provider, though he clearly had charm. He often went missing for days or weeks on end—living under hedges, according to Rose, but she would only have known what he told her. Occasionally, the police would bring him back. Until then, she and the two children lived 'on the parish'—provisions made under the old Poor Laws, until the welfare system was founded in the next decade.

Ern died in 1944 from the stomach wounds he received after the D-Day landings. In 1947 Rose married Regimental Sergeant Major David McEwan, and the following year I was born. A wedding photograph shows her tense, uncertain smile. My father also left school at 14—the family's poverty forced him to abandon his scholarship, and four years later, unemployment on the Clyde forced him into the recruiting office. His lack of formal education sat unhappily all his life with his ferocious intelligence. There was always an air of frustration and boredom about him. He was a kindly man, but he was domineering too, with a Glaswegian working man's love of the pub—and the sergeants' mess.

The drunkenness distressed Rose but she never dared challenge him. She was always frightened of him, and so was I. When I came to early adolescence, I was like her, too tongue-tied to face down his iron certainties. I was at boarding school anyway, and in my mid-teens began to spend my holidays abroad with friends. After that, I drifted away, and saved my darker thoughts for my fiction, where fathers—especially the one in *The Cement Garden*—were not kindly presented. Our most serious clash came some years later, when I was in my twenties and visited my parents in Germany. Rose had nothing to do all day at home but polish the furniture. When she was offered an afternoon job running a tiny barracks library that lent out paperback thrillers to the troops, David turned the job down on her behalf. His firm view was that having a wife who went out to work would reflect badly on him. Two years after our row, the job came round again and, moving with the times, he relented.

In my twenties I was often defending, or trying to defend, Rose against David, or promote her cause somehow. The effect on my writing was fairly direct, though I think at the time I had no clear sense of the connection. I read *The Female Eunuch* in 1971 and thought it was a revelation. The feminism of the 1970s spoke directly to a knot of problems at the heart of our family's life. I developed a romantic notion that if the spirit of women was liberated, the world would be healed. My female characters became the repository of all the goodness that men fell short of. In other words, pen in hand, I was going to set my mother free.

At home, there was violence in the air. There always had been, but only now could I really see it for what it was, and begin to judge it. My father, I know, felt he had a right to it, and it was no one's business but his own. When I was visiting my parents in the late 1970s, Rose told me the latest. I was inclined to believe her and offered to talk to David. The idea horrified her. It would make things worse when I went. That week he gave me, as a late birthday present, an Olivetti portable typewriter. I was grateful—my old machine was falling apart. But the first thing I wrote on it, in a tiny bedroom upstairs, was a letter to my father which I gave to Rose to keep. She was to give it to him if she was threatened again. In it I told David that I loved him. I also told him that hitting Rose was a criminal act, and that if it happened again, I would come from England and see both the military police and his commanding officer. It turned out she destroyed the letter the week after I left. She said she couldn't sleep at night knowing it was in the house. Matters went on much as before, and what settled the problem in the end was only mellowing age, illness, and growing dependency.

The memory of another letter from that time still makes me smile and wince, and remains a caution. Speed kills. Late one Friday morning, just before leaving my flat, I typed an indignant few lines to the *Spectator* concerning some slight I thought I had received in its pages the week before. Generally a mistake to complain, but I hadn't learned that yet. I put a carbon in my pocket and hurried off to the Friday lunch in Bertorelli's. At some point in the conversation, as the main course was being served, the *Spectator* article about me came up. I produced my stinging reply, and it was passed around the table, from Clive James to Mark Boxer, Martin Amis to Karl Miller, from Christopher Hitchens to Terry Kilmartin to Peter Porter to Julian Barnes. Gratifying that, having the writers and critics whose opinion I valued most read my letter. There was general silence, then some throat clearing, and a move to change the subject as Jeremy Treglown, who had seen the carbon last, cupped his hand and murmured kindly in my ear, 'There's a dangler in the first sentence.' Dah!—as Amis and Hitchens liked to say. In the first *word*. That indignantly detached participle. 'Sir', would have been the sort of thing, 'Having destroyed my meaning with dishonestly juxtaposed quotation, I find myself perplexed by your reviewer's sudden concession to probity when...' Osso bucco never tasted so vile.

It is springtime, 2001, and I collect Rose from the nursing home to take her out to lunch. Sometimes she knows exactly who I am, and at others she simply knows that I am someone she knows well. It doesn't seem to bother her too much. In the restaurant she returns to her major theme; she has been down to the cottage in Ash to see her parents. Her father was looking so unwell. She's worried about him. Her mother is going to come up to see her in the nursing home, but doesn't have the bus fare and we should send it to her. There is no purpose in telling Rose that her father died in 1951, and her mother in 1967. It never makes any difference. Sometimes, she packs a plastic carrier bag of goodies—a pint of milk, a loaf, a bar of chocolate, and some knickers from the laundry basket. She will put on her coat and announce that she is going to Ash, to Smith's cottages, to the home where she grew up and where her mother is waiting for her. This homecoming may seem like a preparation for death, but she is in earnest about the details, and lately, she has been convinced that she has already been, and must soon go again. Over lunch, she says that what she would really like is for her mother to come and see her room at the nursing home, and see for herself that her daughter is all right.

Afterwards, I drive her round the streets of suburban west London. This is what she wants, to sit and look and point things out as we cruise from Northolt to North Harrow to Greenford.

'Oo, I really love doing this,' she says, 'I mean, look at me, riding about like Lady Muck!'

As we go along the A40 in a heavy rainstorm, past Northolt airport, she falls asleep. She was always so bird-like and nervous that sleeping in the day would once have been unthinkable. She was a worrier, an insomniac. Soon all her memories will be gone. Even the jumbled ones—her mother, the house in Ash with the plum tree in the garden. It's a creeping death. Soon she won't know me or Margy or Roy. As the dementia empties her memory, it will begin to rob her of speech. Already there are simple nouns that elude her. The nouns will go, and then the verbs. And after her speech, her coordination, and the whole motor system. I must hang on to the things she says, the little turns, the phrases, for soon there will be no more. No more of the mother tongue I've spent most of my life unlearning.

She was animated and cheerful over lunch, but for me it's been another one of those sad afternoons. Each time I come, a little bit more of her has gone. But there's one small thing I'm grateful for. As she sleeps and the wipers toil to clear the windscreen, I can't help thinking of what she said—riding about like Lady Muck. I haven't heard that in years. Lady Muck. Where there's muck there's brass. It must have been in use in the 1930s or 1940s. I'll use it. It's right for the novel I'm finishing now. I'll have it. Then I'll always remember that she said it. I have a character just coming to life who can use her words. So thank you, Rose, for that—and all the rest.

4

Between Waugh and Wodehouse: Comedy and Conservatism

Christopher Hitchens

A joke is, notoriously, not a joke if it needs to be explained, and I often wonder what Americans think they mean when they speak about a distinctly British or English sense of humour. I dare say one knows it when one sees it, or 'catches it on the edge of a remark', if I can annex that phrase from *Chariots of Fire*, which is after all one of the building-blocks of American Anglophilia. The definition of our national humour probably ought to be elusive as well as allusive. It took me many readings to notice what I believe to be the following deep, latent connection.

The Importance of Being Earnest opens like this. We see the curtain rise on the frivolous Mayfair apartment of a frivolous Mayfair bachelor. A piano is playing offstage as the butler lays out the tea-things. The music stops and Algernon Moncrieff enters the room:

> *Algernon:* Did you hear what I was playing, Lane?
> *Lane:* I didn't think it polite to listen, sir.

Not long afterwards, the apartment is convulsed by the arrival of Lady Bracknell, Algernon's Aunt Augusta, one of the most formidable aunts in fiction. Silly and spoiled girls make their appearance; matrimonial complications and financial settlements are the subject matter. Soon, the action is removed to the countryside, where fatuous rural deans are in evidence. Absurd spats and misunderstandings and impostures multiply; in a climactic scene all sundered hearts are united.

What is this faultless three-act comedy, with its young men and butlers and aunts and simpering fiancées and country houses, but the world—one might say the universe—of P. G. Wodehouse? I might add that the dates for this alchemy 'fit' with extraordinary aptness, and that Wodehouse—who spent much of his life in the lighter and more musical end of the theatre business—is justly famous for his use of quotations but never made a single allusion to Wilde. So we have a process whereby Wilde's sparkling and subversive satire mutates into Wodehouse's consoling and ageless balm. There's a ghost here; a fleeting spectre of wit to be pursued through the national unconscious (and I say 'national' with no disrespect to Wilde's Irishness).

In considering this strangely neglected subject, or as Lucky Jim Dixon might have said through empurpled cheeks, this what neglected subject; this strangely what subject; this strangely neglected WHAT? I shall turn first to a review of the latest Little, Brown edition of the work of Evelyn Waugh published in the neo-conservative *Weekly Standard*. The reviewer, David Skinner, had this to say:

Waugh, who converted at the age of twenty six, is often thought of as a Catholic writer. But he was not noted for a Christian temperament. Pointing out the contradiction, Nancy Mitford drew from him the famous rejoinder, 'You have no idea how much nastier I would be if I was not a Catholic. Without supernatural aid I would hardly be a human being.' His biographer Martin Stannard claims that after his conversion, Waugh 'always wrote as a Catholic.' Yet in his comic novels—both those before and those after conversion—one searches long and hard for evidence of a distinctly Catholic mind at work.[1]

[1] David Skinner, 'The Soul of Waugh', *The Weekly Standard*, 3 Apr. 2000, p. 38.

Here, as so often in contemporary American criticism, it would be helpful to have some understanding of the relationship of contradiction—if any—to irony. Irony, which is the cream in the coffee and the knight's move on the board, the gin in the campari, the x-factor, the ghost in the machine, might have assisted Mr Skinner in seeing that his supposed 'contradiction' needs a determinedly literal mind in order to present itself as a real one. Take, first, the idea that Roman Catholic beliefs require a 'Christian temperament', and that this temperament is by definition incompatible with spite or rancour or cynicism. This is, at best, only to assume about Christianity what that religion undertakes or claims to prove—that it is indeed a theology of brotherly love. I'll content myself for now with saying that this would be a very large, not to say generous, assumption.

Further, to write as a Catholic, as late Chesterton (he only became one in 1922, after publishing his most popular books) and Belloc and in a different way T. S. Eliot and Graham Greene and Anthony Burgess (who thought of himself as a lapsed or ex-Catholic) all understood, is to write as a member of a minority in England and to attempt to vindicate the beliefs that have animated that minority—a Christian minority, or perhaps better say a minority among Christians—for centuries of survival. One strongly marked Catholic belief—not unique or peculiar but we would be justified in calling it distinctive—is that of the centrality of original sin. And who can say that Waugh is inconsistent here, as between his writing and his convictions?

'You will not find your father greatly changed,' remarked Lady Moping as the car turned into the gates of the County Asylum.

This brilliant and arresting sentence opens one of my favourite Evelyn Waugh stories, 'Mr Loveday's Little Outing'. Why is it funny? Well, there's the wonderful name of Lady Moping, for a start. Then there is her mournful bugling of the fact—which we can already anticipate—that whatever has brought Lord Moping to the loony bin, it represents no very sharp or abrupt transition from his behaviour and character as it was known to the outside world. (We later learn that he attempted to hang himself in the orangery, with his braces, 'in front of the Chester-Martins'.[2])

Those of you who know the story will also know the echo it contains of the stupidly permissive and progressive prison governor, Lucas-Dockery, in *Decline and Fall* (1928). Lacking the moral anchor that is furnished by a firm belief in the Fall of Man, the authorities in 'Mr Loveday's Little Outing' submit to the sentimental pressure exerted by Lord Moping's irritating daughter, and decide to give the trusty inmate Mr Loveday a second chance. The outcome is as calamitous, for a poor woman out on her bicycle, as it was for the luckless Prendergast in Dartmoor prison. Few can excel Waugh in ability to extract the comic element from random cruelty and caprice: we come across it time and again, with Little Lord Tangent's scratch becoming gangrenous, with the overturned truck in *Scoop* ('Was he hurt?' 'Oh, yes, sir, gravely'[3]), with the misery inflicted by fate—actually so indifferent that it is barely even 'inflicted' in any real sense—on the blameless Tony Last. These, with their knowingness and their flirtation with despair, are the humorous uses of pessimism. A cheap term for this is 'black comedy'; at its best it is a stoic form, very well adapted for conservative purposes in habituating us to the idea or the prospect of the worst, as well as in squashing illusions such as hope in progress. Waugh's non-comic moments in *Brideshead* (1945) and *The Sword of Honour* draw from the same well; 'the modern world in arms' is apprehended by Guy Crouchback as 'the enemy in plain sight' and corresponds perfectly to Waugh's public objection to the British Conservative Party—that for all its brave talk it had failed to turn back the clock by even a single precious minute.[4]

[2] Evelyn Waugh, 'Mr. Loveday's Little Outing' (1935), repr. in *Evelyn Waugh, The Complete Short Stories and Selected Drawings*, ed. Ann Pasternak Slater (London: Everyman, 1998), 179.

[3] Evelyn Waugh, *Scoop* (1938; repr. London: Eyre Methuen, 1978), 233.

[4] The quotation is from Evelyn Waugh, *Men at Arms* (London: Chapman and Hall, 1952), 5, the first in his *Sword of Honour* trilogy, collected 1965.

Evelyn Waugh of course was also a great admirer and pro-
moter of the work of P.G. Wodehouse, of whom he wrote— very
typically—that his stories and contrivances would continue to
release future generations from a captivity that might be more
irksome than our own. He added, rather untypically, that Wodehouse had made a world for us to live in and delight in—a world
that could only be Edenic and thus preceding the fall of man and
original sin.[5] (Oddly enough, one of Bertie's favourite expres-
sions for the pills and blisters who infest his universe is, as well as
'fiend in human shape', 'serpent in Eden'.) Wodehouse's is the
humour of innocence, not pessimism; it can be described as
idyllic because it is as unchanging as Blandings Castle and—if
you make the mistake of excluding any satirical intent—it can be
classified as conservative for that reason.

The guarantee of innocence in Wodehouse is the refusal of the
sexual motive; correctly described by George Orwell as an absolutely tremendous sacrifice for a comic writer to make.[6] And
there's little doubt that it was Waugh's own experience of the
great woe of sexual betrayal that informed his generally *noir*
view of human nature. (There's also little doubt, before I leave
this subject, that Catholicism made Waugh more nasty rather
than less, as well as giving him a moral alibi for his cruelty, to
friends in the real world and to protagonists in the fictional one.)
And, though Wodehouse knew his Bible almost as well as he
knew his Shakespeare, he uses clergymen only as figures of fun

---

[5] See Evelyn Waugh, 'An Act of Homage and Reparation to P. G. Wodehouse',
broadcast over BBC Home Service, 15 July 1961 (first published, *Sunday Times*, 16
July 1961), repr. in Donat Gallagher (ed.), *The Essays, Articles and Reviews of
Evelyn Waugh* (Harmondsworth: Penguin, 1986), 567–8: 'For Mr. Wodehouse
there has been no Fall of Man; or "aboriginal calamity." His characters have never
tasted the forbidden fruit. They are still in Eden. Mr. Wodehouse's idyllic world can
never stale. He will continue to release future generations from a captivity that will
be more irksome than our own.'

[6] See George Orwell, 'In Defence of P. G. Wodehouse', first published in *Tribune*,
16 Feb. 1945, repr. in Sonia Orwell and Ian Angus (eds.), *The Collected Essays,
Journalism and Letters of George Orwell*, 4 vols. (Harmondsworth: Penguin,
1970), iii. 396.

and displays an utter indifference to all religion in every line of his letters and diaries as well as of his prose. (Oh I can't resist—since I mention the formula of 'he knows his'—at one point Madeleine Bassett says to Wooster, 'You know your Shelley, Bertie' and he replies, 'Oh, am I?'[7])

If one inclines to the belief that a pointful joke is almost certain to be at someone's expense, and that humour is a deadly instrument in the right hands, then the hilarity of Wodehouse represents an extreme limiting case. The imperishable moments —the prize-giving at Market Snodsbury grammar school, the laying-low of Sir Roderick Spode—involve acute embarrassment rather than humiliation, and as in a Disney cartoon the fractured teeth or singed fur grow back in time for the next frame. Fate is every bit as capricious in Bertie's and Gussie's world as she is in Basil Seal's, but the element of cruelty is absent. And though it is just possible to see, in the world of Emsworth and Threepwood and Jeeves, a satire on the class system, it is a satire gentle enough for any country-house to keep on the shelves—and rivalled in absurdity only by Waugh himself, who certainly did not desire to see the end of the great houses and titles.

The second great difference is this: Wodehouse solves the problem of progress and modernity essentially by ignoring it. With the exception of one or two shocking and one has to say anachronistic lapses in his post-war output—how one winces when Bertie goes out for a stroll only to be confronted by anti-war demonstrators—he preserves the world he has made, where for example people travel by steamship rather than aeroplane.[8] Waugh, who confronts modernity and machinery and quotes *The Waste Land* and talks about adultery and fornication and narcotics, is not in this sense a reactionary. When he wanted,

---

[7] See ch. 3 of P. G. Wodehouse, *The Code of the Woosters* (1938; repr. London: Everyman, 2000), 58.

[8] Bertie encounters the demonstrators in ch. 2 of Wodehouse's *Aunts Aren't Gentlemen* (London: Barrie and Jenkins, 1974).

later in life, to say what he really thought about the brave new world, he resorted to dystopia—a tactic for projecting existing tendencies to their heartless and soul-less and godless terminus in the nihilistic and the absurd. Dystopia is a very useful weapon in the lampooning of the idealistic or 'progressive'; it always strikes a chord in the English breast as well. Recall Sir John Betjeman's 1945 'The Planster's Vision':

> I have a Vision of the Future, chum,
> The workers flats in fields of soya beans
> Tower up like silver pencils, score on score:
> And Surging Millions hear the Challenge come
> From microphones in communal canteens
> 'No Right! No Wrong! All's perfect, evermore.'⁹

(Worth noting, this, I sometimes think, as anticipating later work of Larkin's like 'Going, Going'.)

Probably few things contributed more, to the great cultural *tendenzwende*, as the Germans say, or sea-change in the *zeitgeist*, than the view that the Left or the 'progressive' element in British society had become humourless. I think I can date this, almost precisely, to the publication just after the 1960s of Kingsley Amis's *Girl, 20 (1971)*. This said farewell to the decade of ostentatious and high-minded good causes as definitely as did Tom Wolfe's *Radical Chic* essay, published the previous year. (It also, like Wolfe, managed to intrude the idea that there was something sinister as well as something boring in the Sixties ethos.) Part of the genius of the novel is its highly sympathetic representation of its central character, a ludicrous old progressive hypocrite named Sir Roy Vandervane, a member in good standing of the stage army of the good and an exemplar of what's sometimes known as the 'Hampstead' set of well-heeled champagne socialists. In his fictional character as a prosperous

---

⁹ These are the concluding lines of the poem, a sonnet, first published in *New Bats in Old Belfries* (1945), repr. in *John Betjeman's Collected Poems* (London: John Murray, 1977), 128.

orchestral conductor, he is a London version of Leonard Bern-
stein. In his manner—endearingly solipsistic, intellectually con-
ceited, and sexually uncontrollable—he put me in mind, as I
think he must have been meant to, of the late Sir Alfred Ayer, the
philosopher for whom the only certain proof of intelligence was
the ability to make other people laugh.[10] His own ability in that
direction or quarter, like Sir Roy's, was rather dependent on
being a very funny, rather than a very humorous, character. He
could make you laugh all right, but often looked a bit baffled
when you did.

At about this time, at the end of the 1960s, Kingsley Amis and
Robert Conquest became the centrepiece of a regular luncheon
group in London, which met originally in an upstairs room in
Bertorelli's restaurant and made sulphurous remarks about the
prevailing *bien pensant* consensus. Other attendees included
Anthony Powell and John Braine, for the fictional contingent,
and Tory satirical pamphleteers like Colin Welch and Russell
Lewis. To be complete, the contingent would have had to, but
did not, include Simon Raven, author of the *Alms for Oblivion*
novel sequence (1964–75) that is sometimes called the poor
man's Powell, and Constantine Fitzgibbon, author of the once-
celebrated but I think now forgotten anti-anti-war dystopia
When the Kissing Had to Stop (1960). Both of these had also
signed, with Amis and Conquest and Braine and others, a notorious letter to *The Times* in 1967, endorsing the British government's support for the Johnson administration in Vietnam. I
once attended a sitting of this lunch; the denizens showed a
marked tendency to begin their remarks with the throat-clearing
preface 'Call me old-fashioned if you will . . .'

If we were to do a rough matrix of British post-war novelists,
plotting them on one graph of right to left and another of degrees
of success as humorists, one would actually have to begin, even if
only to be fair, by eliminating John Braine and Constantine

---

[10] An assertion uttered rather than printed, but often enough to count as a maxim
of Ayer's. I heard it myself.

Fitzgibbon. Then it might go something like this: Kingsley Amis—extremely funny when still quite left-wing (*Lucky Jim*); still fantastically funny when joining right-wing (*Girl, 20*); less funny and more dystopian as positions solidify (*The Alteration*, 1976, *Russian Hide-and-Seek*, 1980); bitter ironist towards the end (*Stanley and the Women*, 1984); elements of self-parody in closing (*Difficulties with Girls*, 1988). Anthony Powell—consistently conservative; consistently if drily amusing and relying very much on understatement rather than satire; less successful when most political. Anthony Burgess —politically unclassifiable except as supporter of restoration of Stuart monarchy; several pointed satires on modernity. Michael Frayn—doggedly and incurably conscience-stricken bleeding-heart liberal; funniest when staying off politics altogether as in *Towards the End of the Morning* (1967), though his masterpiece, *The Tin Men* (1965), flirts with dystopia in satirizing the age of machines and statistics. Frayn is also notable for being the only literary survivor, apart from Alan Bennett, of the 1960s 'satire' movement, when the target of ridicule was the stuffy old regime rather than the canons of levelling and self-pitying political correctness. That would leave us with David Lodge and Malcolm Bradbury, both of them with middle-of-the-road convictions, both working hard on the innocent abroad or lost-in-academia themes pioneered by Amis, with Lodge yet another example of someone trying to be funny while being a Catholic.

'I believe', wrote Evelyn Waugh, 'that man is by nature an exile and will never be self-sufficient or complete on this earth; that his chances of happiness and virtue, here, remain more or less constant through the centuries and, generally speaking, are not much affected by political and economic conditions, that the anarchic elements of society are so strong that it is a whole-time task to keep the peace.'[11] That could have been, and in fact almost certainly was, lifted straight from St Augustine's *City*

[11] Evelyn Waugh, *Robbery under Law: The Mexican Object Lesson* (London: Chapman and Hall, 1939), 16.

of God. It does help remind us, though, that a crucial element of humour may depend on a sense of the absurd, and of the vanity of all human wishes, and even on a sense of tragedy—at any rate on a feeling for universals. Waugh in this way follows Augustine while occasionally forgetting the unnecessary or optional dogma that people are supposed to have souls.

Let me ask a risky question. Is this funny? It is the opening sentence of a Waugh story entitled 'Tactical Exercise':

John Verney married Elizabeth in 1938, but it was not until the Winter of 1945 that he came to hate her steadily and fiercely.[12]

Misogyny can be amusing in itself—at least if you are a man it jolly well can—and often, as in this quotation, reinforces the larger conservative pattern. Waugh's sentence anticipates, for example, some of Kingsley Amis's later 'as against that' formulations: e.g. of a restaurant: the food was very nasty and the wine very poor and the waiters very slow and very rude, but as against that it was extremely expensive. The trick is simply to play for existing expectations—meliorating expectations—and then suddenly negate them, which in turn means a lively awareness of how misguided those prevailing expectations or impressions might be.

In 1965, Gore Vidal gave an address to the Library of Congress entitled 'The Novel in the Age of Science'.[13] Vidal is a renowned wit whose explicitly comic novels have a tendency to farce, but whose world-view might be described as that of a conservative radical. He was ahead of his time in pointing out that:

In the age of science we have come to believe that any problem can eventually be solved by submitting it to the test of orderly analysis.

[12] Evelyn Waugh, 'Tactical Exercise' (1947), in Slater (ed.), *The Complete Short Stories*, 405.

[13] This address, delivered in Feb. 1965, has never been printed, though a recording of it exists in the Library of Congress. My subsequent quotations can be checked against a transcript found among the Gore Vidal Papers in the Houghton Library, Harvard University, a collection recently transferred from the Wisconsin Film and Theater Institute in Madison, Wisconsin (and not yet unpacked and catalogued).

The New Critics of the 1940s consciously initiated the scientific attitude. To them a poem was a machine which could be dismantled by a knowing mechanic; the poem existed in a limbo, with no reality other than the relationship of its parts one to another. This kind of criticism, though useful when applied to metaphysical verse, proved impossible with all but a few novels. Joyce and Kafka were possible subjects for the quasi-scientific approach; Tolstoy and Flaubert were not. Yet the method...one should say methodology... is still with us.

Vidal was prescient in another respect, in anticipating and analysing what has come to be known as political correctness. 'At any given moment there is a kind of novel which is in fashion. At the moment it is the ethnic novel. Jewish writing is in fashion; also books by Negroes. Critical standards are often lowered in the interests of good citizenship. This is not particularly helpful to the cause of literature but it is a natural consequence of important social changes.' Vidal went on to relate the anecdote of a student who handed a story to Saul Bellow, assuring him that he fully intended to put in the symbols later.

What connects these passages is a familiar distrust—the conservative humorist's distrust—of improvement, progress, science (though Kingsley Amis did take a strong interest in that odd soft-option genre known as Sci-Fi). And beneath this distrust, I feel sure, is the inchoate suspicion that science—and indeed modernity—does have designs on literature. Kingsley Amis phrased it like this in an essay, written in 1984, happily enough, entitled 'Television and the Intellectuals':

I sympathise with genuine Luddites, haters of the Twentieth Century, of whom the most eloquent is Peter Simple of the Daily Telegraph, who would like to see the total disappearance of television along with motorways, contraception, frozen food, youth leaders, plastics and certainly psychology, though not I think modern drugs or dentistry—peace to all such.[14]

---

[14] Kingsley Amis, 'Television and the Intellectuals' (1984), repr. in *The Amis Collection: Selected Non-Fiction 1954–1990* (London: Hutchinson, 1990), 255.

It is of interest, then, that one of Amis's most fascinating voyages to dystopia—*The Alteration*—combines all the worst aspects of social engineering and state control with a reversion to the medieval past (perhaps a continuation of *Lucky Jim*'s war on the hell of Merrie England), where the secular arm of an Inquisition is manned by people with the same names as those of living English leftists like Foot and Redgrave. In general, though, and even in this case, the dystopia has as its object the consummation or completion of existing deplorable tendencies. Practitioners have to be careful not to be too specific here—*Russian Hide-and-Seek* supposes an occupation of Britain by the Soviet Union, as had Constantine Fitzgibbon in *When the Kissing Had to Stop*—which is why reactionary futurism, if I may give it a paradoxical name, has always been a better bet.

One way of being seriously conservative is to surrender with a Roman gesture to the barbarians and to say, in effect, Oh very well, have it your own way and see how you like it. This is pessimism cubed, and it is sometimes intended to have a galvanizing or mobilizing effect. For some reason, actually for an obvious reason, dystopian writers ever since Aldous Huxley and George Orwell have preferred to set much of the action in institutions such as clinics, hospitals, or prisons. Evelyn Waugh held to this convention in his 1953 story 'Love among the Ruins' which he subtitled 'A Romance of the Near Future'. The central character, Miles Plastic, a conscienceless and homicidal arsonist, is first met in a model prison where treatment depends on the subtraction or abolition of all moral judgements from the sentencing process. (Kingsley Amis adapted this idea for a satire on sociological lenience entitled *We Are All Guilty*, 1991.) Thus rehabilitated, Miles is found work by the ideal state in a euthanasia clinic, where the old and afflicted clamour and—this being a bureaucracy—queue up to be put down. On one fine day:

Only one old man waited outside, old Parsnip, a poet of the '30s who came daily but was usually jostled to the back of the crowd. He was a comic character in the department, this veteran poet. Twice in Miles's short term he had succeeded in gaining admission but on both occasions had suddenly taken fright and bolted.

'It's a lucky day for Parsnip,' said Miles

'Yes. He deserves some luck. I knew him well once, him and his friend Pimpernell. *New Writing*, the Left Book Club, they were all the rage. Pimpernell was one of my first patients. Hand Parsnip in and we'll finish him off.'

So old Parsnip was summoned and that day his nerve stood firm. He passed fairly calmly through the gas chamber on his way to rejoin Pimpernell.

'We might as well knock off for the day,' said Dr Beamish [earlier described as 'a man much embittered, like many of his contemporaries, by the fulfilment of his early hopes'].[15]

A decade after lampooning them in *Put Out More Flags* (1942), Evelyn Waugh has just gassed Christopher Isherwood and W. H. Auden. This is impressive persistence in a joke—and as I said earlier a good joke is most likely to be at somebody's expense. When Auden actually did die, Anthony Powell was giving breakfast to his house guest Kingsley Amis and exclaimed at the news: 'I'm *delighted* that *shit* has gone . . . scuttling off to America in 1939 with his boyfriend like a... like a... '.[16]

On the continuum between Wodehouse and Waugh—between innocence and experience or from banana skins to full-blown misanthropy—we find Anthony Powell treading, or perhaps better to say veering, very lightly and deftly. Almost as soon as we meet Kenneth Widmerpool—the most terrifying solipsist and philistine in modern fiction, barely redeemed by buffoonery—he stops a thrown banana with his fat face, getting most of it smeared over his spectacles in a public school tuck-shop. This almost Billy-Bunterish moment is counterpointed, however, by innumerable passages of the subtle and the grotesque. Indeed, in

[15] Evelyn Waugh, 'Love among the Ruins: A Romance of the Near Future' (1952), repr. in Slater (ed.), *The Complete Short Stories*, 477–8 (the bracketed description of Dr Beamish comes from p. 458).

[16] See Kingsley Amis, *Memoirs* (Harmondsworth: Penguin, 1991), 151.

The Acceptance World, the third novel of the twelve-volume *A Dance to the Music of Time*, the narrator, Nicholas Jenkins, reflects on the very problem that Powell has in fact set himself:

I began to brood on the complexity of writing a novel about English life, a subject difficult enough to handle with authenticity even of a crudely naturalistic sort, even more to convey the inner truth of the things observed.... Intricacies of social life make English habits unyielding to simplification, while understatement and irony—in which all classes of this island converse—upset the normal emphasis of reported speech.[17]

Powell did not have Kingsley Amis's genius for mimicry or for capturing eccentricities of human speech on the page. But he was a master of irony and understatement, and made the fullest use of the infinite nuances of English conversation. Here is Charles Stringham's ghastly mother, briskly describing his attempts to get back on his feet, specifically as a painter:

'Charles uses gouache now,' said Mrs Foxe, speaking with that bright firmness of manner people apply especially to close relations attempting to recover from more or less disastrous mismanagement of their own lives.[18]

Or—remembering the necessary sensitivity of novelists to scientific 'analysis'—consider the literary critic Bernard Shernmaker:

One of his goals was to establish that the Critic, not the Author, was paramount. He tended to offer guarded encouragement, tempered with veiled threats, to young writers.[19]

V. S. Pritchett, reviewing some early Powell for the old *New Statesman*, wrote that in the 1950s he was 'the first to revive the masculine traditions of English social comedy. He retrieved it on

[17] Anthony Powell, *The Acceptance World* (London: Heinemann, 1955), 32.

[18] Anthony Powell, *Casanova's Chinese Restaurant* (1960; repr. London: Fontana, 1980), 138–9.

[19] Anthony Powell, *Books Do Furnish a Room* (1971; repr. London: Fontana, 1977), 132–3.

behalf of the upper classes. The joke that he is a Proust Englished by Wodehouse has something in it.'[20] Indeed, though he was acutely sensitive to the comparison, Powell did locate Nick Jenkins in Marcel's Balbec at the end of the wartime campaign in Normandy:

Proustian musings still hung in the air when we came down to the edge of the water. It had been a memorable adventure ... At the same time, a faint sense of disappointment superimposed on an otherwise absorbing inner experience was in its way suitably Proustian too: a reminder of the eternal failure of human life to respond a hundred per cent; to rise to the greatest heights without allowing at the same time some suggestion, however slight, to take shape in indication that things could have been even better.[21]

Or as Bertie Wooster once put it in an attempt to capture the essence of bathos, full often had he seen the sun flatter the mountain top with sovereign eye, only to turn into a beastly afternoon.

Understatement and irony are of course the sheet anchor against anomie; a very present help in time of trouble and more durable and trustworthy than any religion. The true comic writer has a sense of this underlying need, which may be at bottom fatalistic and to that extent conservative or pessimistic, but by no means despairing. If the joke must be at someone's expense, then even if it is cosmic it may as well be at one's own.

[20] V. S. Pritchett, 'The Bored Barbarians', repr. in V. S. Pritchett, *The Complete Essays* (London: Chatto and Windus, 1991), 993.

[21] Anthony Powell, *The Military Philosophers* (1968; repr. London: Fontana, 1978), 173.

5

Ladlit

Elaine Showalter

From 1950 to 1999, the fiction genre of Ladlit provided British readers with a romantic, comic, popular male confessional literature. Stretching from Kingsley to Martin Amis, Ladlit was comic in the traditional sense that it had a happy ending. It was romantic in the modern sense that it confronted men's fear and final embrace of marriage, and adult responsibilities. It was confessional in the postmodern sense that the male protagonists and unreliable first-person narrators betrayed beneath their bravado the story of their insecurities, panic, cold sweats, performance anxieties, and phobias. At the low end of the market, Ladlit was the masculine equivalent of the Bridget Jones phenomenon; at the high end of the high street, it was a masterly examination of male identity in contemporary Britain. But by the beginning of the new millennium, the genre was in decline, suggesting both its literary exhaustion and the need for a new story of masculine identity.

The term 'lad' has undergone many permutations of meaning in English literature, from the doomed homoerotic companions of A. E. Housman's Shropshire, to the violent droogs of *A Clockwork Orange* and the developmentally arrested good ol' boys of 1990s popular culture. But the anti-heroes of Ladlit are often losers and boozers, liars, wanderers, and transients. They include the addicts and petty criminals of Irvine Welsh's *Trainspotting* (1993) and its progeny, and the football-worshipping, lager-loving, flat-sharing blokes of Tim Lott, David Baddiel, William Sutcliffe, and John O' Farrell, as well as the underemployed thirtysomething heroes of Nick Hornby and Tony Parsons, and the postmodern urban picaresques of Martin Amis, Will Self, and Hanif Kureishi. In the *New York Times*, Michiko Kakutani headlined her review of Nick Hornby's *About a Boy*, 'Uncommitted Slacker Invents Commitments'.[1]

But at the same time, lads are attractive, funny, bright, observant, inventive, charming, and excruciatingly honest. They are characters who seem to deserve more from life and romance than they are getting; and they are full of rage at those they hold responsible for their dispossession or plight: bosses, parents, girlfriends, male rivals, and Americans. Indeed, while they are addicted to American popular culture (records, detective novels, movies, fast food), lads do not much like Americans. Rob in *High Fidelity* (1995) loves Raymond Chandler, William Gibson, and Kurt Vonnegut; his favourite films are *Godfather I* and *II*, *Taxi Driver*, *Goodfellas*, and *Reservoir Dogs*; his favourite music is Motown and Memphis; and he fantasizes about sleeping with an American. But when he does score he is horrified: American girls talk too much.

Moreover, unlike American Jewish seriocomic anti-heroes—Portnoy, Humboldt, Jerry Seinfeld, and Woody Allen—British lads are obsessed with class distinctions and divisions. Not gentlemen, but not yobs, they defiantly practise the rituals of the working class while aspiring to something better—better education, better jobs, better women. Rob in Nick Hornby's *High Fidelity* says he would like to go to football games, but doesn't like to be with the kind of people who go to football games. Tim Lott's hero in *White City Blue* (1999), declares: 'I'm not a yob at all, come to think of it. . . . Most soccer fans around

---

[1] *New York Times*, 7 July 1988, p. 7.

here stopped being yobs years ago. They read Irvine Welsh
and listen to Classic FM.'[2] Although they overtly despise the
British class system and the cuteness of theme-park England,
lads covertly identify with England's traditional symbols and
styles. In the privacy of his flat, Rob, an uncompromising
vinyl elitist who makes his living selling harsh and recherché
popular records, listens weepily to the Beatles and watches
Brookside.

1. *Laddish Jim: The Frustrated 1950s*

Kingsley Amis's close friend Philip Larkin might have acknowledged Ladlit along with sexual intercourse as one of the pheno-
mena of the mid-century. *Lucky Jim*, written in 1950, was
published in January 1954 and quickly became a best-seller and
trend-setter. 'Looking forward to seeing you at the première of
Lucky Jim on Ice', Amis wrote to his publisher Hilary Rubenstein.[3] He spent 14 shillings on stamps answering a month's fan
mail, and optioned the film rights to the Boulting Brothers for
£200.

To Amis's chagrin, critics were soon to assimilate Lucky Jim to
another 1950s phenomenon, the Angry Young Man. John
Osborne's play, with its scabrous post-Strindbergian anti-hero,
Jimmy Porter, opened at the new Royal Court Theatre in 1956,
and soon pundits were proclaiming the age of anger and post-
war alienation. With the failed Suez crisis and the Hungarian
uprising in the same year, the label seemed aptly to describe a
generation of politically disillusioned young writers. But
Osborne, who was chronically ticked-off if not existentially
infuriated, was also grumpy to be lumped with other writers: 'I
have only met Mr Amis once briefly,' he announced, 'and have
never met Mr Wain nor any of the rest of these poor successful

---

[2] Tim Lott, *White City Blue* (Harmondsworth: Penguin, 2000), 25.
[3] Amis to Hilary Rubenstein, 3 Apr. 1954, in *The Letters of Kingsley Amis*, ed.
Zachary Leader (London: HarperCollins, 2000), 382.

freaks.'[4] John Wain's publishers advertised his books with the line: 'John Wain is NOT an angry young man.'

Jim Dixon, the Lucky Jim of Amis's novel, is actually an angry young lad, a man in terminal adolescence. 'You'll find that the years of illusion aren't those of adolescence,' an older woman tells him. 'They're the ones immediately after it, say the middle twenties, the false maturity if you like, when you first get thoroughly embroiled in things and lose your head. Your age, by the way, Jim.'[5] In the London *Sunday Times*, Humphrey Carpenter described the Amis–Larkin letters as 'characterised by "laddish" sneering at women.... To some extent this laddishness was a symptom of the times. This was the period at Oxford when J. R. R. Tolkien, C. S. Lewis and their fellow "Inklings" met in a pub across the road from Amis's college for hearty male conversation ... gatherings to which no woman was ever admitted.'[6]

But Jim Dixon, and the young Kingsley Amis, would have detested such 'hearty male' gatherings of men Amis regarded as the driest and most tediously donnish of the university set— Professor Bollkeen is his epithet for Tolkien. Lads were not fusty Old Boys, women-haters, or Old Farts, but adolescent men, high-spirited, heterosexual, lovable, anarchic. Somerset Maugham called Jim Dixon, a young man of the new class, 'the white-collar proletariat'.[7]

Subsequent critics have agreed that, as D. J. Taylor writes, '*Lucky Jim*'s interest is at least as much sociological as literary. ... On one level the novel might be seen as a reasonable enough justification of social intolerance. The man whose view of the past and its cultural life is entirely bogus, whose contact with other people is an habitual, woolly-minded double-dealing, is

[4] Quoted in Robert Hewison, *In Anger* (London: Weidenfeld, 1981), 130.

[5] Kingsley Amis, *Lucky Jim* (Harmondsworth: Penguin, 1975), 125. Further references to the novel are indicated in the text.

[6] Humphrey Carpenter, 'The Angry Young Lesbian Fanciers', *Sunday Times*, 16 Apr. 2000, p. 10.

[7] Quoted in Eric Jacobs, *Kingsley Amis: A Biography* (London: Hodder and Stoughton 1995), 151.

easy enough to laugh at; when he controls your destiny, as Professor Welch does Jim Dixon's, then, Amis is suggesting, it is time to take the gloves off.... Jim Dixon is not only Welch's cultural enemy... but his political adversary.... At the time, Amis was a convinced supporter of the Labour Party.'[8] In *The Modern British Novel*, Malcolm Bradbury describes *Lucky Jim* as 'the exemplary Fifties novel. The story of Jim Dixon, the young history lecturer in a provincial university who is inwardly and comically at odds with the Bloomsburified academic, artistic and social culture of his elders, captured a powerful contemporary mood.'[9]

As a novelist, Amis most influenced David Lodge, who writes that the style of *Lucky Jim* 'introduced a distinctive new tone into English fiction. The style is scrupulously precise, but eschews traditional "elegance." It is educated but classless.... It owes something to the "ordinary language" philosophy that dominated Oxford when Amis was a student there.... It is a style continually challenged and qualified by its own honesty, full of unexpected reversals'—which satirically deconstruct clichés and stock responses. At the same time, Lodge suggests, *Lucky Jim* is 'a comic inversion' of Graham Greene's tragic *The Heart of the Matter*, reversing the Catholic emphasis on guilt and pity in Greene, Lewis, and Tolkien. Guilt and pity are the shackles that hold decent men bound to jobs they despise and women they do not love.[10]

To Jim Dixon, the sight of Christine, the elegant girl dating his boss's son, 'seemed an irresistible attack on his own habits, standards and ambitions. Something designed to put him in his place for good' (p. 39). But in addition to his anger and outrage, Jim is also a vulnerable hero, easily undermined and crippled by

---

[8] D. J. Taylor, *A Vain Conceit: British Fiction in the 1980s* (London: Bloomsbury, 1989), 46–7.

[9] Malcolm Bradbury, *The Modern British Novel* (Harmondsworth: Penguin, 1993), 320.

[10] David Lodge, 'Lucky Jim Revisited', in *The Practice of Writing* (Harmondsworth: Penguin, 1997), 86–7, which reprints Lodge's introduction to the Penguin Twentieth Century Classics edition of *Lucky Jim* (Harmondsworth: Penguin, 2000).

feelings of pity, guilt, and shame. He can't acknowledge to himself how shaken he is when Margaret hysterically calls him a 'shabby little provincial bore' (p. 158), although he feels vaguely that 'somewhere his path to Christine was blocked; it was all going to go wrong in some way he couldn't foresee' (p. 164). When he is deeply depressed, Jim self-medicates with alcohol. All of his laddish behaviours seem to be unconscious actings-out of his muffled depression, from his repertoire of hostile faces, to the wonderful scene where he burns, shaves, cuts, and hacks up the bedding at the Welches, as if he were burning down Brideshead, the very essence of the English country house. Much of the comic resolution of the book comes from his happy and successful growing-up—getting a decent job, finding a woman he can love, breaking away with a huge burst of laughter at the follies of the Welches and their dire progeny. Happiness is so unprecedented and unexpected that he has no ready-made facial expression for it: 'Dixon laughed too. He thought what a pity it was that all his faces were designed to express rage or loathing. Now that something had happened which really deserved a face, he'd none to celebrate it' (p. 250). This lad is not an angry young man at all, not an existential rebel or political revolutionary, but rather someone who would prefer to be happy, loved, and settled.

2. *Lucky John: Ladlit in the 1980s*

Kingsley Amis belonged to a transitional generation of British novelists who seemed to be inhabiting a minor and declining form, a traditional novel outclassed by its brawling and innovative American brothers. Playwrights were the literary stars and creative avant-garde of this generation, and Tom Stoppard recalls that to want to be a writer in Britain in the early 1960s was to want to be a playwright.[11] Even by the late 1970s, Bill Buford comments, 'there were only two young novelists whom

---

[11] Quoted in Christopher Bigsby, *Contemporary American Playwrights* (Cambridge: Cambridge University Press, 1999), 370.

anyone was making a fuss over: Ian McEwan and Martin Amis (I know this, because, editing the first issues of *Granta*, I had no young British authors to put in them).... It was easy, I recall Ian McEwan observing... to be a young celebrity writer at the end of the seventies, because there was no one else around. I remember the metaphor he used: the horizon was uncluttered.'[12]

But by the mid-1980s, with the publication of *Granta*'s first defiant list of the best young British novelists—including Salman Rushdie, Julian Barnes, Kazuo Ishiguro, and Graham Swift as well as Amis and McEwan—the horizon had become much more cluttered, almost to the point of gridlock. The revitalization of the British novel was both the result of new voices and new styles, and a resurgence of the spirit of the Lad—the displaced, disturbed, immature picaresque hero journeying to adult commitment.

Martin Amis's *Money* (1984) is both the most paradigmatic British novel of the fast-track greedy 1980s, and the most influential stylistically, technically, and thematically. Its lad anti-hero, John Self, is a director of TV commercials who gets tapped for what seems like a lucrative Hollywood movie deal—either 'Bad Money' or 'Good Money'—but is actually a sting operation and confidence trick—or, as Amis would say, a 'no-confidence trick' that is a metaphor for his life. On one level, the novel is a metafictional tour de force, in which Self gradually discovers that his life has been invaded, controlled, and shaped by a fiction writer named Martin Amis, and then fights to win back his independence. On a second level, it is, as its subtitle announces, 'a suicide note', both a drawn-out saga of self-destruction, and a meditation on suicidal despair that includes a peculiar suicide note in the actual text, purportedly written by John Self, but addressed to Amis's real first wife, Antonia. On a third level, it is a comic dystopian satire of London, New York, and Los Angeles

[12] Buford's comments come from the 'Best of Young British Novelists, 2', *Granta*, 43 (Spring 1993), 11.

which alludes to Oedipus and Othello, as well as Dickens, Dostoevsky, Nabokov, and Orwell.

John Self has all the lad attributes and class hatreds of Jim Dixon. Furiously anti-intellectual to a degree that makes Jim Dixon sound like F. R. Leavis, Self finds reading physically painful. According to Amis, 'he is consumed by consumerism...I also mean him to be stupefied by having watched too much television—his life is without sustenance of any kind—and that is why he is so fooled by everyone; he never knows what is going on. He has this lazy non-effort response which is wished on you by television—and by reading a shitty newspaper. Those are his two sources of information about the planet.'[13] Self's conflicts with his father and father-figures replay the anti-authoritarianism of Dixon as well.

And yet Self is intensely likeable. No critic can be harder on him than he is on himself. He longs for a full-body transplant in California, and loathes his own face: 'a face that can usually face them down, wide and grey, full of adolescent archeology and cheap food and junk money, the face of a fat snake, bearing all the signs of its sins.'[14] In a running gag about auto-eroticism, he identifies with his expensive, useless, perennially broken-down car, the Fiasco; and suffers the perpetual pain of toothache, headache, earache, hangover, and leg-over.

Above all, Self's narrative voice is an irresistible bombardment of inventive and hyperactive language. His description of LA is a miniature verbal wonder that ranges in its rhythms from Nabokov to Jagger:

California, land of my dreams and my longing.... In LA, you can't do anything unless you drive. Now I can't do anything unless I drink. And the drink-drive combination, it really isn't possible out there. If you so much as loosen your seatbelt or drop your ash or pick

[13] Quoted in John Haffenden (ed.), *Novelists in Interview* (London: Methuen, 1985), 5.

[14] Martin Amis, *Money* (Harmondsworth: Penguin, 1985), 9. Further references cited in the text.

your nose, then it's an Alcatraz autopsy with the questions asked
later. . . .

So what can a poor boy do? You come out of the hotel, the
Vraimont. Over boiling Watts the downtown skyline carries a
smear of God's green snot. You walk left, you walk right, you are a
bank rat on a busy river. This restaurant serves no drink, this one
serves no meat, this one serves no heterosexuals. You can get your
chimp shampooed, you can get your dick tattooed, twenty-four
hours, but can you get lunch? And should you see a sign on the far
side of the street flashing BEEF-BOOZE-NO STRINGS, then you can
forget it. The only way to get across the road is to be born there. (pp.
167–8)

Throughout the novel, Amis creates a superrealist but also surreal cityscape in which the hotels are all named for great writers
or great fictional characters, one of many categories of jokes and
allusions that electrify his prose.

Even funnier and more hyperbolic, but also dead accurate, is
the novel's Hollywood subplot, which echoes the theme of gen-
erational rivals in its description of the ageing male sex-symbol's
resentment of younger men. Lorne Guyland (Long Island, Lone
Guy-Land) is a withered old cowboy with delusions of eternal
testosterone, who insists on having three scenes of full nudity in
each of his films, and demands that the script be rewritten so that
he can outfight the fit young actor playing his screen 'son':

I want this whole scene in the nude, we're all nude, that's definite. I
won't sacrifice that, that idea. Now. . . . I'm fucking Butch, right?
And I mean really *fucking* her. The woman's in tears, right out of
control. She's hysterical, John. Then this young *actor* walks in—he's
nude too—for the showdown. And I spring out of bed, naked as I am,
and I just start to tear him to fucking pieces. I'm damn near killing
the guy when Butch, in the nude, starts shouting, 'Lorne! Lorne,
baby! Honey, what are you doing! Stop, sweetheart, please stop!'
And I realize I been—that the *animal* in me, because, John, it's a
terrible world we're living in, John, it's a really crazy, awful . . .
world. So Butch and Caduta lead me away. I'm damn near in tears

on account of what I've done to the guy. Then this young punk comes up behind me and hits me on the head with a car-tool. John? What do you say.' (pp. 110–11)

In fact, this apparently ludicrous and exaggerated scene is a precise description of a scene between Kirk Douglas, Harvey Keitel, and Farrah Fawcett in *Saturn 3*, Amis's only movie credit.

The themes that make *Money* the apotheosis of the Ladlit genre are its subtextual worries about marriage and paternity. Amis provided a gloss on some of these themes in his memoir, *Experience*. 'In 1983 I was finishing a novel, *Money*, which was narrated in the first person by a character called John Self. It would be a ferocious slander of Martin Amis (who was, incidentally, a minor character in the book) if I called *Money* autobiographical. It certainly wasn't the higher autobiography. But I see now that the story turned on my own preoccupations: it is about tiring of being single; it is about the fear that childlessness will condemn you to childishness.'[15] Indeed. Amis was married on the novel's publication day, and his son Louis was born four months later.

Overtly a rover and rogue, a fan of pornography and patron of prostitution, John Self is nonetheless agonizingly aware that at 35 he is getting to be a lonely, dirty old man. Self makes dirty jokes about the forthcoming marriage of Prince Charles and Lady Diana Spencer, but when he watches the Royal Wedding on television with his movie rewrite-man, one Martin Amis, he is overcome with a sentimental sadness that is obviously about himself:

Princess Diana . . . is nineteen years old, just starting out. There she goes now, gathering herself into the carriage while the horses stamp. All England dances. I looked at Martin again and—I swear, I promise—I saw a grey tear glint in those heavy eyes. Love and marriage. The horses ticking down the long slide.

After a while he dropped a toilet roll on to my lap.

---

[15] Martin Amis, *Experience* (New York: Miramax, 2000), 177.

'Do you want a cup of tea?' I heard him ask? 'Or an aspirin? Or a
Serafim? Don't be embarrassed. It was very moving in its way. That's
right, have a good big blow. You'll feel better for it.' (p. 263)

In an interview with John Haffenden, Amis explained that 'the
conjunction of the Royal Wedding and the riots in 1981 seemed
a natural timetable for the book'.[16] But the theme of the wedding is more important to the emotional subtext of *Money* than
it first may seem; it hints at John Self's suppressed identification
with fairy-tale romance.

Many feminist critics have condemned *Money*'s sexism. Laura
A. Doan, for example, argues that 'Self, like the pornography he
devours, denies woman personhood, placing her in the ultimate
state of disempowerment and disembodiment. In fact, Self's
dependence on pornography suggests the crucial nexus between
the woman as pornographic image and his own objectification
of women.'[17] But, in my view, Self needs pornography primarily
as a sex aid, and prefers the handjob to most other forms of
eroticism. For him, the handjob (Amis could have used the
British and Larkinesque term 'wank', but clearly prefers the
American term) is the ideal form of lad eroticism, combining
the dehumanization of sex with a form of work.

Self's ledger of his handjobs (or aborted handjobs) emphasizes
their desperate element of sexual bankruptcy and effort: 'I had
three handjobs yesterday. None was easy. Sometimes you really
have to buckle down to it, as you do with all forms of exercise.'
Sometimes they are almost painful: 'catastrophic, neck-searing'.
He tries to analyse them himself: 'I've got a hunch about these
handjobs, or about their exhausting frequency. I need that
human touch...At least, handjobs are free, complimentary,
with no cash attaching.' The free handjob, of course, is the one
he gives himself. When he tries to buy one, the price goes way,
way up: 'A hundred and seventy-five dollars? For a *handjob*?' he

[16] Quoted in Haffenden (ed.), *Novelists in Interview*, 3.
[17] Laura Doan, in Nicholas Tredell (ed.), *The Fiction of Martin Amis: A Reader's
Guide to Essential Criticism* (Cambridge: Icon Books, 2000), 77.

protests. But that's the street price, and in addition, 'I had to rack my brains to remember a worse one.... Between ourselves, it was one of those handjobs where you go straight from limpness to orgasm, skipping the hard-on stage. I think she must have activated some secret glandular gimmick, to wrap it up quickly.' Most unsatisfactory. The solitary, or regular handjob, is also unsatisfactory, but 'they don't cost five bucks a second. Overheads are generally low' (pp. 103–4). But when Self does meet a woman he loves and admires—the American Martina Twain— he is impotent: 'I've yet to, I haven't, I don't seem to be able to ... There. You've said it for me. They're very difficult. They're not at all easy. *That's* why they're called *hard-ons*' (p. 325).

Self's pathetic sexuality is a symptom of his overwhelming sense of loss, which surfaces intermittently in the midst of his braggadocio. 'You're receding,' a girl tells him when he goes for a haircut. 'We are all receding,' he thinks, 'waving or beckoning or just kissing our fingertips, we are all fading, shrinking, paling. Life is all losing, we are all losing, losing mother, father, youth, hair, looks, teeth, friends, lovers, shape, reason, life. We are losing, losing, losing. Take life away. It's too hard, too difficult. ... Life is so *hard*. Oh, so, it is so—dah. Mah, mother, muh—you never told me, no one said' (p. 273).

This elegiac stammering outburst of sorrow hints at the sources of Self's loss and pain—his mother's death:

I hardly remember her. I remember her fingers: on cold mornings I would stand waiting at her bedside, and she would extend her warm hand from beneath the blankets to fasten the cuff buttons of my shirt. Her face was ... I don't remember. Her face always stayed beneath the covers. Vera was always poorly. I only remember her fingers, her fingerprints, her blemished nails and the mark of the white button on the contours of the tip. Presumably I couldn't fasten my own cuffs. I seemed to need the human touch.' (p. 206)

The memory explains Self's sore, chewed fingernails, so tender that each shirt button feels 'like a drop of molten solder' (p. 15), and a dial phone is a major obstacle. He gnaws his nails to the quick, he becomes addicted to the handjob and to prostitution in search of the lost mother's warm hand. 'I need a human touch. Soon I'll just have to go out and buy one' (p. 67).

Selina Street, Self's 'sack-artist' mistress, makes him an offer: 'Face the facts. Grow up, for God's sake. I'd settle for you. Settle for me. I'd look after you. Look after me. Give me children. Marry me. Make a commitment. Make me feel I have some kind of base to my life' (p. 161). But Self is unable to respond. Only when he is stripped of all his money, illusions, friends, work, can he acknowledge his need for a human touch that comes freely from another person, from a mother figure, Georgina, the first woman he does not automatically reduce to body parts: 'Georgina has got big ... She's got a big heart, that Georgina' (p. 387).

John Self's fall and regeneration are presented in *Money* as comedy rather than tragedy. In an interview with Will Self, Amis decribes the pace of his writing style, and Self comments, 'That's like being a stand-up comic, isn't it? The timing of each exchange suggesting the timing for the next?'[18] For Amis, comedy is the most appropriate and inclusive form of contemporary fiction, the genre of our time. 'Look at my father's last two mainstream novels,' he told John Haffenden. 'They're still in the shape of comedy, but they take on some very sensitive, painful matters.'[19]

3. Funny Jim: Ladlit in the 1990s

While Amis's generation saw themselves as stand-up novelists, the Ladlit writers of the 1990s were often stand-up comedians moonlighting as novelists: Stephen Fry, Ardal O'Hanlon, David Baddiel, Alexei Sayle, Ben Elton. They were based in the manic Lad culture of the decade, typified by the magazines *Viz*,

[18] Will Self, 'An Interview with Martin Amis', *Mississippi Review*, 21/3 (Summer 1993), 147.
[19] Haffenden (ed), *Novelists in Interview*, 6, 7.

Loaded, FHM, Maxim, GQ, Esquire, by cult DJs like Chris Evans, and by the hit TV show *Men Behaving Badly.* The protagonist of these books is the young man on the make, mindlessly pursuing booze, babes, and football. His ineptitude, drunkenness, and compulsive materialism were part of his charm.

But beneath the crass surface, these stories were also about male coming-of-age, the ability to form a marriage and accept parenthood. Lads of the 1990s were no longer able to blame the class and caste system or the ludicrous narcissism of their fathers for their difficulties. All their problems are their own fault. According to Rob in Nick Hornby's *High Fidelity* (1997), 'Here's how not to plan a career: a) split up with girlfriend; b) junk college; c) go to work in record shop; d) stay in record shop for rest of life.' At the same time, they are the most introspective of all the lads, constantly self-monitoring and monologic. Rob sums up his life: 'I'm here in this stupid little flat, on my own, and I'm thirty-five years old, and I own a tiny, failing business, and my friends don't seem to be friends at all but people whose phone numbers I haven't lost.'[20] Matt Beckford, in Mike Gayle's *Turning Thirty* (2000), imitates Rob by looking up all his old girlfriends in an attempt to plot the trajectory of his failure.

As the marriage of Princess Diana was a motif for Martin Amis in the 1980s, so Diana's death was an occasion for Ladlit in the 1990s. In Helen Fielding's 'Bridget Jones' column, still running in the *Independent* in the summer of 1997, Bridget takes a copy of *Vogue*, Milk Tray chocolates, and a packet of Silk Cut cigarettes to Kensington Palace as memorial tributes to Princess Diana. She writes in her diary: 'Really she was the patron saint of Singleton women because she started off like the archetypal fairytale doing what we all thought we were supposed to do, i.e. marry a handsome Prince and she was honest enough to say that life is not like that. Also, it made you feel that if someone so beautiful and gorgeous could be treated like shit by stupid men

---

[20] Nick Hornby, *High Fidelity* (1995; repr. London: Penguin, 2000), 19, 58. Further references cited in the text.

and feel unloved and lonely then it wasn't because you were rubbish if it happened to you. And she kept re-inventing herself and sorting out her problems. She was always just trying so hard like modern women.'[21]

Diana's death appears as a motif in David Baddiel's second novel, *Whatever Love Means* (1999), which takes its ironic title from Prince Charles's notorious disclaimer about his feelings in a 1981 TV interview on the eve of his engagement. The novel begins on the day of Diana's death, with a statement meant to shock: 'Vic fucked her first the day Diana died.' Baddiel's laddish protagonist has hay fever and persuades the woman that his reddened eyes are tokens of his tears of grief; she goes to bed with him believing that he is a sensitive New Man who shares her emotions. In fact, Vic scores while England mourns. 'At first Vic thought he was just exploiting one individual's grief, but then he realized he was exploiting the whole nation's . . . he felt like each day was a bank holiday.'[22] Despite this hard-boiled opener, *Whatever Love Means* is a meticulously plotted medical mystery story, in which Vic's heartlessness is thoroughly punished and reproved, and in which his hay fever too turns out to be a significant clue. Baddiel makes serious use of the public spectacle of Diana's death to analyse the cheapening of human relationships in a culture where women's love and grief are regularly exploited.

Similarly, Tim Lott's *White City Blue* (1999) ends with the hero's meditation on his wedding: 'I have a reason [not to marry], because marriage is a leap in the dark, against the odds. . . . Is my freedom gone? What the fuck is that? A little drop of life between childhood and marriage. It's not all that it's cracked up to be. Marriage is what happens when you learn that life is bigger than you.'[23] Hornby's Rob concludes: 'It's only just beginning to

---

[21] See 'Bridget Jones's Diary', in Brian MacArthur (ed.), *Requiem: Diana, Princess of Wales* (London: Pavilion, 1997), 24.

[22] David Baddiel, *Whatever Love Means* (1999; repr. London: Abacus, 1999), 5, 11.

[23] Lott, *White City Blue*, 275–7.

occur to me that its important to have something going on somewhere, at work or at home, otherwise you just cling on. ... You need as much ballast as possible to stop you from floating away; you need people around you, things going on, otherwise life is like some film where the money ran out, and there are no sets or locations, or supporting actors, and it's just one bloke on his own, staring into the camera with nothing to do and nobody to speak to, and who'd believe this character then?' (p. 59) Michael Adams, in John O'Farrell's *The Best a Man Can Get* (2000), gives up his fantasies about the single life and accepts his responsibilities as husband and father: 'Everyone expected me to say that looking after my children all day was the most wonderfully fulfilling thing I'd ever done. Well, it was certainly the hardest thing I'd ever done, but nothing changed my opinion that small children are boring. But now I understand that having kids and raising a family was hard, because anything really worth achieving is hard.'[24]

4. *The End of Ladlit?*

In an interview shortly after the Los Angeles conference at which I presented this essay, Martin Amis said: 'What is this lads stuff? There was a lecture at this conference called Lads' Lit, and it traced the line between Kingsley and me and Nick Hornby, but I don't think even Nick Hornby is laddish really. I mean lads don't write novels. They're down the pub. Being a writer means that you spend at least half your life by yourself; that's the defining thing. A lad is not a lad by himself, he's only a lad when he's with the lads. You can't walk around in your own house being a lad, can you? It's a communal activity.'[25]

---

[24] John O'Farrell, *The Best a Man Can Get* (2000; repr. London: Black Swan, 2001), 300–1.
[25] Interview with Alan Rusbridger, 'All about my Father', *Guardian*, 8 May 2000.

Of course, the authors of Ladlit novels are not lads themselves; their similarity lies in the themes and techniques of their fiction. But by 2001, the genre was showing signs of decline, perhaps because of authorial self-consciousness about being part of a trend, and perhaps because the formula itself had become named and familiar; there was even a Lad Lit category on amazon.com. 'For a year or two', wrote Rachel Campbell-Johnston in *The Times*, 'lad lit was as fashionable as the era it was set in. Nick Hornby, Tony Parsons, and Tim Lott turned out wise-cracking nostalgia that was snapped up by blokes. But then too many people started to copy them. The genre that they generated has long since gone stale.'[26] Some of the novelists themselves had moved on to darker plots; Nick Hornby's pessimistic fable, *How to Be Good* (2001), disappointed readers looking for more humorous studies of the male psyche. In *Little Green Man* (2001), the poet Simon Armitage attempted a postmodern twist on the genre, to critics' dismay: 'If you're going to write a lads' novel, you really have to go for it.'[27]

At the same time, ageing male novelists including Saul Bellow, John Updike, and Philip Roth were recreating some of the themes of classic Ladlit in stories about elderly roués, still dodging commitment and pursuing gratification—the Viagra Monologues. As traditional distinctions of maturity and coming-of-age collapsed, Ladlit too needed to find new stories to tell.

[26] Interview with Rachel Campbell-Johnston, *The Times*, July 25, 2001.

[27] Phil Daoust, 'Blank Prose', rev. of Simon Armitage, *Little Green Man*, in *Guardian*, 11 Aug. 2001.

6

Enigmas and Homelands

MICHAEL WOOD

> Departure and arrival, both good themes for the novelist,
> were slower then.
>
> Larry McMurtry, *Walter Benjamin at the Dairy Queen*

V. S. Naipaul and Salman Rushdie are often taken as opposites, the terms of a convenient contrast. They are seen as representing different generations, conservatism and radicalism, realism and fantasy, the old-style colonial subject and the new-style global citizen. This chapter is an attempt to explore and diminish this contrast, but there are several questions we need to ask before we can start.

How did we arrive, for instance, at the initial pairing, the presumed common ground which will make the contrast plausible? What do Naipaul and Rushdie have in common, if we suspend for a moment our received ideas about colonial and post-colonial writing? They are both Indian, but what does 'India' mean here? What would a disbelieving Muslim born in Bombay have in common with a disbelieving Hindu born in Trinidad? Their disbelief, perhaps, but that scarcely seems enough to bring them together. They both live in England, but so do several million other people. To start from their Indianness and find a contrast begins to look not only alarmingly easy, but idle. As if we were to take any two dissimilar figures or conditions, and patiently show they were just as dissimilar as we thought, if not more so. As if we were to compare the seventeenth and the twentieth centuries not on the basis of any perceived similarity, but because they are both centuries. Fortunately for me—and for this chapter—there are good reasons for comparing the seventeenth and the twentieth centuries, and for comparing Naipaul and Rushdie. But the reasons, in the case of Naipaul and Rushdie, are not obvious, and the contrast between them dims a little when we look at these reasons. I want to offer a reading of Naipaul's *The Enigma of Arrival* (1987) in the light of certain of Rushdie's ideas about home and the imagination and literature. The writers don't become identical in such a context, but they do become different in different ways, and taken together they have a great deal to say to us about the details of living in the world of empire and its aftermath.

I begin with two fables, the first taken from Rushdie, the second from Naipaul. 'Imagine this', Rushdie instructs us.

You wake up one morning and find yourself in a large, rambling house. As you wander through it you realize it is so enormous that you will never know it all. In the house are people you know, family members, friends, lovers, colleagues; also many strangers. The house is full of activity: conflicts and seductions, celebrations and wakes. At some point you understand that there is no way out. You find that you can accept this. The house is not what you'd have chosen, it's in fairly bad condition, the corridors are often full of bullies, but it will have to do. Then one day you enter an unimportant-looking little room. The room is empty, but there are voices in it, voices that seem to be whispering just to you. You recognize some of the voices, others are completely unknown to you. The voices are talking about the house, about everyone in it, about everything that is happening and has happened and should happen.

Some of them speak exclusively in obscenities. Some are bitchy. Some are loving. Some are funny. Some are sad. The most interesting voices are all these things at once. You begin to go to the room more and more often. Slowly you learn that most of the people in the house use such rooms sometimes . . .

Now imagine that you wake up one morning and you are still in the large house, but all the voice-rooms have disappeared. It is as if they have been wiped out. There is nowhere in the whole house where you can go to hear voices talking about everything in every possible way . . . Now you remember: there is no way out of this house.[1]

In *The Enigma of Arrival*, Naipaul pictures this:

A wharf; in the background, beyond walls and gateways (like cut-outs), there is the top of the mast of an antique vessel; on an otherwise deserted street in the foreground there are two figures, both muffled, one perhaps the person who has arrived, the other perhaps a native of the port. The scene is one of desolation and mystery: it speaks of the mystery of arrival.

And Naipaul, or the Naipaul-like writer in the novel, imagines a story which starts in this port:

My narrator would . . . arrive—for a reason I had yet to work out—at that classical port with the walls and the gateways like cut-outs. He would walk past that muffled figure on the quayside. He would move from that silence and desolation, that blankness, to a gateway or door. He would enter there and be swallowed by the life and noise of a crowded city (I imagined something like an Indian bazaar scene). The mission he had come on—family business, study, religious initiation—would give him encounters and adventures. He would enter interiors, of houses and temples. Gradually there would come to him a feeling that he was getting nowhere; he would lose his sense of mission; he would begin to know only that he was lost. His feeling of adventure would give way to panic. He would want to escape, to get back to the quayside and his ship. But he wouldn't know how. I imagined some religious ritual in which led on by kindly people, he would unwittingly take part and find himself the intended victim. At the moment of crisis he would come upon a door, open it, and find

---

[1] Salman Rushdie, *Imaginary Homelands* (London: Granta Books, 1991), 428. Further references to this book are indicated within the text.

himself back on the quayside of arrival. He has been saved; the world
is as he remembered it. Only one thing is missing now. Above the cut-
out walls and buildings there is no mast, no sail. The antique ship has
gone. The traveller has lived out his life.[2]

Certain resemblances between these two scenes/stories are obvious. There are encounters with other people. There is fear. There
is loss. There is no escape. There is an acceptance of limits
deemed to be unavoidable. Both scenes seem intensely allegorical, cry out for translation into some more worldly, more historical context, something with dates and names and colours
and passions. More precisely, both seem consciously constructed to exclude such a context, to leave it behind, and it is
the sense of that exclusion, that leaving behind which so tempts
us to put the world and the names back.

But there are differences too. A house is not a port. What's
more, the house has elements of a homeland. It contains
strangers, and we are told that we shall never know it all. But
our family, friends, and lovers are also there, whereas the port
city seems to contain nothing the traveller is familiar with. The
house is made bearable by voices and language; the port city
provides a mission and the threat of being sacrificed. There is a
pathos and an irony, a compacted drama, in the port which is not
present in the house. In the house we know there is no way out,
and need only remember the fact if we feel it is slipping away
from us. In the port the sail seems to promise escape, and there
would be no reason to think a port wouldn't have departures as
well as arrivals. But this one has only arrivals. Time has passed
too, since we are told not only that the ship has gone, but that the
traveller has lived out his life. He didn't come to stay, but he has
stayed. That's all there is—or this is all there was.

The largest difference, however, is the simplest: the way we get
into the scene, the putting of the person into the inescapable
place. 'You wake up one morning.' 'My narrator would arrive.'

[2] V. S. Naipaul, *The Enigma of Arrival* (London: Viking, 1987), 91–2. Further
references to this work are indicated within the text.

If we woke up there, we were already there, there was no travel, no arrival. If we arrived, we came from somewhere else. There is an obvious difference between being somewhere and getting somewhere, but the obvious difference may, and in these cases I think does, hide a deeper one: between presenting the world you live in as what there is, a world without a past, and presenting the world you live in as a new country, a place you came to. 'You wake up one morning' might mean you arrived one day but are choosing to forget or underplay the moment and the fact of arrival. Of course it might also just mean you woke up one morning. *The Enigma of Arrival* has a fabulous, casual model for this double mode of interpretation. One of Naipaul's characters is fond of the word 'arrogant', and we are told that it 'was primarily [his] version of "ignorant"; but it also had the meaning of "arrogant"' (p. 217). 'Also had'; the first shall be last.

Let me put a bit of historical flesh on the first of these allegories—Naipaul himself, as we shall see, provides plenty of history for the second. The house with the voice-rooms appears in a lecture Rushdie gave—or rather didn't give, Harold Pinter read it for him—at the Institute of Contemporary Arts in London in February 1990, a year or so after the *fatwa*. In this lecture Rushdie speaks favourably of 'secular fundamentalism' (p. 418), and 'a secular definition of transcendence' (p. 420). 'What I mean by transcendence is that flight of the human spirit outside the confines of its material, physical existence which all of us, secular or religious, experience on at least a few occasions' (p. 421). But there is no transcendence in the rambling house, not even the flicker of it. Something has happened in the course of the lecture. The plea for our non-rational needs has turned into a plea for unbullied speech. The house is the world, it's not in good shape, and the bullies seem to be a large part of it. What makes the place bearable is not the possibility of flight or even change, but the chance of hearing voices 'talking about everything in every possible way'. 'Literature', Rushdie says immediately after inviting us to imagine the house of his fable, and quoting the fable itself, 'is the one place in any society where, within the secrecy of our heads, we can hear *voices talking about everything in every possible way*' (p. 429, Rushdie's italics). This is a modest claim, but modest as it is, there are of course plenty of societies where it is not met. Where the secrecy of heads is not secret; or if it is secret, it is washed out, the secrecy of emptiness.

As I suggested earlier, Rushdie treats this place as home, we are not in exile there. This is because there is, for Rushdie, in a special sense of the familiar phrase, no place like home. There just is no such place as home. In his marvellous little book on *The Wizard of Oz* (1992), he is both scathing and cheerful about the very notion. 'The least convincing idea in the film', Rushdie says. 'It's one thing for Dorothy to want to get home, quite another that she can only do so by eulogizing the ideal state which Kansas so obviously is not.'[3] Not that Kansas, in the film, is unideal. It isn't anything. 'Dorothy looks extremely well-fed, and she is not really, but *unreally* poor' (p. 20, Rushdie's italics). 'If Oz is *nowhere*, then the studio setting of the Kansas scenes suggests that *so is Kansas*' (p. 20, Rushdie's italics). The film is not about getting home but about getting away, 'the human dream of *leaving*, a dream at least as powerful as its countervailing dream of roots'.

[A]s the music swells and that big, clean voice flies into the anguished longings of the song, can anyone doubt which message is the stronger? In its most potent emotional moment, this is unarguably a film about the joys of going away, of leaving the greyness and entering the colour...

'Over the Rainbow' is, or ought to be, the anthem of all the world's migrants... It is a celebration of Escape, a grand paean to the Uprooted Self, a hymn—*the* hymn— to Elsewhere. (p. 23, Rushdie's italics)

[3] Salman Rushdie, *The Wizard of Oz* (London: BFI Publishing, 1992), 14. Further references to this work are indicated within the text.

In this dream, to borrow Naipaul's imagery for a moment, there are only departures, no arrivals and no enigmas. More precisely, only visions of departure, 'anguished longings', as Rushdie says. 'Do you suppose there is such a place, Toto? There must be' (p. 23). Toto doesn't answer, but perhaps he wasn't really being asked.

Rushdie reminds us that Dorothy kept going back to Oz, not only in other movies, but thirteen more Frank L. Baum books. In the sixth book, she takes Auntie Em and Uncle Henry along with her, and becomes a princess.

So Oz finally *became* home; the imagined world became the actual world, as it does for us all, because the truth is that once we have left our childhood places and started out to make up our lives, armed only with what we have and are, we understand that the real secret . . . is not that 'there's no place like home', but rather that there is no longer any such place *as* home: except, of course, for the home we make, or the homes that are made for us, in Oz: which is anywhere, and everywhere, except the place from which we began. (p. 57)

'The truth is' that there is probably more longing than truth in this lyrical paragraph. Or several longings. First, does the imagined world become the actual world for us all? Proust and Wordsworth and many others have thought the imagined world pales before the repeated disappointments of the actual world. Perhaps that is what Rushdie means, but it doesn't seem so. He seems to mean that the imagination takes over. And elsewhere in his work, of course, he does attribute extraordinary powers to the imagination, even in failure. In *Midnight's Children*, India is 'the dream we all shared', and the dream fails because 'in a kind of collective failure of imagination, we learned that we simply could not think our way out of our pasts.'[4] If the imagination had not failed, the implication is, reality would have yielded, given in to the dream. In *Shame* (1983), Pakistan 'may be

---

[4] Salman Rushdie, *Midnight's Children* (New York: Penguin, 1991), 136–7.

described as a failure of the dreaming mind . . . Perhaps the place was just *insufficiently imagined*'.[5]

Second, everyone who survives childhood leaves it behind, but many people don't leave their childhood places: they just get stuck there, and live miserably or happily ever after. Third, how many people have the chance to make up their lives? And finally, what about the implications of the sorrowful and revealing last clause, 'except the place from which we began'. It's not just that there's no place like home. Home can be any place *except* home. Home is the one place it can't be. This is the real point, presumably, of the hymn to Elsewhere. We don't want to leave home, we just want to leave. Home is what we call the place we left; it is what allows us to call our movement a leaving, a departure. Beneath the invented home we leave and the imagined home we find, if we are lucky, there doesn't seem to be too much solid ground. No wonder Rushdie says, in his review of *The Enigma of Arrival*, almost arriving at his own later title, that 'the immigrant must invent the earth beneath his feet' (*Imaginary Homelands*, 149). And the earth that used to be beneath his or her feet too, so that memory itself becomes a kind of novel.

The Enigma of Arrival doesn't suggest that Rushdie is wrong about any of this, only too cheerful, and perhaps too impatient of the interest and sheer intricacy and pain of these movements between lost homes and invented homes or what takes the place of home. And here we can, I think, in the light of the questions I have just asked about the paragraph from Rushdie's book on *The Wizard of Oz*, list some real similarities between the two writers. Both have not only literally left their childhood places but lived substantially in imagined worlds—fictional worlds closely linked to the half-invented worlds they actually inhabit. They have to a considerable extent made up their lives— although a sudden and terrible portion of Rushdie's life was made up for him by others. And they certainly share the double perception that home, in one sense, can only be the place we start from, and that the place we start from, in another sense, can't continue to be home. These things are not true, I would guess, of most writers, or most exiles, or most Indians, or most people who live in England.

Consider these sentences from *The Enigma of Arrival*. The Naipaul-like narrator is talking about his rented cottage in Wiltshire and its surroundings.

> The beauty of the place, the great love I had grown to feel for it, greater than for any other place I had known, had kept me there too long. My health had suffered. But I couldn't say then, and can't say now, that I minded. There is some kind of exchange always. For me, for the writer's gift and freedom, the labour and disappointments of the writing life, and the being away from my home; for that loss, for having no place of my own, this gift of the second life in Wiltshire, the second, happier childhood as it were, the second arrival (but with an adult's perception) at a knowledge of natural things, together with the fulfilment of the child's dream of the safe house in the wood. But there was the cold of the cottage, and the damp and the mist of the glorious river bank; and the illnesses that came to people who have developed or inherited weak lungs. (pp. 83–4)

Rushdie comments on the tremendous sadness of Naipaul's book, and also makes one of those mistakes which enact a real critical insight. He says 'there is one word I can find nowhere in the text of *The Enigma of Arrival*. That word is "love"' (*Imaginary Homelands*, 151). It's an accident of quotation that makes the word appear in the first line of the passage quoted, and of course the quotation does broadly confirm Rushdie's sense of things, even as it proves the detail wrong. The only love here is love for a place, and that place is not home. When Naipaul writes 'being away from my home' here, and writes of 'that loss', he means Trinidad and the loss of Trinidad. He left home to become a writer, and, arriving in England in 1950, took part without knowing it at the time in what he now calls a 'great movement of peoples', 'a movement and a mixing greater than

the peopling of the United States, which was essentially a movement of Europeans to the New World' (p. 130). Not any more,
but let that pass. Naipaul finds love, safety, knowledge, even
happiness in England, but at his second arrival, not at his first; at
his arrival from Gloucester and British Columbia, not from
Trinidad; from disappointment and solitude and the first feelings of cold and illness, not from childhood and family. But he
finds disease too, and he doesn't call this loved place home, even
though he is willing to give it all the attributes of home ('second
life', 'second childhood', 'child's dream').

On the last page of his book Naipaul calls home 'a fantasy'
(p. 318), and it is still Trinidad he is thinking of, which he says
has become 'almost an imaginary place' (p. 311). There is a
divergence between Naipaul and Rushdie here, and a crucial
one—but it looks rather slight. Rushdie is telling us that we can
make a home anywhere except home—anywhere in Oz, nowhere in Kansas. The proposition, as I've suggested, seems
bleaker in the end than it's probably meant to be. Naipaul,
surprisingly, is more optimistic, but, unsurprisingly, more cau-
tious. He is telling us that we can find a loved place away from
home, a place we will love better than home, a second, better
childhood; but it would be a mistake to call it home—not only
because there is only one home, the place we started from, but
because that starting place has, necessarily, vanished or become
fantastic, even as a point of comparison. That was how, for
Naipaul, it came, irremediably, to be home.

The first place, the place we started from, vanishes three times
in *The Enigma of Arrival*. Once materially, historically, because
Naipaul leaves and never goes back except to visit. Second,
again materially and historically, because the place itself is subject to change, whether he leaves it or not. The most lyrical
moments in *The Enigma of Arrival* evoke not the Wiltshire
Naipaul has come to love—*that* appears in prickly, patient,
and haunting, but not lyrical prose—but the Trinidad that is
no more. That he, individually, can't go back in space is one

thing. That they, the Trinidadians, can't go back in time is another.

None of the Indian villages were like villages I had known. No narrow roads; no dark, overhanging trees; no huts; no earth yards with hibiscus hedges; no ceremonial lighting of lamps, no play of shadows on the wall; no cooking of food in half-walled verandahs, no leaping firelight; no flowers along gutters or ditches where frogs croaked the night away...We had made ourselves anew...we couldn't go back. There was no antique ship now to take us back. We had come out of the nightmare; and there was nowhere else to go. (pp. 316–317)

Earlier in the book the antique ship had gone from London, cutting off all chance of departure from the world city, the metropolis. Now it's gone from Trinidad, stranding the migrant Indians forever in their place of migration.

And it is because of this double vanishing of a place called home that Naipaul courts a third vanishing, and wants to find what he calls a philosophy to cope with it. He does this, within the book, in carefully mapped stages: through a love of decay which turns into an embrace of flux; an embrace of flux which turns into unmanageable disarray. I need to trace these stages more slowly.

Rob Nixon writes, very shrewdly, of Naipaul's 'eye for ruin'.[6] Ruin is the romantic form of change, its helpless remains. And decay is ruin in process. 'Already I lived with the idea of decay,' Naipaul writes. 'I had always lived with this idea. It was like my curse: the idea, which I had had even as a child in Trinidad, that I had come into a world past its peak' (p. 26). 'Even as a child in Trinidad' makes the mythology very clear: lateness is all. But then Naipaul in England tries to shake off the mythology, although he still feels its attraction. 'To see the possibility, the certainty, of ruin, even at the moment of creation: it was my

---

[6] Rob Nixon, *London Calling: V. S. Naipaul, Postcolonial Mandarin* (Oxford: Oxford University Press, 1992), 173

temperament' (p. 52). Well, this ratchets the mythology up a notch or two. The world was past its peak as soon as it was made—it was made for that purpose, to *be* past its peak. At one point Naipaul tries to historicize the myth, feeling that arriving in England in 1950 he 'had come too late to find the England, the heart of empire, which (like a provincial, from a far corner of the empire) I had created in my fantasy' (p. 120). But by the end of the sentence the myth has repelled history. How could one arrive too late for a fantasy? Or how could one *not* arrive too late, if the fantasy is all about lateness? 'Like a provincial' is good too. Like a provincial because he is one. But only 'like' one because a little bit of disavowal is taking place. At one point Naipaul writes sarcastically of his 'half-English half-education' (p. 221). But then by the same token he would be only half-provincial and half-uneducated—only half-barbarian, to borrow the term he uses elsewhere.

Later in *The Enigma of Arrival* Naipaul says he 'quickly shed' the idea of decay, swapped it for the idea of flux, 'learned to dismiss this easy cause of so much human grief' (p. 190). He understands that there is something implicitly idealizing about the idea of decay, that it must always, at least in this context or in this mind, create a past or absent perfection which is now spoiled. But of course the idea of flux is just as abstract and easy as the idea of decay, as long as you are entertaining it as an idea, using it to hold at bay not just change but everything unmanageable about the world, what stubbornly remains as well as what irreversibly goes. Perceiving this finally Naipaul says, 'philosophy failed me now' (p. 301). What does he have in place of philosophy? He has the novel he is writing. That is, not another strategy of interpretation or displacement, but what he has when all the strategies are gone: the knowledge that even predicted, mythologized endings cause pain, that the myth served only against the idea of pain, not against the thing itself. The novel doesn't just suffer this insight, of course. It displays it. But it also displays the failure of all theoretical consolations. 'Man is in

love and loves what vanishes', Yeats said.[7] Naipaul describes a
life of attempted avoidance of such love, and a final submission
to it. What vanishes is home; and also everything we put in its
place.

But is *The Enigma of Arrival* a novel? Its subtitle is 'A novel in
five sections', but it is usually thought of as, in Rob Nixon's
phrase, 'a lightly fictionalized autobiography'.[8] Is it possible to
fictionalize lightly? Perhaps it is. I'm inclined to believe fictionalizing is like flying: you're either doing it or you're not. And of
course what Naipaul has done in *The Enigma of Arrival* is rather
different from what we ordinarily take fictionalizing to mean.
He has both transcribed his life and edited it. Leaving Trinidad
for the first time, staying overnight in a New York hotel, the
young Naipaul, hungry and not knowing how to ask for food at
a late hour, eats a roast chicken he has brought with him from
home. 'But I had no knife, no fork, no plate ... I ate over the
waste-paper basket, aware as I did so of the smell, the oil, the
excess at the end of a long day' (p. 105). In a letter to his sister
Kamla, written immediately after his arrival in London, he
describes exactly the same experience. He doesn't mention the
lack of a knife and fork and plate, but that worry doesn't sound
like fiction.

At the same time, much is left out of this account of a writer's
life, which concentrates, as Naipaul says, on 'the writer's journey, the writer defined by his writing discoveries, his ways of
seeing, rather than by his personal adventures' (p. 309). Thus the
writer in this book appears not to have any affective life what-
soever, apart from his rather morbid interest in trees and plants,
and disused farm machinery. He is interested in the Wiltshire
locals, but only in a cagey and self-absorbed way: they look like
projections of pieces of his own anxiety, and are sometimes
openly said to be so. He mentions Robert Silvers, the editor of

---

[7] W. B. Yeats, 'Nineteen Hundred and Nineteen', *Collected Poems*, ed. Richard
J. Finneran (London: Macmillan, 1989), 208.
[8] *London Calling*, 161.

the *New York Review of Books*, but he doesn't mention his wife, Patricia. Only one tiny slip, if it is a slip, gives that particular game away. He writes of 'my room' (p. 196) in the cottage where he lives, apparently on his own. If he really lived on his own, all the rooms would be his.

More important, though, there are readable silences in the book, silences we are not meant to miss. It ends with an account of a ceremony following on the death and cremation of Naipaul's sister, Sati, born in 1934. She died in 1984, the year the book itself marks for the beginning of its writing: 'October 1984–April 1986' (p. 318). Shiva, Naipaul's brother, arrived in Trinidad just after the cremation, and left again soon after V. S. Naipaul arrived. He vanishes from the book with these words, and is never mentioned again: 'Soon an aeroplane took him back to London' (p. 312). Where he died in 1985, also during the writing of *The Enigma of Arrival*. We know this without going outside the book, since it is dedicated to Shiva Naipaul, and gives the dates and places of his birth and death.

> In loving memory
> of my brother
> SHIVA NAIPAUL
> 25 February 1945, Port of Spain
> 13 August 1985, London

Departures and arrivals. Sati and Shiva. The novel is framed by two perfectly non-fictional deaths.

Nevertheless, I think it does mean something to call the book a novel. We usually think of fiction as a matter of truth or lies, an alternative to fact, but there is the sense of fiction as hypothesis. In this light, even an author's actual opinions look more speculative, more discussable, more revealing, if they are given to a fictional character. When Roland Barthes wrote, inside the front cover of *Roland Barthes par lui-même*, 'Tout ceci doit être considéré comme dit par un personnage de roman',[9] he was, I think, signalling something similar. Not a difference in the truth status of what he was saying, but a difference in the kind of speech this was. Insults, for example, can be true or false but they are not philosophically interesting unless they are fictional: otherwise we are too busy just giving them and receiving them. Ideas and opinions are like this too. Nietzsche famously said there are no facts, only interpretations. Well, what he actually said was 'Against positivism, which insists on the phenomenon that there are only facts, I would say: no, facts are just what there are not, there are only interpretations'.[10] Would Nietzsche say something else to someone who insisted on something different? Probably, but that depends on your view of Nietzsche. My suggestion is simply that this historical and fictional Nietzsche is different from, less dogmatic than, the philosopher who doesn't require a context for his or her assertions.

Naipaul, in *The Enigma of Arrival*, is historical and fictional in just this sense. If you run back over the ideas and opinions in the book—about home, about ruin, about lateness, about empire, about provincials and barbarians—you will find echoes and anticipations of them occurring all over Naipaul's other works, often in very disagreeable forms. A moment from a letter to his family in 1951:

The undergraduates in this place are not all dazzlingly intellectual, as you probably think. There are asses in droves here.... The boys in my sixth form, taken on average, are as good—probably better—than most of the people here.

So far, so good: a modest defence of the Trinidadian provinces. But then Naipaul, who is not yet 19, lapses into this Tory fantasy, borrowed perhaps from Evelyn Waugh: 'Gone are the days of the aristocrats. Nearly everyone comes to Oxford on a state

---

[9] *Roland Barthes par Roland Barthes* (Paris: Seuil, 1975).

[10] Friedrich Nietzsche, *Werke, vol. iii*, ed. Karl Schlechta (Munich: Hanser, 1966), 903. My translation.

grant. The standard of the place naturally goes down'.[11] I should add that I went to Cambridge on a state grant just a few years after this, so I'm not likely to be judging these comments neutrally.

But of course in fiction I wouldn't be judging them at all. They would be hypothetical, and therefore, paradoxically perhaps, more human; they would require of me a fuller imagining of the speaker or writer. 'Imagine me,' Humbert Humbert cries out in *Lolita*. 'I shall not exist if you do not imagine me'.[12] He is speaking to an imaginary jury, and within the fiction, the claim is not convincing: he is as real as anyone in the book, more real than most of the characters. But what he says is literally true of himself as Nabokov's invention and of his relation to us as Nabokov's readers. The Naipaul of *The Enigma of Arrival*, similarly, will not exist if we do not imagine him. This imagined Naipaul is not, in my view, less chilly or more lovable than any of his other avatars, and I agree with Rushdie about the immense sadness of the book. But this real, fictional, imagined Naipaul is a thoroughly tentative, vulnerable person, a set of possibilities rather than a finished, unalterable fact. And there is a liberation, even in the midst of sadness, in thinking of what happens to you as a playing out of options rather than a historical doom or the harsh repetition of your own old myths. 'I had come into a world past its peak.' That is a possibility, but in a novel, it is *only* a possibility, what Naipaul calls a way of seeing.

So Rushdie, again, is right to take us to Oz, and there is such a thing as having too much solid ground beneath your feet. Even if there is 'no way out of this house', as in Rushdie's fable, even if 'the antique ship has gone', as in Naipaul's fable, we can imagine otherwise, and without our novelists, we shouldn't do this so well, and perhaps shouldn't know how to do it at all.

[11] V. S. Naipaul, *Between Father and Son: Family Letters* (New York: Alfred A. Knopf, 2000), 59–60.
[12] Vladimir Nabokov, *Lolita* (New York: Vintage, 1989), 129.

7

No Passes or Documents Are Needed: The Writer at Home in Europe

HILARY MANTEL

Jean Baudrillard says we ask ourselves about our identity only when we have nothing better to do. It is, no doubt, a Western luxury, and an indulgence of the intellect. But it is precisely with Western luxuries that I would like to concern myself; I would like to dwell on the collective life of the European imagination, and ask whether and how, born in England at mid-century, writing as the new century begins, I can claim a part of that collective life.

We cannot take credit for our European identity. It stands outside the process of historical definition. It was created before history began, by the movements of shifting land masses, crumpling and folding into each other. The tectonic shifts that gave birth to Europe placed rocks from different origins side by side, and near enough to the surface for their resources to be accessible; the rise and fall of mountains precedes the rise and fall of cities. Europe had a rich inheritance of metals and minerals, so that she became supreme in the arts of working metal; and she had unique topographical advantages, being blessed with natural harbours, with navigable rivers running deep into the interior of the continent. So, what she mined, she could transport; in time, she could also transport the products of agriculture. Our early identity, then, is intimately linked to the natural world. As soon as we define man as apart from that natural world, the question of our identity, collective and individual, begins to arise. We begin to tell ourselves stories about who we are.

Our small and personal narratives circle around the Grand Narrative, nudge it and jar it and knock it off centre. We draw an imaginary line around ourselves and say, this is my space, my territory, this is where I belong. The attributes of that space decide the way we see ourselves. But our ancestors' space was also imaginary, and we are the children of the physical and mental journeys which they undertook. In our minds each one of us draws a line between homeland and exile. Our identity depends on how we locate ourselves, in time and space, along this line.

It is very hard for one writer to speak for other writers. The discipline is solitary and resistant to analysis. So you will forgive me if I speak a little of my own life, and where I grew up, and how my consciousness as a novelist has evolved. When we stay at home—unless we are living through an ethnic war, or an intellectual crisis of self-definition—we are content just to be. When we travel abroad, our hosts ask us to account for ourselves, define ourselves. When I speak or read abroad I am sometimes described as a British writer, sometimes as an English writer. To me, the first description is meaningless. 'Britain' can be used as a geographical term, but it has no definable cultural meaning. As for calling me 'an English writer'—it is simply what I am not.

I was born in England in 1952 into a post-war society that was both anxious and complacent. Anxious, because the struggle since 1939 had been so hard; complacent, because—as my elders would have put it—England had *won again*. We had not been invaded. The gaunt old virgin Britannia had once again spat in

the eye of the European rapist. The island status, the separateness of Britain, or England, was essential to her understanding of
herself. For generations, our historians had proceeded as if
'Britain' and 'England' meant the same. Scottish children learnt
Scottish history, and English history. But English schoolchildren
did not learn Scottish history. They learned English history
alone—and they called it *British* history.

Historically, the English have not bothered to define themselves. They just *are*. It is other people who, in their view, have
the problem of definition. English nationalism is not recognized
to exist. The clashes between England and Ireland were not, in
the past, seen as a battle between English nationalism and Irish
nationalism. They were seen as a result of the Irish nation's stubborn refusal to recognize that it was, for all practical purposes,
English. It would be amusing, if the results had not been so
bloody.

I grew up in a village in the north of England, a descendant of
Irish immigrants who had come over to work in the textile mills.
My mother was a textile worker, as was her mother before her.
As a small child, I grew up in what was essentially an Irish
family, surrounded by Irish people who were old. By the time I
was 10 almost all of them were dead. My consciousness of being
Irish seemed to die with them. Where have they gone, those old
people? There is a place in my head, where I sit down with them.

But in what sense could I call myself English? I was born on
the northern tip of the Peak District, a country of mountains and
moorland, of few people and many sheep. It was not the town,
so was it the country? I had seen the English countryside in
picture books. There were trees, cottages of golden stone, cottage gardens bright with flowers. This bleak and treeless terrain
where I lived was—obviously—some other place. Very often, at
our church, we sang a hymn called 'Faith of our Fathers', which
celebrated the Roman Catholic martyrs of the Reformation, and
included the ambitious prediction that 'Mary's prayers | Shall
bring our country back to thee.' Even when I was quite young

I used to think how comical it would be if the police marched in and arrested us; for, whereas Protestants pray for the reigning monarch and the status quo, we appeared to sing along in hopes of the mass destruction of the House of Windsor. After this event, and the mass re-conversion—after we were once more in communion with our European brethren, the hymn promised us this: 'England shall then indeed be free.' (Was it 'indeed', or 'at last'? By its nature, this seminal text of my youth is absent from dictionaries of quotations. I try to think who I could call, to sing it to me down the phone, but I don't know anyone who wouldn't be unreliable or embarrassed: like the mathematician of Browning's poem 'I feel chilly and grown old'.)

As I grew up I came to see that Englishness was white, male, southern, Protestant, and middle class. I was a woman, a Catholic, a northerner, of Irish descent. I spoke and speak now with a northern accent. And if I tell an Englishman my date of birth and my religion and ancestry, I am telling him, without needing more words, that my family are working people, probably with little education. All these markers—descent, religion, region, accent—are quickly perceived and decoded by those who possess Englishness, and to this day they are used to *exclude*. You are forced off centre. You are a provincial. You are a spectator. If you want to belong to Englishness, you must sell off aspects of your identity.

Possibilities of self-redefinition were presented to me. I could become educated, go and live in the south if I liked, abandon my faith and change my accent. I did some of these things. The American novels I began to read had taught me that literature did not proceed entirely from the torture chambers of the imagination; having spent my teenage years with Dostoevsky, I was more than happy to meet Updike and Lurie. But most of the US literature I encountered was, as it happened, East Coast and WASP-ish; and the Jewish novelists, in their moral sophistication and urban poise, seemed more central to the culture than the WASPs themselves. So if American novels entertained me, they hardly expanded my means of self-construction. Though I was grateful for a state-sponsored schooling that had lasted much longer than that of anyone else in my family, I had not really been educated, rather brought up to pass exams. My knowledge of Latin evaporated the minute I walked out of the exam room at 15, and I had never learned Greek. My lack of knowledge of classical literature still embarrasses me. At no conscious level could I link myself to the ancient idea of Europe, to the defining myths, to the common culture that is shaped by our inheritance from Greece and Rome.

And yet they must have been pervasive, I think: in the water or in the air; or let's say that the crumbs from that inheritance had fallen to me from the table of pan-European Romanticism. For when I began to write, at the age of 22, I defined myself from the first as a European writer. The first book I wrote was *A Place of Greater Safety*, which is a novel about the French Revolution, set in Paris. It was not the first book of mine to be published; it occupied me for many years, and was not published until 1992. I had never been to Paris when I began to write. This did not matter. In my dreams of Europe, I had found the keys to the gate of an unknown city. For the constant and passionate imagination, no documents or passes are needed. It did not seem to me that I was writing of dead people or events that were distant and frozen. I was working at a transformative moment in the history of Europe. I was then the least alienated of beings. I was at one with the work I did. By writing a novel one performs a revolutionary act. A novel is an act of hope. It allows us to imagine that things may be other than they are.

In 1977 my husband was appointed to a post in Southern Africa, with the Geological Survey of Botswana. I took the notes for my French Revolution novel with me, carrying Europe in my suitcase. And strangely, in Africa for the first time I found I was living in a European community, amongst personnel and aid workers who were Scandinavian, Dutch, German: and within an émigré community which was Portuguese, Indian, and Afrikaaner; and among the local Tswana people. I felt English for the first time, because I was told I was English. When you go abroad, a caricatured version of your nationality is waiting for you, the product of other people's myths. In one sense, it is easier to choose your identity when you are at home than when you are abroad. When you are abroad, others will see you twice your natural size; they will define and label you.

Also, five years spent in Africa made me think about the question of what a nation is. There is a view in which nationhood is defined by language, custom, religion, tradition, and aspirations to territory, if not actual ownership of it. This view was very appealing, in the nineteenth century, to small nations ruled by larger nations, who wished to assert their right to self-determination. But we know that definitions of nationality extend beyond the borders of any territory. There are migrant nations—most obviously the Jews, but also of course those Europeans whom economic hardship drove in their hundreds of thousands during the last century to found new communities in the USA. And there are 70 million people in the world who claim Irish descent.

My experience in Africa encouraged me to think about the translucency of national identity. The identity of the Tswana people was hard to locate. Their language had found written form only in the nineteenth century. The way it was spoken varied greatly from place to place—so there was no agreement, for example, on how to pronounce the name of Botswana's capital city. The Tswana identity seemed independent of territory. It flowed over borders. When Europeans travelled from the free, democratic republic of Botswana across the border to apartheid South Africa, they suffered a major psychic convulsion. In my naivety, I imagined, when I went to Botswana, that this crossing would be even harder for a black person. After a while I realized that it was not so. To them, the border did not look like the border. Your name was recorded in a book as you passed, by some self-important official who did not understand that the terrain was the same, and that your relatives were on both sides. The grotesque formulations of racial identity, imposed by white South African officials, were their own, temporary affair, a passing madness. Tswana identity was old, and it was mythical, and it was beyond the reach of apartheid legislation.

By contrast, the English are literal-minded about borders. For obvious reasons, they do not make a territorial identification with the continent of Europe. A stretch of water cuts them off. If you are in England, you can easily dismay your fellow citizens of Europe by a chance remark: by speaking of 'crossing to Europe'. You are speaking geographically, of course. You do not mean to imply that you are not 'in' Europe. Nevertheless, the unfortunate turn of phrase has some significance. It is difficult, from the point of view of a small offshore island, to develop a sense of the integrity of Europe. I remember a few years ago visiting Passau, in Germany, and standing at the riverside at the point where one could take a boat either to Amsterdam, or to Vienna. I felt, suddenly, a childlike moment of wonder: ah, Europe *connects*. I could have worked it out from the atlas. But it is a small thing to look at a map, and a greater thing to feel for yourself how a map relates to life. Not every English-born person has been able to experience such a moment. My grandfather's generation left those British islands only to fight in wars, wars which redrew the map of continental states but left the returning islanders lonely and injured and confirmed in their separateness.

But now, from England, it is possible to travel with your car through a tunnel or step on a train and be, in every sense, in Europe. I do not think that there can ever have been an item of government transport policy that reaches so far into the imagination as the Channel tunnel. Our sense of ourself is altered, and for once, not by some great discontinuity, not by a fracture but by a process of linking up, of connection. There is no heroic sea voyage, no airport formalities, no moment of take off, no traumatic parting from one's own solid earth: only the business of changing platforms at a London station. It is a small miracle, a psychic transformation made possible by engineers.

Let me return for a moment to the story I tell myself about my own identity. In 1982 I went to live in Saudi Arabia. I am mindful that the roots of European culture are not only in Greece and Rome but in the Byzantine empire and the Arab world, that they are not just Christian and Jewish, but Islamic. I tried to use my time in the kingdom to learn what I could of Islam, both in theory and in practice. Saudi Arabia is a recent nation, constructed in the last century, with an identity imagined for it— and not very thoroughly imagined. Slavery was not abolished until 1962, and the official inauguration of education for women came a few years later, and occurred against violent opposition. In my time in Jedda it seemed the kingdom was a society devoted entirely to trash consumption, to instant desires instantly gratified: a nightmare growth leaked from the test-tube of some mad, superhuman social scientist. In Jedda it was possible to buy almost anything, but you could not buy a bookcase. If you went into what was called a 'book-store', it proved to be a stationery shop. You could buy empty notebooks, blank books, pens. Were these empty pages for the books yet to be written? Were these pens the instruments for writing them? I am afraid not. This society had passed straight from pre-literacy to the video age. From there it has passed to the age of information. The proliferation of information does not necessarily involve the proliferation of meaning. My experience in that society, with its culture of claustrophobia and powerlessness, left my own sense of identity bleached out, stretched thin. It gave me some idea of what it is to exist in a culture where, as a woman, I have not even the right to be seen, and it gave me a profound sense of identification with those whose being is veiled and whose tongue is silent.

In 1986 we returned to England. I published several novels. But it is well known that in mid-life we take our packs upon our

backs again and set off on the second part of our road. In the
course of writing my last novel, *The Giant, O'Brien*, I was led
back to Ireland. My book was based on the true story of an Irish
Giant, a man called Charles Byrne, who was a little under 8 feet
tall: who journeyed to London, at the end of the eighteenth
century, to exhibit himself as a monster, and who died there,
and who was dissected by the Scottish surgeon John Hunter. His
bones are hanging up even today in a London museum: an awful
symbol to remind us of how the body of Ireland is cut apart.

In the course of my writing I felt a great sadness about the loss,
for me, of the Irish language. I was aware my mouth was empty,
but I was aware also that my brain was crammed with newly
minted myth. If you are a member of the Irish diaspora—and
perhaps most of all, if you are an American or Australian of Irish
origin—you are a victim of the Celtic Revival of the late nineteenth and early twentieth century. This movement was an
attempt of a type familiar to us in Europe, an attempt to reach
back to a mythical time and place, where the world was perfect
and whole, where the Celts were a pure race, and the Irish
language was a pure language. It was a sham, but it was seduc-
tive. It fed into the current of Irish nationalism—the chief language of which, of course, is English. It was, however, a lasting,
commercially rewarding sham, and it has taken on a new energy
in recent years, with the rediscovery of a 'Celtic' brand of music
which seems to embrace many of Europe's outlying, forgotten,
misty regions, and give them a common identity, and at the same
time set them defiantly apart from the mainstream. My own
shelves, I should admit, are stacked high with recordings of this
music, from Ireland and Scotland, from Brittany and Galicia; in
pursuit of the togetherness offered by otherness, I too have made
the cash registers ring. The new-minted 'Celtic' culture offers the
thing that is extremely attractive to the exile: a spurious sense of
belonging. To be Irish has, recently, become suspiciously fashionable; though you are excluded from fashion, I think, if you
are a Northern Irish Protestant. But if we ask 'who are the

Irish'?—and consult our history and not simply our emotional need for self-definition—they are not only Celts but Vikings, Normans, Anglo-Saxons, and Spanish and Scots. When Mary Robinson became President of Ireland, she put a candle in her window, perpetually burning, to light the exiles home. I found myself thinking it must be a very high-tech candle, for you could see it blazing on the sunniest day. It needed to be bright, for there was a long way to guide us home. About four years ago I visited Tromso, in Norway, one of the most northerly towns in the world. There, under the midnight sun, I felt instantly at home. Within its severe geometry, its black trees reflected in icy water, I felt more myself than I had felt anywhere before. It was a feeling I had not sought, that I had never expected, and that I have never lost. On my next visit to Dublin I bought from the National Museum a copy of a Viking armlet which had been excavated on a Dublin archeological site. To my own satisfaction, I had come home, in Ireland and in Europe. I had added another episode to my story of who I am; though it is powerful to me, I know it is a confabulation. And now I hardly ever go out without this symbol on my wrist, because at the beginning of the twenty-first century I am a primitive person, and not so secure as to leave my current place of residence without a marker to lead me 'home'.

In my lifetime Ireland has changed her idea of herself, perhaps even more than England has. Ireland finds herself, as a country within the European Union, in a state of unprecedented prosperity, and also fully recognizing and celebrating the European dimension of her history. The year 1998 saw the bicentenary of the rising of the United Irishmen, an attempt by both Protestant and Catholic Irishmen to throw off British rule, with military aid from France. The rising was a heart-breaking catastrophe. It led to mass slaughter of a helpless population, and is a source of continuing bitterness and misunderstanding. But to commemorate this dreadful event, modern Ireland has built a beautiful exhibition centre in Enniscorthy, and planted trees of liberty in the grounds. There, to my personal joy, the story of Ireland's struggle for freedom was set in a European context. The tragedy does not diminish, but collective memory is honoured, truth is served, and myth gains in force.

Ireland's sense of connection to Europe is something the English are slow to acquire. Among novelists writing just now, Michèle Roberts brings a polished Anglo-French sensibility to her work. Tim Parks, a long-time resident of Florence, wrote first with an expatriate's eye, but now infuses his unsettling narratives with a transnational jitteriness. Barry Unsworth, whose early themes were slavery and colonialism, has lived for many years in Italy; a studious, clever, but unpretentious writer, he is one of our most intelligent commentators on cultural mythology, and one of the most remarkable novels published in England recently has been his *Losing Nelson* (1999). It tells the story of a modern-day man, a writer, who is obsessed with the glorious deeds of Nelson, reckoned the greatest of England's sea commanders, and who is writing a glorifying biography of him. Yet he cannot write his book, he keeps stopping. He cannot get past one shameful episode in Nelson's early career: his betrayal of the revolutionaries of Naples, to whom he had offered safe conduct, but whom he betrayed back to the hangman. This episode, Unsworth sees in a European context. He believes it to be of great consequence in the history of southern Italy. To my dismay, and no doubt to his, the critics largely ignored the central point of his book. He dared to displace the Anglocentric view, and sacrifice an English hero to our common European humanity. It is still such a frightening enterprise, for some, that they are almost literally unable to read what he has put on the page.

All the same, the country where I was born has changed enormously from that scared and insular post-war nation. The young are pro-European, without having to think about it. The European Community is one of the givens of their world. The British parliament at Westminster has formally devolved a share of power to Scottish and Welsh assemblies. The English sense of identity is beginning to fracture. This is a healthy development. No one now would speak of an English writer, if he meant a Scottish writer. Generations of emigration from the former empire have made Britain a pluralist, multi-ethnic, multi-faith society, and now, like the rest of western Europe, she is host to waves of refugees from disaster-stricken territories to the east. These migrant communities will have to reimagine themselves. We are all, as I have tried to show, members of imagined communities. In the century ahead, shall we transcend nationalism, or accommodate it? There is a sense in which a postmodern world must be a post-nationalist world. But the idea of a nation will be with us for a long time yet, for historically, nationalist ideals have provided ideologies of resistance and emancipation, and in the present sorry state of Europe I do not think we can reasonably ask thwarted and injured peoples to do without their nationalist ideals, or to ask them to bask in the light of a sunny cosmopolitanism—for them, the day has not yet dawned.

The greatest hope of minorities, I think, is that they can find a refuge in an imagined Europe of the regions: not in a superstate, a Europe created on the model of past nation states, but within a Europe of diversity in which plural identities can flourish: in which a man is free to define himself as a member of such a group or nation, but also to define himself as a European. Meanwhile I think it is the role of writers and artists to make sure that the idea of a nation is not regressive, not repressive, not injurious to the freedom of others. Can this be done? It is artists and writers who deal in symbol and myth, in the manipulation of our psychic realities. Myth is what can be collectively remembered, collectively imagined. I do not think you can separate what is remembered from what is imagined. Myth is a psychic resource which can energize us for better or worse. It is our way back into history, a substitute for lost languages and a mirror we hold to long-vanished faces: see, we say, they were just like us. Myth is a kind of sacred history. It seems to incarnate a truth that goes beyond fact. It appeals to our origins among the gods, before we were merely human. It can offer symbolic consolations for the catastrophes that befall a people: in our heads, the wrongs of history are undone. Nations use their myths to affirm and re-affirm themselves. In times of war, occupation, and diaspora, they provide at least an illusion of continuity. In times of prosperity they provide an assurance of a god-given right to thrive and to expand. They can be a malign ideological mechanism: they can be used to exclude and excuse, or they can lead a whole people to adopt a lexicon of martyrdom and hopeless sacrifice. The transnational myth of revolution can do that too: in the last two centuries there has been a powerful quasi-religious idea running through the European consciousness, to the effect that the blood of the strong can somehow nourish the weak.

But myth can also be empowering and redemptive. The stories we tell ourselves, or which we appoint writers to tell us, can show us a better self, a self in potential. Myths are concerned with making possible on an imaginary level that which is not possible in our empirical experience. Behind every nation or state there is the state-that-might-have-been. Myth expresses a need for rootedness and identity, but it also allows us to continue to exist when we are uprooted; it allows us to uproot ourselves and still live, to take a seavoyage from our own identity.

Myth is in constant movement and change. It re-creates itself through constant multiple reinterpretation, through countless acts of telling and reading and writing. As writers, we have certain options, which we carry into the new century. We can, for example, like Samuel Beckett, repudiate the images of collectivity, seeing them as sentimental compensation for our individual isolation and misery. Beckett, notoriously, preferred to live in France at war rather than in Ireland at peace. But the émigré sensibility can become nothing more than affectation, an empty piece of provocation; you can choose to be an exile only because others stay at home. More fruitful, perhaps, is the example of James Joyce, who shows that we can free ourselves from tribal constraints without abandoning ourselves to the despair of solitude. Joyce chose to blend Hellenic symbols with Irish symbols, to draw strength for his work both from a local culture and the culture of continental Europe. Among twentieth-century novelists he is one of the greatest, most enriching examples of how a European identity may be imagined.

At the beginning of the century, we want to carry our past with us, without being bowed under its weight. We want history to be our guardian angel, an airy companion who walks beside us into the new millennium. The creative imagination is a place of safety for the dead, where they can show their faces and be recognized. We have to conjure the people of the past, summon them back to life, so they can lead us to our future. At the beginning of the new millennium, the god that artists must invoke is Janus, the double-faced god, the guardian of gates and doors. It is the duty and privilege of the novelist to look both outward and inward, to the past and the future, to the particular and the universal, to the parish and the world. My greatest wish for the writers of the new century is that they will find a capacity to be both at home and on a journey; that they will find that Europe is our *Heimat*, and our home away from home.[1]

[1] An early version of this essay was delivered as a talk in 1999 at the Institute of Continuing Education in Barcelona, as part of a Seminar on Cooperation and Diversity in European Culture.

8

Penelope

WENDY LESSER

There is a kind of rereading in which you go over and over a piece of writing (a paragraph, a page, a few stanzas) to try to figure out why it has the effect on you that it does. This kind of rereading is obsessive and a bit tedious; it may be especially dull for the onlooker who does not share the obsession. Though the purposes of the two actions are quite different, it has in it something of Penelope's nightly unweaving of her daily work as she waits for Ulysses' uncertain return. She is trying to keep time still and at the same time move it forward. Something similar may be said of the obsessive rereader.

While I was asking myself why it was that the novels of Penelope Fitzgerald had such a profound effect on me, I came across the following remarks by Tom Stoppard. He was writing in the pages of the *New York Review of Books* about his first encounters in the 1950s with the plays of Beckett and Pinter, which he contrasted with John Osborne's *Look Back in Anger*:

The point was I could see what Osborne was up to and how it might be done. But with *Godot* and *The Birthday Party* the case was entirely different. I couldn't see how it was done. I couldn't see exactly what was done, either. Each play was simultaneously inspiring and baffling. It broke a contract which up to that era had been thought to exist between a play and its audience. There had seemed to be a tacit agreement, up to then, that if you could be bothered to show up to watch something up there, then the thing up there had certain obligations toward you, such as the obligation to give you the minimum information you needed to make sense of the whole.

Waiting for Godot redefined the minimum, for all time, or at least up to the present time. *The Birthday Party*, differently, did the same. And although both authors had done this cruel thing to me, I trusted them and, dimly, I knew why I trusted them.

The easiest way to explain why is simply to state that Surrealism, Dada, and that whole family of cruelties from previous generations seemed to me (and still seem) to be intrinsically worthless (though sometimes enlivening, as a fight in a pub might be enlivening), and *this* was not *that*. It was not irrational. It was not arbitrary. It did not make its effects by dislocating narrative or thought process or the connections between things. 'Early Modern' attempts to advance the state of the art, in Zurich and Paris, seemed merely childish by comparison. But these new plays were baffling in a different way. The narrative line was pure, so pure that you lost sight of it some of the time, pure as a spider's thread: when it seemed to be broken, a small shift showed it still there. These plays, so unlike Shakespeare, did the thing that makes Shakespeare breathtaking and defines poetry—the simultaneous compression of language and expansion of meaning.[1]

Something similar seems to me to apply to the novels of Penelope Fitzgerald—I mean the late, great novels written from 1986 onward: *Innocence, The Beginning of Spring*, and *The Blue Flower*. And while one doesn't necessarily want to subscribe to Stoppard's full-scale attack on the 'Early Modern' (in which I detect overtones of the philistine English antipathy to Picasso), the contrast he sets up does say something about Fitzgerald's work as well. For one of the reasons it's so easy to

---

[1] Tom Stoppard, 'Pragmatic Theatre', *New York Review of Books*, 23 Sept. 1999, p. 10.

mistake what Penelope Fitzgerald is doing is that her fiction does not resemble any kind of typical 'experimental' writing. Nothing in the sentence structure or the plot outlines alerts us to the fact that the narrative contract has been broken. For the most part—*The Blue Flower* may be an exception here—we can read along as happily as if we were reading a standard old-fashioned novel. (Though what *is* a standard old-fashioned novel? Jane Austen? Daniel Defoe? Miguel de Cervantes? The genre fails to materialize.) The only problem arises at the end, when we are unexpectedly left hanging in some strange way. 'What was *that* all about?' we may then ask ourselves, like the early patrons of Beckett's plays.

This is what happened to me with my first Penelope Fitzgerald novel, before I had any idea who she was. I read *The Gate of Angels* in early 1992, when it first came out in America, and I didn't get it. I must have liked it well enough, because I kept the hardback copy on my shelf (the same shelf where I was later to accumulate everything Penelope Fitzgerald wrote: even her biographies of Edward Burne-Jones and Charlotte Mew, and *The Knox Brothers*, her wonderful family portrait of her father and his siblings). But I read it as if it were a normal Anglo-Saxon comic novel by one of the other Penelopes (Mortimer, say, or Lively), with a neat plot and cleverly shallow characters. As such, it didn't quite add up. It wasn't very funny, for one thing. It had a lot of extraneous bits about science and religious faith. And the novel ended just as the two main characters ran into each other by chance (or whatever the science/faith equivalent of chance is) in the street outside a Cambridge college. Were they going to get married or not? Would they be happy or unhappy together? Why was I being ejected from the story just here, when nothing decisive had been resolved? I hadn't a clue.

This is why I recommend starting with *The Blue Flower* and working backward. And in general, when people ask me what Penelope Fitzgerald novels to read, I tell them to read the ones set outside England. *Offshore*, which won the Booker Prize in

1979, is very satisfying in its way; *At Freddie's* has enormous virtues, including one of the best child characters she ever wrote (and she is excellent at children); and *The Gate of Angels* is much, much better than I thought it was the first time I read it. But nothing compares, for me, with the three great novels set in other places and other times. And it is through looking closely, obsessively, at passages from these three novels that I will try to unravel Penelope's work. I will not be successful; no one ever is, in my experience. But I will give it a try.

Friends of mine—Arthur Lubow in the *New York Times Magazine*, Joan Acocella in the *New Yorker*, Kerry Fried in the Internet pages of amazon.com—have tried before to explain her magic. Because of their general-circulation audiences, my three friends were required to approach Fitzgerald mainly through personal facts about her life—the fact that she hadn't started writing fiction until age 60; the fact that her marriage, which produced three children, had not been happy, though she wrote her first novel to entertain her husband on his deathbed; the fact that she had, in real life, actually lived on a houseboat in the Thames like the heroine of *Offshore*, and taught at a children's theatre school like the characters in *At Freddie's*, and had an uncle who lost his religious faith at Cambridge in 1912, just like Fred Fairly in *The Gate of Angels*. Such facts are the fruits of the Profile, the Interview, which is the only way large audiences ever want to hear about a living writer. Fortunately, I am not bound by these requirements. In any case, as a way of explaining how the novels operate on us, that approach doesn't seem to work (particularly with a writer as sly as Penelope Fitzgerald, who has said some improbable things to interviewers, possibly to amuse herself). So I will intrude rudely on the books instead, standing closer to them than is polite, quizzing them in a way that normal reading etiquette would disallow.

But before I attempt to determine how Fitzgerald creates her magical effects, I should perhaps say what I think those effects are. Let me, at any rate, list three of them. One is her uncanny ability to write from within an alien culture. As my sister says, 'Each time I read a Penelope Fitzgerald novel, I learn where she grew up'—that is, in eighteenth-century Germany, early twentieth-century Russia, 1950s Italy, or whatever. Fitzgerald does not write historical novels, for even the best historical novels aim to elucidate another time for us, mediating (however subtly) between our period and that other one, so that we are always aware of the distance. With Penelope Fitzgerald's works, there is no sense of distance: she is in that other time, and so are we.

The second curious quality is the fact that all of Penelope Fitzgerald's novels have a certain authorial wit, but the wittiness does not seem to come from the narrative voice, the sentences in between the dialogue. Rather, it seems to emanate from the characters themselves. We never see her poking fun at her characters, amusing us at their expense; we have no sense of an author laughing from on high. On the contrary, the central people in Penelope Fitzgerald novels seem to share her sense of humour. Yet this is not because they have a detached, ironic, uninvolved perspective on their own lives; they are not angels, or devils. They are as humanly unconscious as the rest of us, as likely to make mistakes and misinterpret things, but they do so with a particular note of levity they share with their author.

The third element I detect in Fitzgerald's greatest novels is something that I can only describe as a skewed relationship to the passage of time. Normally, we think of novels as presenting us with a slice of life, whether a brief slice (*The Beginning of Spring*, say, covers a few months in 1913) or a lifetime-sized slice (for instance, the relatively brief lifetimes conveyed in *The Blue Flower*), or even two separate slices (as in *Innocence*, which begins with an anecdote from sixteenth-century Italy and then leaps to 1955). But none of these summaries even begins to suggest how Penelope Fitzgerald uses time in her novels. It is as if there are two entirely separate time schemes: the one chronicled by the words on the page, which end abruptly and resolutely fail to give us everything; and then the other one around or behind or between those words, which is filled with the richness of the characters' inner lives, their histories before we met them, their fates after they leave us, and a million other things we can only imagine. In Fitzgerald's work, these two timelines have no predictable relation to each other. It is not as if one comes after the other, or sits in front of the other, or stands in for the other. We are given only one of them directly, in the author's words, and yet the sense of them both is equally strong. It is very much the way you feel standing in front of a Vermeer painting: he gives you a single moment in time, almost a snapshot of a fleeting moment, and yet there is a feeling of timelessness to his work as well, as if that one moment—of weighing something in the balance, of playing a single note on a keyboard, of glancing briefly out a window, of looking up from a letter—were an eternity in its subject's life.

But now let me try to show you what I mean.

The passage I've chosen from *The Blue Flower* comes from near the beginning of the book. All we know, at this point, is that we are visiting the home of the Hardenberg family in the small German town of Weissenfels, on wash day. Since wash day occurs only three times a year (we learn in the book's second sentence that 'the household had linen and white underwear for four months only'), we have a sense that this story is set somewhere in the past, but it is not until the fifth chapter that we are given any dates (1738, 1769), and not until chapter 6 that the author firmly locates the action in 1787. 'Firmly' is not, come to think of it, a word I would associate with anything about this novel: its revelations are intense but filmy, attenuated almost to the point of invisibility, like that spider's thread of a narrative Stoppard discerned in Beckett and Pinter. It is not until the book's Afterword, in which we also learn of the early deaths of all the characters, that the novel actually identifies Fritz von Hardenberg with the romantic poet Novalis, author of an unfinished work about the Blue Flower. (I say 'the novel' as if it were a discrete item, but there are preliminary attachments—an Author's Note explaining the historical sources, an epigraph from 'F. von Hardenberg, later Novalis'—that pave the way, warning us of what we are about to take in. Fitzgerald is as experimental, in her own way, as Cervantes, and the things we have come to think of as publishing artefacts are actually part of her art.)

In Chapter 3, which is called 'The Bernhard', we begin to sense the unusual nature of the Hardenberg family, and in particular its smallest member. The Bernhard, as this chapter opens by telling us, is actually August Wilhelm Bernhard von Hardenberg, the youngest of Fritz's six siblings. In this scene, his sister Sidonie is gently instructing him about how to behave to Fritz's newly arrived guest, Herr Dietmahler.

He was now more than old enough, Sidonie thought, to understand politeness to a visitor. 'I do not know how long he will stay, Bernhard. He has brought quite a large valise.'

'His valise is full of books,' said the Bernhard, 'and he has also brought a bottle of schnaps. I dare say he thought there would not be such a thing in our house.'

'Bernhard, you have been in his room.'

'Yes, I went there.'

'You have opened his valise.'

'Yes, just to see his things.'

'Did you leave it open, or did you shut it again?'

The Bernhard hesitated. He could not remember.

'Well, it doesn't signify,' said Sidonie. 'You must, of course, confess to Herr Dietmahler what you have done and ask his pardon.'

'When?'

'Well, it should be before nightfall. In any case, there is no time like the present.'

'I've nothing to tell him!' cried the Bernhard. 'I haven't spoiled his things.'

'You know that Father punishes you very little,' said Sidonie coaxingly. 'Not as we were punished. Perhaps he will tell you to wear your jacket the wrong way out for a few days, only to remind you. We shall have some music before supper and after that I will go with you up to the visitor and you can take his hand and speak to him quietly.'

'I'm sick of this house!' shouted the Bernhard, snatching himself away.

Fritz was in the kitchen garden patrolling the vegetable beds, inhaling the fragrance of the broad bean flowers, reciting at the top of his voice.

'Fritz,' Sidonie called to him. 'I have lost the Bernhard.'

'Oh, that can't be.'

'I was reproving him in the morning room, and he escaped from me and jumped over the window-sill and into the yard.'

'Have you sent one of the servants?'

'Oh, Fritz, best not, they will tell Mother.'

Fritz looked at her, shut his book and said he would go out and find his brother. 'I will drag him back by the hair if necessary, but you and Asmus will have to entertain my friend.'

'Where is he now?'

'He is in his room, resting. Father has worn him out. By the way, his room has been turned upside down and his valise is open.'

'Is he angry?'

'Not at all. He thinks perhaps that it's one of our customs at Weissenfels.'

Fritz put on his frieze-coat and went without hesitation down to the river. Everyone in Weissenfels knew that young Bernhard would never drown, because he was a water-rat. He couldn't swim, but then neither could his father.[2]

There are so many things to notice here: the way we are made apprehensive that Bernhard will actually have drowned (an apprehension that is not fulfilled now—but in the Afterword we learn that in real life 'The Bernhard was drowned in the Saale on the 28th of November 1800'); the way the character of the wilful, somewhat spoiled, very original and endearing child is sketched in just a few lines; the way no line of dialogue is exactly the expected response to the previous line, so that we are constantly

---

[2] Penelope Fitzgerald, *The Blue Flower* (London: Flamingo, 1995), 8–10.

kept slightly off balance. But mostly I want to focus on how Penelope Fitzgerald has captured and conveyed her setting here: the way she has observed the most telling details during her apparent visit to late eighteenth-century Germany, so as to be, in Henry James's phrase, the kind of novelist on whom nothing is lost. This is a world in which the towns are separate countries, almost, so that a German from a few hundred miles away might not be able to tell the difference between local customs and family idiosyncracies. (This is also a family in which jokes about such possible confusions are considered amusing.) It is a world where people wear 'frieze-coats', and are punished by having their jackets turned inside out, and have music performed before supper.

The language throughout is ever so slightly un-English, slightly German sounding, but it does not sound like a translation—rather, it sounds as we imagine German would sound in our minds if we knew it as fluently as we know English. It is English functioning as German while still retaining the flexibilities of English. This is especially clear in the phrase 'The Bernhard', which is used by both the author and Sidonie *about* Bernhard, though he is never addressed that way directly. Its sense in English is clear enough—a kind of family joke, a singling-out of the youngest, oddest child—and there are even English examples of a similar usage in children's nicknames (*The Piggle*, for instance, is a D. W. Winnicott case study about a little girl). But something about the phrase made me also wonder about Der Bernhard. I asked a friend born in Germany whether a definite article would ever be used with a name that way, and he had a vague memory, from his mother's childhood, of that being the case. When he checked with an adult German speaker, he learned that such a phrase had a very particular connotation, as in 'Oh, that Bernhard! That is so typical of him.' This is one of those authorial gifts we needn't fully receive to enjoy. That is, you can still get a kick out of the name 'The Bernhard' even if you don't know the German habit of speech, but if you do know it, the phrase is made even richer.

So much for Penelope Fitzgerald having grown up in Weissenfels during Goethe's time. But she was also, apparently, in Moscow just before the Russian Revolution. *The Beginning of Spring* (probably my favourite of her novels, for reasons I can't quite pin down) deals with a cluster of English people who have lived in Russia for several generations. They have English first and last names but Russian patronymics, as in 'Frank Albertovich' and 'Selwyn Osipych'. The main character, Frank Reid, runs a printing business in Moscow, a family-owned press called Reidka's. There is a special interest, I find, that attaches to novels focusing on the printing or paper business: I'm thinking of Arnold Bennett's *Clayhanger*, for instance, or Balzac's *Lost Illusions*. It's not that I enjoy the self-reference as a piece of Borgesian cleverness—more that it's always of interest when an artwork points, however indirectly, to the processes of its own making.

At the beginning of *The Beginning of Spring*, Frank's wife, Nellie, leaves him, and at the end she returns. In between there are complications with a potential governess, Miss Kinsman, and wonderful if brief glimpses of the three children, and a great deal else about Frank's life in Moscow, including his relations with his long-time employee, Selwyn. Here he is talking with Selwyn, roughly in the middle of the book; I intrude on them in mid-conversation.

'... I'm speaking of the sexual impulse, Frank, and its gratification.'

'Well, I thought you must be,' said Frank.

'At that time I thought that both men and women benefited from a multiplication of joyous relationships. But I had come to see how wrong that is. My predicament was, then, how to act in order to cause as little pain as possible and, above all, what I should tell the human beings concerned.'

'I don't know what you had to tell them,' said Frank.

'You would have been as puzzled as I was?'

'I'm puzzled as it is.'

'But I haven't distressed you by what I've been saying? You haven't taken offence?'

'How could anyone take offence at you, Selwyn? You might as well take offence at a drink of cold water.'

Selwyn gave a melancholy smile. 'We must go back to the subject later.' He seemed reluctant to leave, a symptom which Frank recognized at once. At length he said, in a lowered voice, almost reverent voice, 'How is it going, Frank? Has it been set up?'

He meant, Frank knew, the *Birch Tree Thoughts*. 'I'm trying to get the loan of some European type, Selwyn, you know that. Sytin's have some, but they won't lend it. We may have to try in Petersburg. Tvyordov will set it up for you, he won't mind what language it's in, and of course the boy won't be able to read the proofs, but I can leave that to you. We can hand-print it on the Albion.'

'The punctuation may give trouble, I know that. It happens that I'—he took a manuscript notebook out of his breast pocket, opened it—but it seemed to open itself at the required place—and handed it to Frank, who, aware that he hadn't been grateful enough for Selwyn's ready sympathy over Miss Kinsman, took it and read aloud:

> 'Dost feel the cold, sister birch?'
> 'No, Brother Snow,
> I feel it not.' 'What, not?' 'No, not!'

'Are you sure that's right, Selwyn?'

'What would you say is amiss?'

'I'm not quite sure.'

'Wasn't I successful in conveying my meaning?'

'It seems a bit repetitive.'

Selwyn took back the notebook, as though he did not like to see it in less expert hands, and Frank, saying that he'd lock up, was left alone in the darkened building, to look through the various offers of his paper suppliers.[3]

I think you can hear how Russian this feels, compared to how German the section from *The Blue Flower* felt. The idea of a 'melancholy smile' is quintessentially Russian, as is the rather

---

[3] Penelope Fitzgerald, *The Beginning of Spring* (London: Flamingo, 1988), 77–8.

Dostoevskian discussion about how to exist in the world without hurting other people. (Selwyn actually describes himself as a disciple of Tolstoy. Whatever.) These characters are simultaneously Russian in their directness of speech and English in their reticence; either alone would be a difficult enough trick for an author to pull off, and both at once seems miraculous.

But what I mainly want to focus on here is the humour. This inheres not only in the hilarious verses themselves (as Selwyn suggests, though without exactly meaning to, it's the punctuation that makes them particularly funny), but in the whole combination of delicacy, wit, and genuine puzzlement that colours Frank's dealings with his eccentric friend. 'I'm puzzled as it is' has the ring of a punchline, though it is also true. The snippets of authorial humour that we get—Selwyn's 'almost reverent' voice, the way Selwyn is described as not liking to see his notebook 'in less expert hands'—are of a piece with the bits of Frank's humour that come through to us in the dialogue: faintly amused, patient, unwilling to inflict a direct insult, and nonetheless aware that two people's perspectives can differ in a way that seems laughable to one and highly serious to the other. Are Frank's understated responses to Selwyn the result of purposeful tact, an incomplete understanding of his own feelings, or a typically English brand of restraint? Probably all three. The main point is that nowhere can we pin down a purely mocking moment, a moment at which Frank sets himself wholly above Selwyn or Penelope Fitzgerald sets herself wholly above either of them.

The last passage I will focus on comes at the very end of *Innocence*, and I'm afraid I will need to quote a few pages to give you the full idea. But first I must set the stage a bit. I don't want to spoil the beginning of the novel for you by repeating the wonderful anecdote that is given there; you need only know that it is a strange little allegory, set in 1568, about the aristocratic Ridolfi family and its cruelly kind prejudices against outsiders. By the third chapter, we have skipped forward to 1955, and the rest of the novel considers one of the last surviving Ridolfis, a young Florentine named Chiara who has been educated in England. Somewhat against her family's wishes, she marries an idealistic young doctor named Salvatore Rossi. Their backgrounds could not be more different. Salvatore's family is from the South, rather poor but very proud, and politically left wing (he remembers a childhood visit to the communist Gramsci in prison, which has in part fuelled his idealism). Though they unmistakably love each other, Chiara and Salvatore have severe difficulties living together, and toward the end of the novel they separate. It is not clear, either to them or to us, whether this break will be permanent.

Salvatore, in despair, goes to the Ridolfi country property— the same estate on which the initial sixteenth-century anecdote is set. The family farm is now run by Chiara's cousin Cesare, a rather silent, solitary fellow who has long been secretly in love with Chiara. Perhaps suspecting this, or perhaps not, Salvatore asks Cesare to help him commit suicide. It will be best for Chiara, he urges, if he is simply taken out of the way. But he needs Cesare's help, and has come to ask for it:

' . . . To turn to practical matters, I have an adequate life insurance policy with Previdenza, the beneficiaries of course are my mother and Chiara, but in the event of my suicide the company pays out nothing.'

'That's not in my policy,' said Cesare.

'Probably not, it's occupational, Previdenza includes it only for journalists, doctors, artists, speculators and degenerates. It follows, however, that if I were to put an end to myself this evening, your evidence would be necessary as to its being an accident. What do you feel about this?'

'On the whole I feel sorry for you.'

'You wouldn't try to prevent me?'

'I don't know.'

They went out together through the front door, acknowledging that this was a formal occasion of sorts. The night was pitch dark and starless, breathing relief after the disagreeable heat of the day, and like all country nights it was unquiet, with rustlings and creakings. The fragrance of the viburnum, which this year had flowered exceptionally well, followed them relentlessly round to the back of the house.

'I'll go ahead,' said Cesare. 'There's usually something to fall over.'

There follows a longish scene out in the shedlike office, dealing mainly with the selection of the appropriate gun. In the end, at Salvatore's request, Cesare hands him the shotgun, which Cesare usually uses, as he says, only to shoot vermin.

Salvatore thanked him, and Cesare left him there and walked back again around to the front of the house. A very slight breeze was now getting up, as it often did at this time of night. He went into the entrance hall, leaving the doors open behind him, and as he passed the painted cassone, running his hand along the top, he heard the telephone begin to ring.

'Cesare, it's Chiara.'

'Well, I know your voice,' he said. 'Where are you?'

'I'm speaking from the Riomaggiore, from the Ricasoli house where I'm staying, it's so good of them to look after me, but Cesare, Salvatore rings me up every evening and this evening he hasn't, and I can't get him at the flat, or the hospital, or at the Gentilini.'

'Why should you think he's here?'

'I don't, I'm just asking you what to do, come sempre.'

'Well, he is here.'

'He's come to talk to you, he's lonely, I knew it.'

'I don't know whether he's lonely or not. He wanted a gun.'

'But he never has a gun.'

'I know, he wanted to borrow one of mine.'

'But what for?'

Cesare considered a little, and said, 'He said he was thinking of shooting himself.'

Chiara, so often misguided, so rarely knowing the right thing to do, now, by a miracle, did know. She said nothing at all. The unexpected silence had its effect on Cesare. After waiting a moment and finding out that she did not ring off, he went out once again. He had meant to spend the evening in peace, sitting in his dining-room.

This time the corner of the back yard seemed to have sprung to life. There were disputing voices. The office door was still open, the weak light poured out, the dog, who never barked, who had not barked when Cesare's father was killed or when the orphans arrived, was barking now. The disturbance was irritating.

'Signor, dottore, that gun does not belong to you.'

Salvatore said something in a low voice, like a sufferer, and Bernardino cried, 'It's not his to give. If it was daylight, you would have to acknowledge that everything up to the north wall of the second olive grove is mine.'

Cesare stepped into the light, took the shot-gun, broke it once again and unloaded it.

'Salvatore, you're wanted on the phone. It's your wife. She's speaking from Riomaggiore.'

Salvatore threw up his hands.

'What's to become of us? We can't go on like this.'

'Yes, we can go on like this,' said Cesare. 'We can go on exactly like this for the rest of our lives.'

Leaving Salvatore to go back by himself, he put the little gun into its correct rack. As soon as the cupboard door was shut the old dog settled off to sleep again. Bernardino disappeared, either into the large spaces of the country night or more probably into the kitchen entrance. Cesare put out the light and locked up. He didn't mind tedium, he was trained to it, but it struck him that he didn't want to walk in and out of his house any more on this particular night.

As he turned the corner Salvatore was coming into the courtyard to find his Vespa. He called out that he was going back to Florence and would be starting first thing in the morning for Riomaggiore.[4]

And that is how the novel ends. There are many moments on this last page that could have offered a firmer, more resounding ending—Cesare's remark about going on exactly like this for the rest of their lives (which would probably be the closest thing to the stated point of this novel, or any Penelope Fitzgerald novel,

[4] Penelope Fitzgerald, *Innocence* (London: Flamingo, 1986), 220, 221–2.

that we're ever likely to get); or even, if one were to prefer a dying-fall final note, the line about Cesare's not wanting to go out any more on this particular night. But Fitzgerald chooses instead to end on a sentence that is at once a new beginning and an inevitable repetition of what came earlier. We know that when Salvatore and Chiara get back together they will have exactly the same problems as they had before; Cesare knows it; even they know it. Yet we could not have wished Salvatore dead, even if it solved those problems. We want them to get back together again and we also don't want it. In a way, this whole novel—but particularly this ending—is an elaborate working-out of the last line of *The Bostonians*, where James says of his heroine's tears, 'It is to be feared that with the union, so far from brilliant, into which she was about to enter, these were not the last she was destined to shed.' But though I love Henry James with all my heart, and have always loved that sentence, I must admit it seems melodramatic in comparison to the Penelope Fitzgerald version.

I have not mentioned the obvious Italianness of the tone here, which one can locate partly in those run-on strings of sentences that sound so much like rapid Italian speech. Nor have I said anything about the humour (also very Italian): the digression about insurance policies, for instance, or the almost slapstick way in which Salvatore's salvation depends partly on a neighbourly dispute about boundaries. Let us take all those virtues for granted, now, in these late novels by Penelope Fitzgerald. What I want to focus on here is the skewed slice-of-time aspect, the way the book manages to encompass both the events it actually describes and those it does not.

It's not just that the novel ends abruptly, before we find out whether things have turned out well or badly. (They have turned out well *and* badly, as they have a habit of doing in Penelope Fitzgerald's world, and in ours.) It isn't simply that we can't know what happens after the novel ends. There are all sorts of other things we can equally never know. Did Cesare's return to the office save Salvatore, or had he been saved already by Bernardino? Would Salvatore actually have killed himself, if left alone, and did Cesare believe he would do it? Would Chiara ultimately have been happier if Salvatore had died at this point? How would Cesare have answered her if she had said something reproachful to him instead of keeping silent?

I find it somehow perfect that the key moment of the climactic scene in a Penelope Fitzgerald novel should be a moment of spontaneous silence. It is in those wordless moments—the ones between the lines, or before the lines begin, or after they end— that her stories have their secret life. What she gives us on the page, she manages to suggest, is only a small part of what is really there.

I have gathered from various sources that Penelope Fitzgerald is considered, or has considered herself to be, a religious writer, a religious person. This may well be the case. However, I would not have supposed it from reading her novels. To me, they are the work of a pure agnostic. And by this I mean not just someone who feels we can't ever know that God exists, but also someone whose God, if he did exist, would never be able fully to know *us*.

Afterword

On Saturday, 29 April 2000, at a conference at the Huntington Library in Los Angeles, I delivered something like the above as a lecture. I say 'something like', because the lecture was not written down: it was delivered impromptu, with the aid of a page of notes and the three books I planned to quote from. I thought that occasion would be sufficient unto itself, a way to disseminate the Penelope Fitzgerald virus into a roomful of eager, friendly listeners. It is only in the aftermath that I have felt impelled to write my talk down.

The day after I returned from the conference, on 1 May, I received an email from the conference organizer, my friend

Zachary Leader, who had just flown back to his home in London. 'I'm sorry to have to tell you', he wrote in passing, 'that this afternoon's papers are reporting the death of Penelope Fitzgerald.' And over the next couple of days I got many similar notes of condolence, as if I had in some way been connected to her.

I never met Penelope Fitzgerald, but her death at 83 was a shock to me, as it was to the many people I know who loved her work. It is not just that we will miss the future work, the novels that will remain unwritten because death has stolen their author. It is also that we'll miss the notion of her as a living, continuing presence—not unlike those women in Vermeer paintings, or the characters in her own novels, who seem to go on forever even as they are locked in a particular moment. As an author, of course, she will always have this kind of presence for her new readers. But to those of us whose lives overlapped with hers, she was more than an author; she also served as a special kind of literary guide. Many of the old, good books I discovered for the first time in the last few years— from L. P. Hartley's *Eustace and Hilda*, through Alberto Moravia's *The Woman of Rome*, to James Farrell's *The Siege of Krishnapur*—were recommended by Penelope Fitzgerald, either in print (she reviewed a Farrell biography for the *TLS*) or through indirect word-of-mouth (my friend Arthur, who met her, passed along her recommendations of Moravia and Hartley).

I did not know Penelope Fitzgerald, but she affected me as if I did, and when I spoke about her in Los Angeles she felt very alive to me, very immediately present. I had the sense, up at the podium in front of the conference audience, that I had to live up to what she asked of me, as a reader and a critic. It made me nervous, but it also gave me courage, as if I had a strong ally. Yet when I read the obituaries that came out on 2 May, they said she died sometime on the previous Friday, so she was already dead when I stood at that podium. It is in a useless attempt to reverse that process—to overcome my consciousness of her death and make her live once again for me—that I have written down what I said about her at that brief moment out of time when I thought she was still alive.

9

Why Christopher Isherwood
Stopped Writing Fiction

KATHERINE BUCKNELL

In 1938, William Somerset Maugham told Virginia Woolf that
Christopher Isherwood '[held] the future of the English novel in
his hands.'[1] Isherwood had already published *Mr. Norris
Changes Trains* (1935), *Sally Bowles* (1937),[2] two other novels,
and his fictionalized autobiography *Lions and Shadows* (1938),
and he had also written three plays and most of a travel book
with W. H. Auden with whom he would shortly emigrate, in
January 1939, to the United States. Two decades later, when
Isherwood and his companion from 1953 onwards, the Ameri-
can painter Don Bachardy, visited Maugham in the south of
France, Maugham said over lunch, 'you threw it all away.'
Maugham went on to say that Isherwood had thrown it all
away 'for personal happiness and for Vedanta. "And," said
Willie, "I envy you." '[3]

Maugham had a point about personal happiness and Vedanta.
Sated with literary and social success and disillusioned both by

---

[1] See entry of 1 Nov. 1938 in *The Diary of Virginia Woolf*, ed. Anne Olivier Bell
and Andrew McNeillie, 5 vols. (London: Hogarth Press, 1977–84), v. 185.

[2] Later incorporated into *Goodbye to Berlin* (London: Hogarth Press, 1939).

[3] Isherwood, unpublished diary, 15 Sept. 1960.

his own pseudo-political commitment and by the crisis ending of his relationship with his German boyfriend, Heinz Nedder-meyer, Isherwood had left for America dreaming of a new boy he was already half in love with and hoping to find a more authentic way to live. At first everything had seemed to fall into place. He moved from New York to California, where he settled down with the boy and paid their bills by writing for the movies, and he was initiated into the Vedanta sect of the Hindu religion in July 1939. The Second World War pushed him into an extreme acting out of his long-held pacifist and his newly adopted religious beliefs: he parted with the boy, for various reasons, and lived for a time as a novice monk, performing voluntary work under the auspices of the Quakers. But writing had become difficult.

During the war Isherwood produced only a few short stories and one slim, exquisite novel, *Prater Violet* (1945), which looked back to his European experiences and to his last years at home in London. After that, it was nine years before he published *The World in the Evening* (1954), the novel that changed Maugham's (and probably others') view of him for the worse. It looked as though his career was petering out. He even neglected his diary for nearly half a decade after the war ended. During this period, Isherwood lived with an outspoken photographer, William Caskey, with whom he was destined not to find personal happiness; the two of them drove each other, through drink and argument, to the edge of despair before parting. Thus Isherwood came to recognize that domestic sta-bility was for him an essential prerequisite to writing anything at all, and he managed to establish a home by himself. The play *I Am a Camera* (transformed in 1966 into the musical *Cabaret*) helped to secure him financially, and at last, in February 1953, the promise of personal happiness appeared in the form of Don Bachardy, then an 18-year-old college student.

The experience of falling in love with Bachardy is what first made Isherwood feel that he might give up writing fiction. He

recorded in his diary a glimmering intuition that life was going
to interest him more:

—the nice smell of redwood as I lifted the garage door. And the
feeling of impotence—or, what it really amounts to, lack of inclin-
ation to cope with a constructed, invented plot—the feeling, why not
write what one experiences, from day to day? And then, as I slid my
door back, this sinking-sick feeling of love for Don . . . and the reality
of that—so far more than all this tiresome fiction. Why invent—
when Life is so prodigious?

Perhaps I'll never write another novel, or anything invented—
except, of course, for money.

Write, live what happens: Life is too sacred for invention— though
we may lie about it sometimes, to heighten it.[4]

Perhaps it was inevitable that Isherwood's long quest to find a
right way to live would eventually take over as the subject of his
writing. His background was minor gentry, and his mother's
diaries afford a view of a milieu in which passing the time
well—painting, music, theatrical entertainments, travel—
along with writing diaries and letters about doing so, was the
central pursuit. Friends like Auden or Edward Upward, sons of
hard-working doctors, were obliged to earn a living almost
immediately upon leaving university; as a young man, Isherwood had a small income from his family. Perfecting his personal life was a privilege of his class, perhaps the only such
privilege he did not discard, despite the fact that after his emigration to America, he, too, had to earn a living and worked
compulsively most of the time on movie projects and on his own
writing. But in the end, personal happiness and Vedanta called
upon Isherwood to commit himself publicly to the gay liberation
movement and to Ramakrishna. The detachment of the novelist
gave way to deep engagement. During the last third of his career,
Isherwood stopped writing fiction and instead tried to tell the

---

[4] See entry of 20 Apr. 1953 in Isherwood, *Diaries Volume One: 1939–1960*, ed.
Katherine Bucknell (London: Methuen, 1996), 455–6.

true story of his own life as a way of explaining and testifying to his beliefs.

Maugham could not have known in 1960 that Isherwood had three novels yet to appear—*Down There on a Visit* (1962), which was already half finished, *A Single Man* (1964), probably Isherwood's masterpiece, and *A Meeting by the River* (1967). As if in response to Maugham's criticism, these three novels address the themes of the personal life and of religious belief—the inner life, as Isherwood's hero, E. M. Forster, might have called it. *A Single Man* in particular advances the tradition of the English novel in the cultural setting of Isherwood's new movie-obsessed homeland. It is modelled on Virginia Woolf's *Mrs Dalloway*, and it is about the right length for a screenplay; indeed Isherwood, by then an experienced writer for the Hollywood studios, first conceived of *A Single Man* as a film.[5] Nonetheless, by the end of the 1960s, Isherwood did give up writing fiction and while still at the height of his powers turned solely to autobiography, producing *Kathleen and Frank* (1971), his memoir of his parents, *Christopher and His Kind* (1976), a retelling of his life during the 1930s, and *My Guru and His Disciple* (1980), about his relationship with Swami Prabhavananda.

Isherwood had always been an autobiographer of sorts. All of his work—novels, travel books, memoirs—adapts his personal experience in varying ways, usually drawing from the diaries he began to keep steadily in the early 1920s. At his public school, Repton, he was trained as a historian, and he won a scholarship to read history at Cambridge. Cambridge history seemed dull; Isherwood left after writing joke answers on his Tripos papers. Nevertheless, a historian's impulse to record lies behind much of his writing. Take the famous passage near the opening of *Goodbye to Berlin*: 'I am a camera with its shutter open, quite passive, recording, not thinking. Recording the man shaving at the window opposite and the woman in the kimono washing her

---

[5] He called the proposed film 'The Day's Journey'; see *Diaries Volume One: 1939–1960*, 16 Dec. 1954, p. 475.

hair. Some day, all this will have to be developed, carefully printed, fixed.'[6] The modern, mechanical process of 'recording' gestures toward documentary realism. Of course, as Isherwood well knew, even photography is interpretative. As he also knew, writing down his observations changed them. Isherwood the writer was never passive, never not thinking. His own sort of history writing was subjective, intuitive, psychological. He had a journalist's instinct for knowing where to go and whom to observe and talk to, and he rendered his personal impressions with a historian's sense of the interconnection between the popular psyche and the facts of political and social change. His characters were drawn as eccentric, unique individuals, and yet they somehow epitomized and stood for a whole epoch.

Isherwood's appearance as a narrator in so many of his stories highlights for the reader his implied view that the storyteller is never entirely objective. The Isherwood narrator is not necessarily 'unreliable', but he intervenes between the reader and the reality he undertakes to represent—sometimes more, sometimes less. As has often been remarked, Isherwood's 1930s narrator is a bland, sexually neutral figure. This is partly because as a homosexual, Isherwood could not give a forthright account of himself in print until well into the second half of the century. There are homosexual characters in his early novels, but references to their sexuality are obvious only to readers who are looking for them. Some characters are portrayed as heterosexual although their real life originals were homosexual, as with 'Mr Norris' and Gerald Hamilton. In the 1970s, Isherwood explained that it would have caused scandal and probably legal difficulties if, during the 1930s, he had tried to write overtly about homosexuals—in particular, about himself as a homosexual. He feared to embarrass his mother or to have his allowance cut off by his uncle. But, more importantly, he feared to alienate the reader; he

---

[6] *Goodbye to Berlin*, p. 13; later included in *The Berlin Stories* (New York: New Directions, 1954).

wanted the reader to identify with the narrator as an ordinary figure and to share in the narrator's perceptions of the subject matter. In *Mr Norris Changes Trains*, for instance, attention would have been shifted away from Mr Norris 'if Christopher had made his Narrator an avowed homosexual, with a homosexual's fantasies, preferences and prejudices. The Narrator would have become so odd, perhaps so interesting, that his presence would have thrown the novel out of perspective.'[7]

A Single Man, with its odd, interesting homosexual main character, George, is the novel that Isherwood dared not write in the 1930s. George with his homosexual's fantasies, preferences, and prejudices indeed commands the whole book, and he is more closely based on Isherwood's own personality than any other Isherwood character. When Isherwood got stuck in an early version of the novel, called *The Englishwoman*, Bachardy, as Isherwood recorded in his diary, 'made a really brilliant simple suggestion, namely that it ought to be *The Englishman*—that is me. This is very far-reaching.'[8] Thus, Isherwood moved beyond imitating *Mrs Dalloway* toward making something new in the lyrical form Woolf had invented. He had praised *Mrs Dalloway* abjectly and repeatedly in his diary,[9] but after Bachardy's suggestion, Isherwood didn't mention Woolf's novel again. The personality until then concealed behind the Isherwood narrator figure now emerged as a fully developed fictional character, a middle-aged, gay Englishman, teaching literature at a southern Californian university, mourning his lover killed in a car crash and

---

[7] Isherwood, *Christopher and His Kind* (New York: Farrar Straus and Giroux, 1976), 186; (London: Methuen, 1977), 142.

[8] Isherwood, unpublished diary, 18 Sept. 1963. His diaries record that Bachardy offered numerous suggestions about his work, including inventing many of Isherwood's titles. Recently Bachardy said that Isherwood often made him serve as a kind of medium: 'I felt he used me to tell him what he already sensed or knew about where he should go' (Convensation with Katherine Bucknell, 11 June 2001).

[9] For instance, he called it, 'one of the most beautiful novels or prose poems or whatever that I have ever read. It is prose written with absolute pitch, a perfect ear. You could perform it with instruments. Could I write a book like that and keep within the nature of my own style? I'd love to try.' Unpublished diary, 22 Aug. 1963.

entering into a playful new friendship with a young, straight male student.

In October 1963 and again in November 1964, Isherwood wrote in his diary that he felt certain *A Single Man* was his masterpiece.[10] He also remarked that, despite its sour reception, he felt good about having written it, 'Not so much as a work of art but as a deed. I feel: I spoke the truth, and now let them swallow it or not, as they see fit. That's a very good feeling, and this is the first time that I have really felt it.'[11] A long and tortured process led up to this feeling. During the 1930s, the challenge of disguising his homosexuality perhaps gave his work an erotic charge that accounts for some of its special qualities: half-repressed hilarity, intensely cerebral linguistic enthusiasm, self-conscious charm. Then as the years went by, the same challenge had begun to twist his work out of shape. In the 1940s and 1950s, he started and restarted *The World in the Evening* (for years with the working title *The School of Tragedy*) but never felt sure of the identity or the sexuality of his main character and never felt sure how to tell his story. In his diary at the time, he remarked of 'Stephen Monk', 'he has got to be me . . . it must be written out of the middle of *my* consciousness,'[12] but looking back in the 1970s he ridiculed the aspiration of his younger self: 'How could he write out of the middle of his consciousness about someone who was tall, bisexual, and an heir to a fortune?'[13]

Although *The World in the Evening* was more explicit and more sympathetic about its homosexual and bisexual characters than any of Isherwood's previous books, Isherwood had to manipulate his publishers in order to achieve this degree of artistic candour. He wanted to include two homosexual love scenes, and he knew that he would be asked to modify them, so he deliberately wrote them more strongly than necessary in

[10] Isherwood, unpublished diary, 31 Oct. 1963 and 23 Nov. 1964.
[11] Isherwood, unpublished diary, 7 Sept. 1964.
[12] *Diaries Volume One: 1939–1960*, 17 Aug. 1949, p. 414.
[13] *Lost Years, A Memoir: 1945–1951*, 200.

order, subsequently, to be seen to be complying with his publishers' requests. Stephen Monk's guilt over his past sexual sins seems strident because Isherwood could not depict the actual nature of the sins. Then, in order to make Monk's hysteria seem justified, Isherwood also had to exaggerate the puritanical character of the Quakers among whom Monk was living. Monk's same-sex affair is marked on his side by coy reluctance and on his lover's by sulkiness so embittered as to make the lover seem unlovable. Boldly, Isherwood included two 'good' homosexual characters, Charles Kennedy and Bob Wood, who are settled in a long-term relationship and who are pointedly depicted as contributors to society: Kennedy is a doctor; Wood volunteers for the army when the Second World War begins. Even more boldly, Isherwood has Wood say about the war: 'Compared with this business of being queer, and the laws against us, and the way we're pushed around even in peacetime—this war hardly seems to concern me at all.' Still, Wood joins up, telling Monk, who is a pacifist: 'I can't be a C[onscientious] O[bjector] because, if they declared war on the queers—tried to round us up and liquidate us, or something—I'd fight. I'd fight till I dropped. I know that. I'd be so mad, I wouldn't even feel scared. . . . So how can I say I'm a pacifist?'[14] These are sentiments Isherwood admired, even though, as a pacifist, he did not share them.

Isherwood's new boldness in *The World in the Evening* may have been inspired partly by reading *The City and the Pillar*, which Gore Vidal sent him in 1948 before it was published. He was even more impressed by John Horne Burns's *The Gallery*, Calder Willingham's *End as a Man*, and Willard Motley's *Knock on Any Door*, all published in 1947 and all containing striking passages about homosexuals.[15] Change was in the air. In 1948,

[14] *The World in the Evening* (New York: Random House, 1954), 281; (London: Methuen, 1954), 310–11.
[15] Isherwood met Gore Vidal in Paris soon after reading the typescript of *The City and the Pillar*—Vidal's bitter tale of an adolescent same-sex romance that evolves into an unrequited, rage-inducing love—and they became lifelong friends. He met Burns in 1947, and later noted that he wished he had had time to know him

Alfred Kinsey published *Sexual Behavior in the Human Male*; his ten years worth of interviews suggested among other things that as many as 37 per cent of men had had at least one homosexual experience after the onset of adolescence. Above all, the war altered the circumstances of many homosexuals, certainly in America. It is a cliché that persistent nearness of death and of one another (for instance, on board ship or in crowded military digs) liberates human beings from sexual reticence; certainly, Isherwood's own accounts of the war years depict busy sexual activity, in many forms, among military personnel on the move and civilians on the edge. Mobilization also brought about significant long-term demographic shifts, and homosexual men who moved from small towns to larger ones, to ports and urban centres, were able to establish not only contact and relationships but even a new sense of group identity.

Such trends are illustrated in Isherwood's diary, which tells, for instance, how William Caskey's naval career ended with a 'blue discharge', neither honourable nor dishonourable, after he was implicated in what Isherwood called 'a homosexual witch-hunt'.[16] If anything, this strengthened Caskey's rebelliousness and his sense of common purpose with his homosexual friends. Toward the end of the war, Caskey arrived in Santa Monica with a 'sister', Hayden Lewis, a civilian naval clerk from a tiny rural community in Alabama, who had lost his job in the same scandal. Lewis found a boyfriend, started a business with him, and settled near Los Angeles for several decades. Isherwood enormously admired Caskey's outspokenness about his homosexuality, and Bob Wood in *The World in the Evening* is partly

better. *End as a Man* he called, 'an exciting discovery and the beginning of Christopher's (more or less) constant enthusiasm for Willingham's work.' (*Lost Years*, 176n.). Of *Knock on Any Door*, he wrote, 'Christopher was much moved...when he read it; this was *his* idea of a sad story. He fell in love with the hero and wrote Willard Motley a fan letter' (*Lost Years*, 140n.). Motley's hero, a heterosexual petty criminal who hustles as trade part time, embodies the defiance of authority which often captivated Isherwood in his real-life acquaintances.

[16] *Lost Years*, 43.

modelled on Caskey, who 'declared his homosexuality loudly and shamelessly and never cared whom he shocked. He was a pioneer gay militant in this respect—except that you couldn't imagine him joining any movement.'[17]

In 1949, Isherwood himself was drawn into a bohemian circle known as The Benton Way Group—artists, intellectuals, social workers, teachers, mostly from the Midwest—who lived together in a kind of pre-commune. Many of them were active homosexuals. Among their leading lights were the poet and social critic Paul Goodman, the philosopher David Sachs, and the scholar and writer Edouard Roditi. Evelyn Hooker, the psychologist who made her career studying the gay community in Los Angeles and who, in 1956, was among the first ever to present research demonstrating that homosexuals were as well adjusted psychologically as heterosexuals, was also involved with The Benton Way Group and became a close friend of Isherwood's. The group's all-night parties were fuelled by highbrow talk about love and the homosexual in modern society. Thus, Isherwood came into contact again with something like the organized radical impulse of Magnus Hirschfeld and the Institute for Sexual Science, which had launched his sexual liberation in Berlin in the 1930s but which had been persecuted and then obliterated by the Nazis and the war.

Gay liberation was the only movement for social change to which Christopher Isherwood ever felt personally and entirely committed. He had strong Communist sympathies during the 1930s, but he never joined the party. His regret at not having been able to commit himself, like his friend Edward Upward, to the revolutionary cause of the workers in Europe and England is evoked in *Prater Violet* (1945). His far more complex feelings, including guilt, about the detachment with which he observed the rise of the Nazis is the concluding preoccupation of *Goodbye to Berlin* and haunts *Down There on a Visit*. His diaries are laced

[17] Ibid. 54.

with related anxieties about being away from England during the war. But the fact is, only the predicament of the homosexual really engaged him. As he wrote in the early 1970s, 'Christopher was certainly more a socialist than a fascist, and more a pacifist than he was a socialist. But he was a queer first and foremost.'[18] The only consideration which ever restrained Isherwood's involvement in the gay movement was the fear that he might embarrass Swami Prabhavananda. Swami accepted Isherwood's way of life, but his congregation was entirely susceptible of being shocked. Nonetheless, Isherwood and Bachardy participated in gay rallies and parades. In April 1971, Isherwood noted in his diary that he was attracted to the idea of himself as 'one of the Grand Old Men of the movement',[19] and in July, the same year, he recorded that he felt compelled, now, to mention his homosexuality to everyone who interviewed him.

Isherwood had first come across a published statement that he was a homosexual in January 1971 when an English fan sent him a clipping from such an interview: 'The article says I am a homosexual, quite flatly, without further explanation. I think this is the first time anyone has said this right out in print. I'm glad he did. It sort of prepares readers for my remarks in *Kathleen and Frank*.'[20] In *Kathleen and Frank*, he presented himself *in propria persona* explicitly as a homosexual for the first time and made clear that his new commitment to the gay movement was both political and intensely personal. In fact, after a visit from one gay activist, he altered a passage near the end of *Kathleen and Frank* to make it more aggressive, incorporating, for example, the phrase, 'heterosexual dictatorship'.[21]

---

[18] *Lost Years*, 190.

[19] Isherwood, unpublished diary, 19 Apr. 1971.

[20] Isherwood, unpublished diary, 13 Jan. 1971. The interview, with Brendan Lehane, was conducted during the spring of 1970 when Isherwood was visiting England. The piece appeared in *The Daily Telegraph*, 7 Aug. 1970.

[21] Isherwood, unpublished diary, 30 Dec. 1970. The activist was Michael Silverstein, who, according to Isherwood, believed 'a revolution is inevitable'; see unpublished diary, 28 Dec. 1970.

Kathleen and Frank was first conceived in 1966 as a special kind of autobiography in which Isherwood could explore the family romance which had produced him and which still continued to unfold within him. It was to be a psychological account shaped in particular by the theories of Carl Jung, whose own autobiography Isherwood frequently referred to in his diary:

The book should be preoccupied with the concept of autobiography as myth, following Jung's remarks at the beginning of his autobiography, and there should be a lot of examples of how myth is created out of the materials of experience.[22]

In a sense, Isherwood set out in this new book to be his own psychoanalyst, and he began to unpick and to explain away the fictions he had created in his earlier writing. As soon as he began working on *Kathleen and Frank* he decided to reread two of his early books to remind himself exactly what his youthful myths had been.[23] The preparation and writing of *Kathleen and Frank* brought him increasingly into contact with facts. 'I realize more and more clearly I am going to rely heavily on my Mother's diaries.'[24] He reread them all, roughly seventy volumes, and copied out passages from them and from his father's letters and other family papers; the finished memoir is loaded with quotation. Such a dutiful handling of primary material would have been inconceivable in his youth, when he destroyed his own diaries once he had written the books based on them. After reading his mother's diaries about the years of the marriage up to Frank Isherwood's death (almost certainly in May 1915, when Isherwood was 10), he observed, 'I feel that I know Frank for the first time.'[25] And he recognized that his youthful myths about his parents had fulfilled psychological

---

[22] Isherwood, unpublished diary, 22 Jan. 1967.
[23] *The Memorial* (London: Hogarth Press, 1932) and *Lions and Shadows* (London: Hogarth Press, 1938).
[24] Isherwood, unpublished diary, 7 Apr. 1967.
[25] Isherwood, unpublished diary, 6 Aug. 1968.

needs powerful enough to obscure certain objective facts—facts which now re-emerged and called for a different kind of attention:

One thing that Don found exciting was the idea that I really didn't know my father at all, and that the myth about him was created for my own private reasons—i.e. that I needed an anti-heroic hero to oppose to the official hero-figure erected by the patriots of the period who were deadly enemies. Therefore it would be most interesting to show how certain aspects of my father had to be supressed, because they were disconcertingly square; eg his references in his letters to 'real men' etc.[26]

Writing *Kathleen and Frank* changed Isherwood for good. Afterwards he felt again, as he had briefly felt when he fell in love with Don Bachardy in 1953, that his reactions to real experience were more vivid and more intense than anything he could invent. But he had found that writing accurate history was a more severe discipline than writing fiction because he could not alter the facts to conform to his artistic needs. Here's what he wrote in his diary at Thanksgiving 1970, not long after completing *Kathleen and Frank*:

Have I given up all idea of writing another novel, then? No, not necessarily. The problem really is as follows: The main thing I have to offer as a writer are my reactions to experience (these are my fiction or my poetry, or whatever you want to call it). Now, these reactions are more positive when I am reacting to actual experiences, than when I am reacting to imagined experiences. Yet, the actuality of the experiences does bother me, the brute facts keep tripping me up, I keep wanting to rearrange and alter the facts so as to relate them more dramatically to my reactions. Facts are never simple, they come up in awkward bunches. You find yourself reacting to several different facts at one and the same time, and this is messy and unclear and undramatic. I have had this difficulty many times while writing *Kathleen and Frank*. For instance, Christopher's reactions to Kath-

---

[26] Isherwood, unpublished diary, 22 Jan. 1967.

leen are deplorably complex and therefore self-contradictory, and therefore bad drama.[27]

Around this time, Isherwood began to write the sexually explicit memoir of his life immediately following the Second World War which was published posthumously as *Lost Years: A Memoir, 1945–1951*. He called it a reconstructed diary because he was trying to build up a day-to-day record of the stressful, alcohol-sodden years with Caskey which had ended in writer's block and personal despair. He used his pocket appointment books to remind himself of events, and he called upon friends for their letters and recollections. Despite being forced to rely partly on his own incomplete memories, he was once again, as in *Kathleen and Frank*, trying to establish a factual, chronological record of objective events. The reconstructed diary is sexually explicit partly because, for the first time ever, it could be. In 1971, well into the cultural and sexual revolution spawned during the 1960s and two years after the riot outside the Stonewall bar in Greenwich Village which launched the gay-liberation movement, Isherwood felt comfortable committing to paper— though not then for publication—details of sex acts which were still widely illegal. Since the end of the 1950s, censorship laws in the USA had been gradually relaxed; the courts had increasingly required the post office to deliver magazines formerly ruled obscene and had permitted publication and sale of books that might once have attracted a ban. Even the Production Code, governing censorship of films, gave way during the 1960s. Isherwood could, without much risk of penalty, record the true habits and attitudes of the homosexual milieu in which he had long lived in semi-secrecy.

The reconstructed diary proved in part to be a preparation for writing *Christopher and His Kind*, the book which made Isherwood a hero—even an icon—of the gay-liberation movement. For *Christopher and his Kind*, he refined his new autobiograph-

---

[27] Isherwood, unpublished diary, 26 Nov. 1970.

ical method, trying to compromise between invention, which now felt burdensome, and 'brute facts' which he had found awkward to arrange when writing *Kathleen and Frank*. He called the finished memoir a 'a non-fictitious novel'.[28] As with *Kathleen and Frank*, he built from recorded observation toward myth, and he again called upon Jung as his model:

I am basing the opening on my diary, but already I am expanding the material and, I dare to hope, beginning to see how I can work away from mere narrative. My inspiration is Jung's resolve 'to tell my personal myth.' Therefore, I shall try to dwell only on the numinous, or the magical and the mythical.[29]

His planned subject was his years in America, but, ruled as he now was by historical chronology and by fact, he found that he first had to go back in time and explain why he had come to America to begin with. Put plainly, he had come because he was a homosexual, and at last it was possible to say this in print and to lay to rest both the public criticism and the private guilt that had resulted from his departure from England on the eve of the Second World War:

My difficulty is that I want to have the book start with our departure for America. But I have now realized that I can only put our depart-ure in perspective if I begin with Germany—why I went there—'to find my sexual homeland'—and go on to tell about my wander-ings with Heinz and his arrest and the complicated resentment which grew out of it, against Kathleen and England, Kathleen *as* England.[30]

As with *Kathleen and Frank*, he worked from primary docu-ments—diaries and letters written during the 1930s, including the few diaries of his own that he had not already destroyed. He also drew on published memoirs like Stephen Spender's *World within World* (1951).

---

[28] Isherwood, unpublished diary, 22 Sept. 1976.
[29] Isherwood, unpublished diary, 14 Sept. 1973.
[30] Isherwood, unpublished diary, 29 Oct. 1973.

Christopher and His Kind sold faster than any of his other books. When he went to sign copies at the Oscar Wilde Bookshop in Greenwich Village, a line of mostly young men formed around the block: 'I had such a feeling that this is my tribe and I loved them.'[31] Isherwood never felt as easily affectionate toward his fellow Hindus, and perhaps this is partly why writing about his religious beliefs proved to be as difficult as—perhaps more difficult than—writing about his homosexuality. All his post-war fiction addresses religion in some way, but he tended to handle Hindu themes obliquely. In *Prater Violet* and in *A Single Man* he uses the imagery of narrow paths, mountain peaks, and rock pools in the ocean to evoke a higher, spiritual plane, where the themes of fiction, like all the concerns of Maya, are left behind. The last section of *Down There on a Visit*, 'Paul', presents the Isherwood narrator's conversion to Vedanta as the inevitable outcome of his nightmare journey among the lost in Europe, but rather brilliantly avoids saying why. The narrator adopts the cynical, world-weary tone of the much-travelled and entirely disillusioned Isherwood of the Berlin days or *Prater Violet*, and he shows no sign of spiritual joy or religious conviction. His religious activities are conducted like a seance: spiritual powers are conjured and proven to exist, but their meaning and purpose remain unclear. Nowhere does the narrator mention Swami Prabhavananda—who refused to assist in the religious conversion of Paul's real-life original, Denny Fouts—and he hardly mentions love. Love, though, was at the centre of Isherwood's own religious belief, and so was Swami Prabhavananda.

In the winter of 1963–4, Isherwood accompanied Swami Prabhavananda to India, where he experienced a personal crisis about appearing in public to talk about Vedanta. After speaking at a Parliament of Religions held in Calcutta, he wrote in his diary that he could never do such a thing again:

[31] Isherwood, unpublished diary, 23 Dec. 1976.

I was swept by gusts of furious resentment—against India, against being pushed around, even against Swami himself. I resolved to tell him that I refuse ever again to appear in the temple or anywhere else and talk about God. Part of this resolve is quite valid; I *do* think that when I give these God-lectures it is Sunday religion in the worst sense. As long as I quite unashamedly get drunk, have sex, and write books like *A Single Man*, I simply cannot appear before people as a sort of lay minister. The inevitable result must be that my ordinary life becomes divided and untruthful. Or rather, in the end, the only truth left is in my drunkeness, my sex, and my art, not in my religion. For me religion must be quite private as far as I'm publicly concerned. I can still write about it informatively, but I must not appear before people on a platform as a living witness and example.[32]

Another diary entry records telling this to Swami anxiously, even hysterically, in order to make a strong impression and free himself quickly from further obligation. The episode harked back to Isherwood's personal struggles during the 1940s and 1950s, when he had occasionally returned to the monastery (at Ivar Avenue and at Trabuco) and used it as a sort of spiritual drying-out clinic in times of domestic crisis. But in India, he settled once and for all the degree to which he could be Swami's disciple and also remain himself, and the resolution of this long-standing question about his religious identity informs *A Meeting by the River*, his last work of fiction. Isherwood transcribed whole passages from his diary of the India trip into the novel.

A Meeting by the River, like 'Paul', depicts two characters engaged in a struggle over belief, 'the temptation of any saint by any satan'.[33] The characters are brothers, and the catalyst for their struggle is the decision of one brother, Oliver, to become a Hindu monk. The second brother, Patrick, offers Oliver a free ticket back to real life: England, a career, perhaps an affair with his wife. But he offers out of competitiveness and a need to

---

[32] Isherwood, unpublished diary, 31 Dec. 1963.
[33] Isherwood, unpublished diary, 4 Jan. 1966.

justify his own duplicitous life as a bisexual married man who
cheats on his wife and misleads his lover. The conflict between
the brothers reflects the conflict between two impulses in Isherwood's own life toward the sacred and the secular.[34] As Paul tells
the narrator in *Down There on a Visit*, 'Either be a proper monk,
or a dirty old man.'[35] In fact, Denny Fouts made this remark to
Isherwood in September 1943 when Isherwood was still living
as a demi-monk in the monastery at Ivar Avenue and trying to
decide whether or not he would leave.[36] But if Isherwood
learned anything from his unhappiness during the subsequent
years with Caskey, it was that for him there was no such simple
choice. He would always be both of the brothers, both a monk
and a dirty old man. Achieving a balance between the sacred and
the secular life was to be his daily, long-term struggle. At the
crisis of *A Meeting by the River*, Oliver has a vision of his Swami
which enables him to see his own world and his brother's world
as one in Swami's love. Once he has had this vision, he no longer
feels any compulsion to choose between two different ways of
life. Isherwood's own real-life Swami accepted Isherwood as he
was, yet he never ceased to try to tempt Isherwood back to the
monastery.

A Meeting by the River is, in some respects, a vehicle for a
religious debate. It is overridingly cerebral and includes only one
important action, the taking or not taking of a religious vow.
Isherwood knew this from the outset: 'the setting of this narrative shall be, as it were, "mental." I am emphatically *not* writing
about the humours and quaintnesses of the Orient. This is not a
realistic novel.'[37] In some respects, it is hardly a novel at all. As

[34] The personalities of the brothers are not based on Isherwood but on other real-
life figures. The monk, Oliver, is partly modelled on John Yale, later Swami Vidyat-
mananda, and Patrick is partly based on Frank Taylor and on Stephen Spender.

[35] *Down There on a Visit* (London: Methuen, 1962), 333; (New York: Simon and
Schuster, 1962), 301.

[36] Isherwood, *Diaries Volume One, 1939–1960*, 15 Sept. 1943, p. 316: 'Either
make up your mind to be a monk or a dirty old man.'

[37] Isherwood, unpublished diary, 20 Mar. 1965.

with *The World in the Evening*, Isherwood planned to tell the story through diaries and letters which would reveal the inner thoughts of the characters, but he referred in his diary to the burden of making it all up: 'I need to invent so much about the offstage characters.'[38] He borrowed a little from the real-life diary of John Yale, a friend who took his brahmacharya vows at Belur Math in the winter of 1963–4.[39] And indeed, by the time he finished *A Meeting by the River*, Isherwood had already begun to immerse himself in the real-life diaries and letters of his parents. Thus, he was on the brink of the new kind of writing that would occupy him for the rest of his career.

In 1968, after the publication of *A Meeting by the River*, Isherwood had an idea for one more novel—about his relationship with Swami Prabhavananda—and at the time, he was extraordinarily excited:

I felt that spooky thing, the sense of a vast terrain of almost virgin subject-matter, waiting to be explored; and the gasp with which one recognizes and says to oneself, but *that*—that would *have* to be a masterpiece or nothing....[40]

But when he next mentioned the book in his diary, he had completed *Kathleen and Frank*, and he had begun to think that a book about Swami should not be be a work of fiction but a work of fact. Also, he had come to recognize that any narrative about his religious life would have to include an account of Swami's response to his homosexuality:

The idea of a novel about Swami and me no longer seems so appealing. Surely it would be better from every point of view to do this as a factual book? Well of course there is the difficulty of being frank without being indiscreet: but that difficulty always arises in one form or another. For example, it is absolutely necessary that I should say how, right at the start of our relationship, I told Swami

---

[38] Isherwood, unpublished diary, 2 Apr. 1965.
[39] See unpublished diary, 25 Oct. 1965.
[40] Isherwood, unpublished diary, 6 Oct. 1968.

I had a boyfriend (and that he replied, 'Try to think of him as Krishna,') because my personal approach to Vedanta was, among other things, the approach of a homosexual looking for a religion which will accept him. Another difficulty, far more serious, is that the book couldn't be truly complete until after Swami's death.[41]

Isherwood needed to know, materially, how Swami's death would affect him before he could write about their relationship because he had to see if his belief, his sense of the thing Swami had revealed to him, would still be there once Swami himself was gone.

Prabhavananda died on 4 July 1976, and Isherwood immediately planned to write about him. At first, he relished telling how Swami had enabled him to face old age and death with joy— death which had terrified Isherwood unreasonably in youth:

Perhaps the best thing about [the book] will be its final passage, a description of me in old age and of what Swami means to me now that he is dead and of how I view my approaching death and of the phenomenon of happiness near the end of life.[42]

But when the time came, the need for privacy in religious matters which had swept over Isherwood in Calcutta warred with the need to offer himself as a living witness and example of what he professed to believe. The scepticism of his old English friends, the scepticism which in youth he had shared with them and which, in its extreme form, had led them to rebel against all forms of authority, stopped him being able to write:

What is holding me up? Is it that I feel an obligation to declare that Don and I are somehow 'saved...?'
This block which I feel is actually challenging, fascinating. It must have a reason. It must be telling me something.
Am I perhaps inhibited by a sense of the mocking agnostics all around me—ranging from asses like [John] Lehmann to intelligent bigots like Edward [Upward]. Yes, of course I am. In a sense, they are my most important audience. Everything I write is written with a

---

[41] Isherwood, unpublished diary, 26 Nov. 1970.
[42] Isherwood, unpublished diary, 18 Feb. 1977.

consciousness of the opposition and in anwer to its prejudices. Because of this opposition, I am apt to belittle myself, to try to disarm criticism by treating it with a seriousness it doesn't (in my private opinion) deserve. I must not, cannot do this here. I must state my beliefs and be quite intransigent about them. I must also state my doubts, but without exaggerating them. Yes, that's it. I must give the reader a glimpse of myself in a transitional stage, between Swami's death and my own.

The doubts, the fears, the backslidings, the sense of alienation from Swami's presence, all these are easily—too easily—described. One mustn't overemphasize them. What's much more important is a sense of exhilaration, remembering, 'I have seen it,' 'I have been there.'[43]

Isherwood's 'consciousness of the opposition' is virtually unchanged from his youth; it shaped all his writing in different ways throughout his career. Non-fiction demanded and permitted that he concentrate more on his subject than on the opposition; he could not, as he learned with *Kathleen and Frank*, rearrange the facts to make them more dramatic, he could not alter the material in order to entertain, to captivate, to persuade the audience. His devotion to Swami Prabhavananda and to Ramakrishna urged him to tell the truth, and this is perhaps the way in which his religion most influenced his writing. Truth-telling became the greatest possible virtue:

When Swami used to teach me that purity is telling the truth I used to think that this was, if anything, a rather convenient belief for me to have, because it meant that I didn't have to be pure but only to refrain from lying about impurity. Well, that's the minimum or negative interpretation. But thinking about it in relation to Ramakrishna, I saw this: that the greatness of Ramakrishna is not expressed by the fact that he was under all circumstances 'pure'. No. And even if he was pure, that didn't mean he wasn't capable of anything. You always feel that about him—there was nothing that he might not have done—except one thing—tell a lie.[44]

[43] Isherwood, unpublished diary, 23 Oct. 1977.
[44] Isherwood, unpublished diary, 16 Oct. 1961.

At the time that he wrote this passage in his diary, Isherwood was in the midst of preparing his biography of Ramakrishna, which took him about a decade to complete (it was finally published in 1965). His careful labours on this sacred history reveal his fundamental confidence in objective facts. In his life of Ramakrishna, Isherwood abjured 'emotive words', preferring to handle the mysteriousness of his subject simply as a phenomenon. 'A phenomenon is always a fact, an object of experience',[45] Isherwood wrote, and he relied on the facts of Ramakrishna's life, reported in the plainest style he could muster, to draw their own response from the reader. His other writing followed in this direction to a certain degree, growing plainer in style in proportion to the spiritual importance of what he had to say. In his lifetime, his plainest published prose appeared in *My Guru and His Disciple*, which incorporates long passages from his diaries, unrevised and unadorned.

Like Auden and like Edward Upward, Isherwood was celebrated in youth for a near fantastic stylistic brilliance— engaging, effortless, playful, precociously knowing. But the abundance of quasi-mystical imaginative energy in the early writing of these three friends evaporated in the heat of mature conviction. Auden's Christianity, Upward's Marxism, Isherwood's Hinduism and his committment to the gay movement called for sober, earnest handling, and each of them in different ways moved toward a perhaps surprising, solemn committment to tell the truth, unromantically, without illusion. Isherwood worried as he began *Christopher and His Kind* that his writing style had become too heavy, but he was concerned above all with content: 'When I reread my earlier work, I feel that perhaps my style may have lost its ease and brightness and become ponderous. Well, so it's ponderous. At least I still have matter, if not manner.'[46] In the end, fiction itself had to go. Nonetheless, he can be seen as an originator of the documentary and autobio-

---

[45] *Ramakrishna and His Disciples* (London: Methuen, 1965), 1.
[46] Isherwood, unpublished diary, 2 Nov. 1973.

graphical fiction now widely practised in various forms as well as of the present interest in non-fiction, especially autobiography and memoir. It has been observed that one younger friend, Truman Capote, modelled Holly Golightly in *Breakfast at Tiffany's* (1958) on Sally Bowles; then Capote turned from fiction to write *In Cold Blood* (1966), as if he had reflected, by studying Isherwood's career, that to achieve importance as a writer, he needed to address a real historical crime as Isherwood had done in writing about the Nazis in *Goodbye to Berlin*. Other examples of Isherwood's influence on younger writers abound; by now his work is part of the cultural atmosphere.

IO

Shaping Modern English Fiction: The Forms of the Content and the Contents of the Form

VALENTINE CUNNINGHAM

'What sort of novel shall I write?' the beginning novelist Iris Murdoch enquired of herself in her diary in October 1949 (three years and seven months before her first published novel *Under the Net* appeared):

> Vague reduplication of my own situation must be rejected...A tale of someone making a choice!...Some simple frame. In form of a diary? (cf. *La Nausée*) Half in Paris, half in London—some ex-lover confidant in Paris. The task—to break a liaison, achieve something intellectual? Introduce a 'rub'—of the Xavière variety...Some cool other female in London. Light on relation with women. How shall religion come in?[1]

Such reflections, incitements, *aides-mémoires*, densely people novelists' work-books, not least as they plot the next fiction.

[1] Peter J Conradi, *Iris Murdoch: A Life* (London: HarperCollins, 2001), 380: this, along with Conradi's gathering of Murdoch's critical-philosophical texts, *Existentialists and Mystics: Writings on Philosophy and Literature* (London: Chatto and Windus, 1977), and his *The Saint and the Artist: A Study of the Fiction of Iris Murdoch* (London: Macmillan, 1986; 2nd edition 1989; paperback HarperCollins, 2001), is the essential guide to Murdoch's work.

And, characteristically, Murdoch's are a complex mixture of form and content. Here she thinks setting, location (Paris, London) and characters (lover, lovers, an ex-lover, a confidant, intellectual(s), a cool other female, religious people), and event (choice, task, liaisons, intellectual achievements, a hero's light relations with women, possible developments in religious concerns, hampered developments—a 'rub'). She thinks fictional models, Sartre's *La Nausée* (1938; translated 1949), Simone de Beauvoir's *L 'Invitée* (1943)/*She Came to Stay* (1949) (in which the character Xavière appears); *Hamlet* is on her mind (Hamlet talked of the 'rub' of not knowing what awaited you after death, an ignorance which prevented you committing suicide: *rub* is an impediment, a metaphor from the game of bowls). And these models imply, of course, the usual entanglements of form and content: existentialist and Hamletian choosing, the rubs of thought and circumstance, in a Sartrean diary frame. Arrestingly, though, thought about *frame*, the formal shape that these erotic inter-city, cross-channel existentialist doings will be cast in and communicated through, comes very early in the note. Will this novel take the form of an autobiography? The plot will involve someone making a choice: there's a person, a character, envisaged in action, the stuff of a Sartrean plight which could be done as autobiography. But this time the writer will go for the 'form of a diary'.

In point of fact, Iris Murdoch never wrote this novel, at least not in this form. *Under the Net* (1954) is not cast in the shape of a diary; it's a first-person narrative in the autobiographical-confessional mode. But what's important here is that the question of which model of fictional narrative to adopt—which shape, which frame for the story, which formal device or devices, which narrative machine or gadget, or gimmick even (as Martin Amis might, and does, say)[2]—has to come in very early, and is utterly fundamental. When you change the metaphor, said

[2] e.g. *Money* (1984; repr. Harmondsworth: Penguin, 1986), 265.

George Eliot most cannily in *The Mill on the Floss*, talking of ways of picturing minds (the mind of Tom Tulliver, dim at Latin studies, was in question), you change everything.[3] And so it is with fictional form: change the frame, change the form, the formal model, and everything changes.

Noticeable about the course of English fiction is how many fictional models got rapidly tried out at the beginning of the tradition, in the earnest quest for the best ways of accessing the observations, the truths (even), about people and society, about personal and social ethics, religion, economics, about history, mind, language and culture, and so on, all of which novelists saw as the business of the new era for story. There was Bunyan's puritan biography method (*The Pilgrim's Progress*), and then Defoe's diary-puritan autobiography-personal testimony mode (*Robinson Crusoe*), and Swift's autobiography-travelogue-utopian story combo (*Gulliver's Travels*), then Richardson's epistolary model (*Pamela, Clarissa*), and Henry Fielding's picaresque 'Cervantick' comic-epic in prose (*Tom Jones*), and the novel as mock encyclopedia (*Tristram Shandy*), and so on. What's the aptest model for what he wants to write, asks Fielding in *Joseph Andrews*: topography, chorography (writing about particular regions), biography? He settles (in *Joseph Andrews*, in the chapter entitled 'Matter Prefatory in Praise of Biography') for biography, the 'written life'. But formal 'experiment', as these trials are often labelled, never stopped. 'There is an order in every way appropriate,' James Joyce told his friend Frank Budgen about *Ulysses*, thinking of his own questing for 'the perfect order of words in the sentence', but also mindful of his novel's larger formal shaping, its parodic structural imitation of the plot of the *Odyssey* of Homer.[4] And his search for perfect

---

[3] George Eliot, *The Mill on the Floss* (1860), Book Second, 'School Time', ch. 1, 'Tom's "First Half"', The World's Classics edn., ed. Gordon S. Haight, introd. Dinah Birch (Oxford: Oxford University Press, 1996), 140.

[4] Frank Budgen, *James Joyce and the Making of 'Ulysses', and Other Writings*, ed. Clive Hart (London: Oxford University Press, 1972), 20.

order never stopped. Many novelists, of course, settle for some given mode. Which is how genres of fiction build up, and why there's so much routine work at any given moment of fictional history. But it's no accident that we think of fictional importance and significance as in some fashion related to a certain innovative way with form. We prize innovation, 'making it new'. But above all, I think, we prize formal aptness, form and content partnering each other appropriately. The order 'in every way appropriate'.

Vexingly, of course, Joyce did not specify what that appropriateness was, nor how we might define (let alone attain) that 'perfect order' of the sentence. Taking their longer views, literary historians come up with historical-sociological suggestions, ever ready to attach changes in fictional form to historical shifts, to developments in what Marxists classically label the economic base, to altering theories of language and the person, to the death of God, or the end of 'Grand Narratives'. So that Defoe's plot of fortune-making is thought of as apt to his mercantile-puritan era ('religion and the rise of capitalism'), and eighteenth-century picaresque to the era of the stagecoach, and the epistolary novel of the eighteenth century to contemporary stirrings of domesticated bourgeois female consciousness, and the mature, connected-up Dickensian plot to the great agglomerations of people in the Victorian city and to speeded-up railway communications, and George Eliot's highly deterministic ethical plots to her interest in contemporary sociology, and modernist plots of epistemological hesitation, refusal, and general unknowing (Henry James, Joseph Conrad, Virginia Woolf) to collapses of confidence in the old Christianized legal and moral order and the rise of new psychology-led scepticisms, and so on and so forth. All of which kinds of mechanistic explanation as to how alterations in fictional form, the comings and goings of form, might be motored—this envisioning of fictional form (and content) in a deterministic relationship with history and the context—undoubtedly have their attraction.

And it is perfectly possible to come up with instructive explanations along these lines for the great variety of modern British fictional form. For example, to link the mid-twentieth-century plots of those Roman Catholic converts Evelyn Waugh and Graham Greene, novels variously conversionist, believer-oriented, miracle-inspecting, or doubting and heretical, to the anti-modernist reaction which drove many intellectuals to become Roman Catholic Christians. Or to see William Golding's arresting parable mode in *Lord of the Flies* (1954) as reflecting a felt need to turn the fictional clock back to allegory, an allegory about Original Sin and evil, as the only way of aptly confronting the recent *Hitlerzeit* and the atomic age. To see Martin Amis's controversial backwards-proceeding narrative in *Time's Arrow: or, the Nature of the Offence* (1991) as reflecting a sense of how the truly incredible Nazi horrors utterly disrupted conventional linear narration ('No poetry after Auschwitz'), demanding extreme formal alternatives for their telling. To read Samuel Beckett's retreat from the comparative fullnesses of *Murphy* (1938) or the Trilogy—*Molloy* (1950), *Malone Dies* (1951), and *The Unnameable* (1952)—or *Watt* (1953), to the rapidly dwindling minimalisms of the later, jotty, fizzling-out, nearly extinct texts (e.g. *For to End Yet Again, and Other Fizzles*, 1976) as related to the wide challenging of faith in logos in the later twentieth century. To take Julian Barnes's essayistic mode (*Flaubert's Parrot*, 1984, *A History of the World in* $10\frac{1}{2}$ *Chapters*, 1989) as postmodernism's denials of the truthfulness of the merely fictional. To ascribe the so-called magic realism of Angela Carter and Salman Rushdie (an archangel drops in on Thatcher's London in his *The Satanic Verses*, 1988; a woman can grow wings and fly in her *Nights at the Circus*, 1984) not just to a desire to cash in on the practices of South Americans such as Gabriel García Marquez or of the German Günter Grass, but to a persuaded participation in the intensely sceptical modernist movement of carnivalized *post-histoire* (in which old-fashioned history claims and historiographical practices get collapsed into the merely rhetorical, into metaphor, blatant poeticity). To see Angela Carter's investment in what T. S. Eliot (talking of *Ulysses*) called 'the mythical method', her revisionary fairy stories in *The Bloody Chamber* volume (1979), her terrifying mythic re-enactments (*The Magic Toyshop*, 1967, for instance, with its central updating of the story of the rape of Leda by the swan), as part of the great modern movement to rehistoricize the genesis and essence of the Novel, to relate these not to the age of sectarian puritan capitalism, but to the broader fictional church of story-telling, going all the way back to archaic times and ancient myth.[5]

But while there are, doubtless, always particular historical circumstances, utterly contemporary interests, drives, ideologies which can be argued as compelling formal choices and strategies, there's no denying the historical fact that, once instituted, for whatever ascertainable reasons, formal models and devices hang around, and remain available to future practitioners, long after the alleged circumstances of their particular birth and evolution appear to have altered. The menu of tried-out forms stays in place, more or less, for the latest newcomer. And whatever strict determinists might think—and fictional modes do indeed come and go, seemingly in tune with historical moments—choice of forms, at least in our present time, does seem pretty free; though it's true, and inevitably, perhaps, that our current formal freedoms, our operating on a formal self-service canteen basis, also gets historicized by critics as a feature of an alleged historical postmodernity. Certainly recent English fiction goes in for a plethora of modes, picking and mixing with liberal aplomb. Now Martin Amis does first-novelist's autobiography (*The Rachel Papers*, 1973), now big urban satires (such as *Money: A Suicide Note*, 1984, and *London Fields*, 1989), now

---

[5] For the relation of the novel to sectarian puritan capitalism see the grand old Ian Watt thesis in in *The Rise of the Novel* (London: Chatto and Windus, 1957); for the broader fictional church see Margaret Ann Doody, *The True Story of the Novel* (London: HarperCollins, 1997). For Eliot quotation see footnote 20.

Time's Arrow, putting back the Nazi clock, now his pastiche of a hard-bitten New York cop novel (*Night Train*, 1997). Now Angela Carter claims she's writing a 'pataphysical' novel (after she's heard of Alfred Jarry), *The Infernal Desire Machine of Doctor Hoffman* (1972), now she's ploughing a Foucauldian furrow and building a large section of *Nights at the Circus* around the sort of panopticon prison she's come across in Foucault's *Discipline and Punish* (1975), now she's doing modern fairy, now the novel as cinema (*Wise Children*, 1991).

Freeloading pastiche, *hommage*, parody, replay are everywhere. Amis's *Money* waltzes elaborately in the arms of Shakespeare's *Othello* (and Verdi's *Otello*). Graham Swift's Booker Prize-winning *Last Orders* (1996) is a modern Canterbury Pilgrimage after Chaucer, a story of men travelling via Canterbury to deposit their dead friend's ashes in the sea; it also carefully imitates the structure of William Faulkner's *As I Lay Dying* (1935) in a pastiche so carefully built on the bones of the Faulkner that it got sensationally accused of plagiarism by one observant/unobservant critic.[6] Jeanette Winterson (*Boating for Beginners*, 1985) and Michèle Roberts (*The Book of Mrs Noah*, 1987) redo Bible stories. The great London-lover Iain Sinclair revives the novel as a text of Dickensian-documentary topography, mapping London, especially sinister, criminal, Jack the Ripper, Kray Brothers London (as in *White Chappell, Scarlet Tracings*, 1987, and *Radon Daughters*, 1994) with deft acknowledgements of the not dissimilar proclivities of his friends Peter Ackroyd, Mr London History himself, in *English Music* (1992), *The House of Doctor Dee* (1993), *Dan Leno and the Limehouse Golem* (1994), and Michael Moorcock, the Sci Fi writer, in his London documentary mode, as in *Mother London* (1988). You can, it is clear, now do the novel, the serious novel (what literary prize arrangers and the posh newspapers know as 'literary'

---

[6] John Frow, Australian Marxist, now Professor of English, Edinburgh University. See *The Times, Independent, Guardian*, 10 March 1996, and Valentine Cunningham, 'Fiction 96', *Literature Matters*, 22 June 1997, pp. 1–4.

fiction) in almost any way that comes to mind, or, to go on using the Joycean term, that seems to you appropriate. The novel can indeed be allegory, or essay, or fairy story, or cartography, or Sci Fi with J. G. Ballard, or Crime Story with Michael Dibdin, or anatomy textbook with Jeanette Winterson (*Written on the Body*, 1992), or retro-Gothic with the lovely chilling Patrick McGrath (*Blood and Water*, 1989, *The Grotesque*, 1989, *Spider*, 1991, *Dr Haggard's Disease*, 1993). The formal field could not be more open.

This freedom to choose is, as Iris Murdoch would put it, utterly necessary. There's no proceeding without some idea of form. This is the essential prefatory step (which is why on the threshold of the English novel prefaces proliferate, as in the novels of Henry Fielding, prefaces pointing out available models, and justifying the novelist's chosen formal take—biography, comic-epic-in-prose, 'Cervantick strain', and so on). It's a poser, of course, every time (except for copy-cat repeaters). Fat or thin? Compendious, a fictional pantechnicon, encyclopedic like *Tristram Shandy* or *Ulysses*, or Rushdie's mighty gathera, or Angela Carter in her uncorseted mode, or Lawrence Norfolk in his *Lemprière's Dictionary* (1991) and *The Pope's Rhinoceros* (1996)—what Italo Calvino in his *Six Memos for the Next Millennium* (1992) celebrated as *multiplicity*?[7] Or exiguous and spartan (as taut as later Beckett or an Angela Carter short story or an Ian McEwan novel)? What sort of a beginning will it be; what kind of middle is to be in prospect; even more what kind of ending? Do you go for closure, that *bête noire* of structuralist critique, the finality of the judgement-day climactics of trad realist novels, nicely epitomized in the detective story (that ectype of traditional plotting)? Or go for closure-busting openness, an indeterminate ending in the wake of European practitioners such as Alain Robbe-Grillet and his inverted detective story *Les Gommes* (1953)/*The Erasers* (1964)—a

[7] Italo Calvino, 'Multiplicity', Memo 5, *Six Memos for the Next Millennium*, trans. Patrick Creagh (London: Jonathan Cape, 1992), 101–24.

resistance to closure most extremely illustrated in Britain by B. S. Johnson's anarchic novel *The Unfortunates* (1969), consisting of loose sections, bits of text in a box, which readers were supposed to read in any order they chose (public librarians hated this practical manifesto against the 'clapped out' connected linear narration, for obvious reasons: bits kept getting appropriated by borrowers); and most popularly provided by John Fowles's *The French Lieutenant's Woman* (1969) with its 'you choose' double ending, but indulged in quite widely by less obvious experimentation flirts—like Iris Murdoch in *The Black Prince* (1973), with its four postscripts by characters of the novel, each offering different revised versions of the story?

Determining formal determinations, then. As witness Iris Murdoch in that 1949 notebook meditation. A moral philosopher greatly taken by the existentialist novel (her first book would be *Sartre: Romantic Realist*, 1953), she considers following in the formal footsteps of Sartre and Simone de Beauvoir, i.e. producing yet one more 1940s plot, a novel very much of 1949. At the same time she weighs the attractions of two of the very oldest novel forms of all, autobiography, the I-narrated 'written life', and the journal. And of course every formal shape ever tried out thus far lay before her as it does for every other novelist. She would come rapidly to settle for big, 'spread out', omniscient narrations, tributes to the clientele of F. R. Leavis's *The Great Tradition*, the so-called classic-realist novel. Later on she would occasionally try out different forms—the epistolary and the telegraphic (*An Accidental Man*, 1971); the self-reflexive Shandyesque novel, with an editor and revisionist postscripts (*The Black Prince*); an autobiographical novel full of formal concern about its status as autobiography, a kind of throwback to eighteenth-century metatextualities (*The Sea, The Sea*, 1978). Perhaps these 1970s novels reflect a certain unsettlement caused by persistent charges against her of formal repetitiveness, the making of a self-duplicating 'Murdochian' novel, and prompting some experimenting, a sort of formal self-renewing. And to be sure, it was in the early 1970s that she responded to such criticism in *The Black Prince*, with its Murdoch lookalike novelist Arnold Baffin, who is astutely put down by his critical daughter Julian, and by his friend Bradley Pearson in a coshing review—lambasting his over-production, his never blotting a line, his producing yet again 'the mixture as before', yet one more Murdochian affair about a stockbroker who wants to become a monk, who has long debates about religion with the sister of his abbot-to-be, climaxing in the felling of the abbot by a huge bronze crucifix at the altar during mass ('Bradley Pearson's Story', pt. II).[8]

Baffin responds painedly to these criticisms. 'You, and you aren't the only one, every critic tends to do this, speak as if you were addressing a person of invincible complacency, you speak as if the artist had never realized his faults at all. In fact most artists understand their own weaknesses far better than the critics do.' Which is certainly Murdoch's own voice, the

---

[8] The problem of referencing Murdoch novels is extreme. There is no standard edition. All her novels were published by Chatto and Windus. Until 1976 paperback versions were published by Penguin. In that year, amidst great fuss, Granada (Triad Panther paperbacks) scooped Penguin to the paperback rights, beginning with *A Word Child* (London: Chatto and Windus, 1975). Granada then reissued all the Murdoch backlist as their paperbacks. Within a decade the paperback rights were back with Penguin. A new series of paperbacks is now in progress from Vintage, with new Introductions by assorted critics. This will eventually comprise a sort of Collected Edition. Most of the earlier paperbacks have gone out of print, like all but the most recent Chatto and Windus hardbacks. Giving page references to any particular printed version is not, therefore, very useful to the average reader, who may, like me, have a random mixture of old and new versions. So where chapter references exist I give those. A difficulty with this solution is that Murdoch more or less abandoned chapter divisions with *An Accidental Man* (1971), which has no marked divisions at all, and after that went in for rather large sectional divisions, modelled, often, one guesses, on the Acts of drama and the Movements of symphonies. *The Sea, The Sea* (1978), for instance, is divided into the large blocks 'PreHistory', 'History', and 'Postscript', *The Book and the Brotherhood* (1987) into 'Midsummer', 'Midwinter', and 'Spring'; and so on. *A Word Child* is divided into weekdays. Chapters, if that's what they are, reappeared with *Jackson's Dilemma* (1994). I refer quotations from these later novels to whatever of these large section heads is available. For chapter-less, section-less *An Accidental Man* I give Penguin page references (to be as helpful as I can!).

voice of the interviewee who regularly accepted objections about her failures to live up in practice to her theories about the ethical grandeur of the novel ('Every book is the wreck of a perfect idea'). But what Baffin won't give way on is the decisions he's made as to mode and method. 'If one has a thing at all one must do it and keep on and on trying to do it better.' And whatever the truth of Pearson's objections—and he is indeed the ventriloquial voice of Iris Murdoch's many disgruntled readers—there's no denying the seriousness, the principledness of the theoretical basis Iris Murdoch tries to proceed on. And in fact Murdoch's extended discussions of the novel are as captivatingly serious as any coming from a practising novelist in modern times—easily ranking with those of Henry James, or Virginia Woolf, or, for that matter, Italo Calvino.

Formal questions greatly inflect her many discussions of the novel, of the twentieth-century fictional scene, her anticipations of the novels she wants to write, her sidelights on the fiction she does write, just as these thoughts about fiction keep on being central to her philosophical meditations on the nature of things, morality, God. She wants to do moral philosophy in fiction, to write 'spiritual adventure stories' (in the phrase of the hollow sage Effingham Cooper in *The Unicorn* (1963), ch. 12). The subjects of her moral philosophy have their form, she says. The concept of *redemption*, for instance, which 'can exist without God', 'has strong emotional appeal, but also structure'.[9]

And the fictional form she desires will coincide with the forms of her moral philosophy. 'Art, especially literature, has in the past instinctively operated as a form, the most profoundly accessible form, of moral reflection' (*MGM*, 89). What's wrong with modernity is precisely its disconnecting of art from morality, which entails the loss of our sense of form and structure in

[9] *Metaphysics as a Guide to Morals* (London: Chatto and Windus, 1992), 131. Further citations given within the text are abbreviated to *MGM*.

the moral world itself.[10] This allegation comes in what is perhaps the most potent of her polemical essays, 'Against Dryness'
(1961)—it's certainly by far the most republished one.[11] The
trouble with so much modern and modernistic fiction, she
claims in this piece, is formal failure, its unnerved retreat from
the large moralized human scopes of the great nineteenth-century realists. The modern novel is 'either crystalline or journalistic', either simply too small ('small myths, toys, and crystals', a
'small quasi-allegorical object') with no room for the life of
characters or for extended ethical investigation; or it's big but
feeble, big in the wrong way, a 'degenerate descendant of the
nineteenth-century novel, telling with pale conventional characters, some straightforward story enlivened with empirical fact',
merely 'a large shapeless quasi-documentary object'. The world
is big, 'aimless chancy huge', its immense variety 'unsystematic
and inexhaustible', as she puts it in her lecture of 1967, 'The
Sovereignty of Good over Other Concepts'.[12] And Iris Murdoch
in her role as published moral philosopher, and the better characters in her fictions, and her narrative voices, keep declaring
this vastness—the world as huge *jumble*, a *muddle*, a *mess*,
rubble even, *messy, contingent, utterly contingent*. Tiny fictions
are simply too small to register this variety. It's not just that the
House of Fiction is honourably big, but that every novel in it
should be big, open to the world, to things, to the human, the
ethical world of choice and dilemma. 'Tinification', what in
The Italian Girl (1964) engravers are said to perform (ch. 4,

---

[10] Murdoch and moral form are touched on in Maria Antonaccio, 'Form and
Contingency in Iris Murdoch's Ethics', in *Iris Murdoch and the Search for Human
Goodness*, ed. Maria Antonaccio and William Schweiker (Chicago: University of
Chicago Press, 1996)—a most impressive gathering of discussions of Murdoch as a
moral philosopher by moral philosophers, including her greatest philosophical fan
Martha C. Nussbaum.

[11] 'Against Dryness', *Encounter* (Jan. 1961); *Existentialists and Mystics*, 293.

[12] This lecture was first collected in *The Sovereignty of Good* (London: Routledge and Kegan Paul, 1970) and later in *Existentialists and Mystics*. The moral being
accepts 'the inexhaustic detail of the world' ('Vision and Choice in Morality' (1956),
in *Existentialists and Mystics*, 87).

'Otto and Innocence'), is a formal error of huge moral proportions. Only misguided persons complain about the quantity of
'heterogeneous' *stuff* in the great novels—as does Anna Cla-
vidge, just escaped from her convent in Part I of *Nuns and
Soldiers* (1964), and deplorably out of touch with novel reading.
Sartre's problem, we're told in *Sartre: Romantic Realist*, Iris
Murdoch's own critical preface, or prelude, to her fiction, is his
'impatience, which is fatal to a novelist proper, with the *stuff* of
human life'.[13] The truthful, ethically responsible novel will
('Against Dryness') be full, rich, amplitudinous, 'spread-out',
'substantial', its people presented in 'a rich receding background'. Small forms, crystalline fictions, small 'moral tales',
allegories, eighteenth-century throwbacks, are all ways of im-
aginatively resisting, trying to control, the world's mess. They're
trying to keep mess and contingency at bay, and so are dubiously
consolatory, a kind of fantasy, deforming the world, a deform-
ation which in her view is a negation of proper moral form. 'All a
muddle', those despairing words of Stephen Blackpool in Dickens's *Hard Times*, are adopted as a badge of moral courage for
Murdoch and her characters. Accepting the muddle of things is
morality itself. 'Was this paralysed muddling on from moment
to moment what moral thinking at its most difficult was really
like?' thinks Ludwig in *An Accidental Man* (1971).[14] The implied answer is that it is.

The large, jumbled, well-stuffed forms of Murdoch's advo-
cacy and admiration inevitably involve, then, a certain kind of
character, dictate the celebration of a certain sort of *dramatis
personae*, a certain sort of action and plot. And novels paying
attention (that favourite notion of Murdoch's taken from
Simone Weil)[15] to the reality of real people, 'real impenetrable

[13] *Sartre: Romantic Realist* (1953; repr. London: Fontana, 1967), 118.
[14] (Harmondsworth: Penguin, 1973), 378.
[15] Starting perhaps with her review of Simone Weil's *Notebooks*, 'Knowing the
Void', *The Spectator*, 1956: in *Existentialists and Mystics: Writings on Philosophy
and Literature*, ed. cit., pp. 157–60. See in addition *attention* in the index to
Existentialists and Mystics; also *MGM*, 52, and extensively.

human person(s)' in their large social scene, registering 'the absurd irreducible uniqueness of people' (as the Sartre book has it)[16] in their mess and contingency, are doing good, are being good. This is where goodness lies, which should be the goal not only of the person, but of the novelist. By 'allowing others to be through him', the novelist becomes the analogue of the good man. Recognizing 'the otherness of the other person' is goodness because it is love, it is liberalism (it grants the other his freedom to be).[17] And only thus does the ethical continue in a world without God. This is the only transcendence there is now. 'We need', Murdoch said ('Against Dryness', again), 'to picture, in a non-metaphysical, non-totalitarian and non-religious sense, the transcendence of reality'. 'Virtue is *au fond* the same in the artist as in the good man in that it is a selfless attention to nature'.[18] All of which sounds pretty close to Joyce's notion of the epiphanic of the ordinary, close also to George Eliot's programme of Feuerbachian humanism, in which the sacramental, the transcendent, are now only possible as experiences of the ordinary world when it is seen through properly alerted, truly attentive eyes. 'So that aesthetic situations', at least ones conducted on the Murdoch plan, 'are not so much analogies of morals as cases of morals.'[19]

It's a recipe for fiction quite astounding in the nature and range of its claims, deftly knitting together, as it does, a model of fictional form, a model of the artist, a model of the human and of the ethical in a post-God era, and a model of reader-effects. It is

[16] *Sartre: Romantic Realist*, 118.

[17] For Murdoch as a liberal theorist and practitioner (and for the connections between her theory of the liberal novel and that of her husband, John Bayley) see, variously, A. S. Byatt, *Degrees of Freedom: The Novels of Iris Murdoch* (London: Chatto and Windus, 1965); Bernard Bergonzi, *The Situation of the Novel* (London: Macmillan, 1970); Patrick Swinden, *Unofficial Selves: Character in the Novel from Dickens to the Present Day* (London: Macmillan, 1973); and Richard Freadman, *Eliot, James and the Fictional Self: A Study in Character and Narration* (London: Macmillan, 1986).

[18] 'The Idea of Perfection', *The Sovereignty of Good*, 41; *Existentialists and Mystics*, 332.

[19] Idem.

colossally ambitious, arrogant even, as a kind of Platonized revisiting and redoing of all of Aristotle's great map of poetics. Pursuing it is the only way, Murdoch suggests, of doing what T. S. Eliot claimed Joyce's 'mythical method' did, namely 'making the modern world possible for art'.[20] It is, not least, Murdoch's way of having fiction cope with what is for her the largest, most looming and oppressive moral problematic of her time, namely the Holocaust, the *Hitlerzeit*. 'The material of art is contingent limited historically stained stuff', she wrote (*MGM*, 85). History's stains mightily stained her imagination. The troubles of Ireland were never far from this Anglo-Irish Protestant woman's thinking (as witness two of her very best novels, both set in Ireland, *The Unicorn*, and *The Red and the Green*, 1965). The Vietnam War became a topic for her in the early 1970s in *An Accidental Man*. But the most concerning of all historical stains was the Nazism that eliminated in death-camps the loved ones of the Jewish men she knew and loved, that had driven those friends into exile, that ensured the death of her beloved Frank Thompson on active service in the Balkans, that engendered the misery of displaced persons, which she witnessed at first hand in Austria as an UNRRA (United Nations Relief and Rehabiliation Administration) officer (the details are all in Conradi's *Life*). Only large and greatly humanist fictions could cope with modern evil. The small mythicizings she abhors, the ones whose tinifications resist the large jumble of the world, are prevented by their formal 'self-satisfaction' from imagining evil. 'Our inability to imagine evil is a consequence of the facile, dramatic and, in spite of Hitler, optimistic picture of ourselves with which we work. Our difficulty about form, about images—our tendency to produce works which are either crystalline or journalistic—is a symptom of our situation' ('Against Dryness' once more).

The programme was impressively clear, and in the massive fictional œuvre of 26 volumes (27 if you include the short story

---

[20] T. S. Eliot, '*Ulysses*, Order and Myth', *The Dial* (Nov. 1923), in Frank Kermode (ed.), *Selected Prose of TS Eliot* (London: Faber and Faber, 1978), 178.

Something Special, published separately only after her death, in 2001) she pursued it with extraordinary vigour. No novelist comes more highly self-programmed—not George Eliot, not Virginia Woolf. The fictional product—its forms, its contents—is geared in almost every aspect to what the theory predicated. And the most striking result is indeed formal; the fullness, the extreme fatness, the largeness and largesse which she advocated, she indeed performed. Her only really slimline novel, *The Italian Girl*, stands out as peculiarly anorexic (when anorexia came to public notice, it was quickly latched on to as a fearful thing, a model terminal affliction, for several of Murdoch's young women, like Tamar in *The Book and the Brotherhood*, 1987). And Murdoch's many fat containers come simply packed with people and stuff. They're dense with particulars. It's no surprise that a repeated worldly frame is the city, mainly London. Murdoch is one of our best novelists of London. This locale, the most awing of man-made creations for the nineteenth-century novelists she admired, is the great people-container she repeatedly maps, traverses, celebrates. From her first novel, *Under the Net*, the very affectionately dwelt-on London streets, pubs, churches, the river Thames set Murdoch's favourite scene. It's a crowded scene, home of the original English fictional crowd. Her novels act as its A–Z guide.

And the inhabitants of these novels devoted to the great good-bad urban place come in appropriate crowds, small crowds, but still throngs, tribelets, clans, families, local allegories of the great human tribe. Murdoch's favourite opening is a meet-the-family occasion, an encounter with '*les cousins et les tantes*' (as the Ebury Street mob of friends, colleagues, lovers is known in *Nuns and Soldiers*) who are to be the novel's subject group. Here in the opening minutes of *The Book and the Brotherhood* come the middle-aged chums reassembling at an Oxford Summer Ball—'your little group', as the Classicist Levquist says to his old pupil Gerald when he pops in on Ball night (pt. I, 'Midsummer'); they're the *Gesellschaft* who've clubbed together to finance philosopher David Crimond's Big Book. The novel's opening time is a time for family trees—as in *The Red and the Green*, or *The Philosopher's Pupil* (1983): 'As there are quite a large number of McCaffreys in the story that follows, I might, before conclud-ing these introductory remarks, give a brief account of the family.' Her people keep being assembled, named, catalogued —at Sunday lunch in *The Nice and the Good* (1968), for instance (ch. 12)), or at the Quaker meeting in *The Philosopher's Pupil*. 'Present were Brian, Gabriel and Adam, William Eastcote and Anthea, Mr and Mrs Robin Osmor, Mrs Percy Bowcock, Nesta Wiggins, Peter Blackett, Mrs Roach the doctor's wife, Nicky Roach the doctor's son, now studying at Guy's Hospital, Rita Chalmers, wife of the Institute Director, Miss London who was a teacher at Adam's school, Mr and Mrs Romage who kept a grocer's shop in Burkestown, and a Mrs Bradstreet, a visiting friend who was staying at the Ennistone Royal Hotel and taking the cure for a condition in her back' ('The Events in our Town'). These striking cast-lists—there's another arresting one at the clan party arranged to meet Peter Mir in *The Green Knight* (1993) (pt. III, 'Mercy')—read as defiant: they're the kind of group portrait assembly Murdoch well knew was mocked rigid in Beck-ett's novel *Watt* as a no longer useful epistemological exercise. But here they are, the cousinage, checked in for us as all present and ready for the games of family musical chairs Murdoch's plots consist of—the wife-swappings, serial adulteries, fallings in and out of love, the incests, the whole glorious kaleidoscope of clan repositionings she so obviously enjoys celebrating.

And these person maps are always coloured in, as it were. Murdoch's family story reminds one of the Happy Families card-game. Here is Mr Bun the Baker, and Mrs Bun, and Jenny Bun their daughter. The occupational labels attached to those Quakers are always attached. Such are the particulars of the person Murdoch's theory insists upon as necessary to our knowing. And the same is true of what they wear as what they do. People must be remarked for their togs—as for their kit generally, their props, their rooms, their dogs (so many dogs!), their meals (those extraordinary meals, dinners of infantile tuck, midnight-feast-in-the-dorm comestibles—baked beans, it might be, or a few roll-mops, cheddar cheese, and Cox's orange pippin apples). Such are the outward and visible signs of the characters we are being led to know—in a materialistic practice of knowing that deliberately keeps alive the bourgeois materialist epistemology of the Victorians.

It is a practice that relies very heavily on the thumbnail sketch of the first meeting. 'Her face had a secret private inward pure dewy beauty which, to me, *blazed* forth. Her hair was mousy-brown and straight and cut in a simple sort of bob. She had a large brow and a rather long bony face, with slightly prominent blue-gray eyes and a long sensitive beautifully shaped mouth. She never wore make-up. Her skin was very fine, as if transparent, and always seemed very slightly moist. Her eyes had a moist bright look and absolutely *shone* with intelligence.' That's Anne Jopling of *A Word Child* (1975) (second 'Friday'), in the kind of all-knowing description that was also greatly satirized by Beckett (Cooper in *Murphy* 'was a low-sized, clean-shaven, grey-faced, one-eyed man, triorchous and a non-smoker', which is alright until you work out that *triorchous* means 'having three testicles').[21] But this is all part of the ostentatious *hommage* to Victorian fiction's confidently unfazed knowings.

And such knowing and representing are what we're to think of as the life-ordinariness which, in the Murdoch theory, novels must take seriously. Thus and thus is the world that 'is all that is the case', in those opening words of Wittgenstein's *Tractatus Logico-Philosophicus* (1922), the book which so clearly haunts Iris Murdoch. (There's no other novelist, I think, who would begin a novel, as Murdoch does her *Nuns and Soldiers*, with the single word 'Wittgenstein'.) 'There is no beyond, there is only here', writes Father Bernard at the end of *The Philosopher's*

---

[21] Samuel Beckett, *Murphy* (1938; London: John Calder, 1963), ch. 4, p. 41.

Pupil in *Tractatus*-echoing words ('What Happened After-wards'). Wittgenstein, we're told, would have liked the banality of Arthur's supper in *A Word Child*—always the same, winter and summer alike, 'tinned tongue with instant mashed potatoes and peas, followed by biscuits and cheese and bananas' (first 'Tuesday'). This is the ordinariness of Murdoch's desire.

Ordinary is of course a much repeated key word. 'Oh the piercing sadness of life in the midst of its ordinariness!' (*A Word Child*, first 'Thursday'). The garden in Oxford's Rawlin-son Road, where Ludwig and Gracie plan to live (*An Accidental Man*) is 'sweet and desolate with ordinariness' (p. 207). The ordinary, the untranscendent real, the humanist world of the down-to-earth detail Murdoch keeps touching in, in her deliber-ate George Eliot–Tolstoy tribute-paying, is where human truth is uniquely. Only novels that register the 'ordinary' are 'in the truth'—as Murdoch characters keep putting it. Which is why, of course, all those Christian believers and clergy and nuns have to lose their one-time faith in Christian transcendence. All those spoiled priests Murdoch can't stop giving us are obeying a contemporary necessity, the dictate of history. 'Do you believe in God?' people keep asking; the answer is invariably No; and No, the enquirer doesn't either. In Murdoch's fiction, as in the theory, the contemplation of God gives place to the desire for the ethical, the good, the good life, perfection even, by other means. The means are contested—as in the two paired and opposed sermons in *The Bell* (1958) about the way to the good life (chs. 9 and 16), and in all the imitation Platonic dialogues and symposia Murdoch keeps arranging—but there's no ambivalence about the fact of the Sovereignty of Good replacing what the Puritans heralded as the Sovereignty of God. Religion, transcendence, the metaphysical are now, in the now of Murdoch's novels, only realizable in the ordinary untranscendent. Which is, of course, a version of a long post-Christian demythologizing tradition going back at least to Feuerbach's *The Essence of Christianity* (1841), which George Eliot translated in 1855 and which fired her every move and mood. 'Metaphysics and the human sciences are made impossible by the penetration of morality into the moment to moment conduct of ordinary life: the understanding of this fact is *religion.*' Thus Father Bernard, again (*The Philosopher's Pupil,* 'What Happened Afterwards'). He's writing from Mount Athos, the famous Greek holy mountain, where, like so many of Murdoch's one-time Christians, he's been contemplating how the ethical, the religious, Christ, might survive the denial of God ('What is necessary is *the absolute denial of God*').

Of course the way of the moral philosopher in the post-God bind is hard. Marcus Fisher's book on morality in a secular age gets stymied (*The Time of the Angels,* 1966)—like most of the numerous Big Book projects in Murdoch. To be sure, David Crimond does finally complete his great synthesis of religion and politics and everything—the book that the 'brotherhood', the *Crimondgesellschaft,* collectively bankrolls (*The Book and the Brotherhood*)—but he's a moral rotter who ends up shooting his friend Riderhood dead.

These post-Christians are often in a moral mess, like Crimond, or like Nick, devilish old Nick, the treacherous betrayer of lover and friend (*The Bell*), or Father Fisher, sadistic and incestuous as well as blasphemous (*The Time of the Angels*).

Devilish, blasphemous (also prayer, miracle, paradise, angel, archangel, hell, demon)—there is, of course, an extraordinarily dense rhetoric in these texts of words from the Christian theology pot. But they lack their once thoroughly transcendent reference. The only Easter Sunday resurrection on offer in *The Red and the Green* is the 1916 Easter Rising of the Dublin insurrectionists—and even that rising is only aborted and disastrous. But what the keen rhetoric of salvation, of goodness, which pervades the absolutely ordinary language of Murdoch's people and narrations ('Oh good!', people keep saying; 'Good!') is evidently there to mark is the persisting reality, in a kind of untranscendentally transcendent discourse, of the essence of the

great moral meanings, struggles, successes, failures. Encounter-
ing the *thingy* (Murdoch's word, in *The Italian Girl*, ch.10)
otherness, the particulars of the world, is where *redemption*
now alone lies. The very survival of that word indicates an
important survival of an old human desire, even of an old experience, but now in its merely untranscendent version.

These Murdoch language survivals are her resort to and dem-
onstration of a version of the old ontological 'proof' of the
existence of God—what you can think, or name, thereby does
exist—which she has quite a lot of time for in her theoretical
writings: an ontological argument now, though, proving the
existence not of God but of *good* and *love* and so on. Accepting,
noting, appreciating the 'wonders of the world' (the phrase from
the end of *Under the Net*) is what saves; redemptive grace lies,
precisely, in the things that Murdoch's texts catalogue as enthu-
siastically as they list their people—the leaves, for instance, that
Tim Reede gathers in *Nuns and Soldiers* and turns into collages
in his redemptive 'time of the leaves' ('handsome plane leaves,
green and brown or the purest yellow, maple leaves which turned tawny and vivid green or sometimes radiant red, and were
often covered with the most elegant spots, curvy oak leaves,
brownest of absolute browns, and the more exotic joys of rhus
cotinus...', sect. 7); or the 'sea of Cox's Orange Pippins' Rose
lays in a loft in *The Book and the Brotherhood*: 'These English
apples...had always seemed to Rose good apples, innocent
apples, apples of virtue, full of the sweet nourishment of goodness' (pt. II, 'Midwinter'). And raptures like these before the
things of the natural world (the Cox's paragraph is succeeded by
one cataloguing the pebbles Rose also stores in her loft) are what
goodness, virtue, holiness, religion are, for now. Such things
turn, in effect, into religious icons, the iconicity of the particular.

And some art can, it's clear, share this absolute, transfigurative
force, as when Edward Baltram, in *The Good Apprentice* (1985),
experiences 'salvation by Proust' when he comes across a Proust
sentence about rainy days: 'a perfectly ordinary run-of-the-mill

sentence in the midst of the narration describing some quite ordinary day's routine at Balbec, not particularly dramatic or significant, an *ordinary day* at Balbec—but Edward might just as well have been looking at the weightiest lines of a holy text or the climax of a great poem' (pt. II, 'Seegard'); or when Dora Greenfield experiences a transforming 'revelation' before Gainsborough's painting of his two daughters in the National Gallery (in *The Bell*, ch. 14), which takes her beyond personal fantasy and solipsism into experiencing the transcendence of art—something *real, perfect, radiant, good*. And a mark of ethical deficiency is being unreceptive to the transcendence which art offers (as is Julius in *A Fairly Honourable Defeat* (1970), who decries the Turners and the 'junk' of European art and literature in the Tate Gallery (ch. 19), or Tim's wicked girlfriend Daisy, in *Nuns and Soldiers* (pt. II), who deplores the prettification in National Gallery paintings). The respect for the otherness of the other person as the essence of good, of love, includes great art just as it also embraces the natural world. The deformed vision is blind, and is not graced.

Just so, the spiritually unaware merely go for a swim, while the awakened ones enjoy the holiness of water baptism. The extraordinary multitude of waters in Murdoch's novels—the sea, rivers, lakes, baths, the Spa waters of *The Philosopher's Pupil*, into which Murdoch's people keep dunking themselves, going for a swim, having a bathe, the waters that are put to use constantly as representing the invitations of contingency, water as wild, chaotic, messy, the swimming that's an essence of the individual freedom Murdoch preaches up—are all of them some sort of version of old Christian baptism. The octagonal room at the Baths in *The Philosopher's Pupil* is known as 'the Baptistry'. 'Over and over, like a mighty sea, Comes the love of JESUS, rolling over me!': that's the chorus voice of the Children's Special Service Mission, the evangelical CSSM, that we hear in *The Red and the Green* (ch. 4), the sung word coming from Murdoch's own evangelical Protestant upbringing. 'Horrible sounds', 'appalling vulgarity', thinks Andrew Chase-White. The old evangelical inundation—and Murdoch's Plymouth Brethren cousins were of course baptizers of adults by immersion (see Conradi's *Life*)—is ripe for the usual rereading.

> Wide, wide as the ocean, high as the heaven above,
> Deep, deep as the deepest sea is my Saviour's love.
> I though so unworthy still am a child in His care
> For His love teaches me that His love reaches me
> Everywhere.

Murdoch used to sing these words in adult life, Conradi tells us, keeping alive her Sunday school memories. Gildas Herne, the former priest of *The Message to the Planet* (1989) sings them (and is just one of the very many Murdoch people who've had such evangelical childhoods).[22] The words remain, this poetry of Christian waters, only the meaning has, as ever, shifted onto the only baptismal waters we're allowed, the waters flooding Murdoch's plots, reminiscent indeed of baptismal water, full of the old transcendent memories and traces, but only offering baptizings of a secular kind.

The waters which can baptize you into freedom are, of course, also extremely dangerous. Many Murdoch people drown in them. Rozanov loses the manuscript of his Big Book in the Baths of *The Philosopher's Pupil*. Other people almost nearly lose their lives in water; they keep needing to be rescued from drowning. Water saves and heals; water is also deadly; so salvation through it is just like Christian baptism was, that old model of death and resurrection. 'The murderous waters of the canal and the blackness of the tunnel had beaten and baptised him back to life': that's Tim Reede, who survives his fearful immersion in a canal in the south of France in *Nuns and Soldiers* (sect. 9). What Murdoch is simultaneously demythologizing and picturing, of course, is the old proximity between good and evil represented in the story of

---

[22] *The Message to the Planet*, pt. I. Slightly misremembered, in fact. The third line should be 'child *of* his care'.

Christian redemption through Christ's death on the Cross and resurrection and its analogue in baptism's modelling of that going down into the grave and rising from it again.

Seeking to make up for what she alleged was the twentieth-century novel's deficient picturing of evil involves Murdoch—and impressively, I think—in this troublingly complex vision of what evil entails. The energies of her approach to the topic of evil undoubtedly gain much from their being a particular kind of heresy, one not uncommonly returning in twentieth-century imagining, namely Manichaeism, a vision of good and evil closely related to Neoplatonism (spirit good, matter bad), a sort of dualism in which the demonic and the good, God and Satan, are equally opposed partners (Thomas Mann's essay 'Bruder Hitler' comes to mind, with its picture of Hitler as a necessary other to, as kin of, the good German, the good Jew).[23]

Power over others, enslaving, subjugating others, is the critical mass of the evil, the particular modern evils, that Murdoch wants us to imagine. And her fiction is extremely good, if that's the word, at presenting evil. Her wicked people are truly malign subjugators and destroyers of others (gaining power over others by spying and voyeurism and exercising it through blackmail are quintessentially large sins in Murdoch's book). They are little Hitlers and Stalins, avatars on the domestic front of the great twentieth-century dictators. They operate in a fictional world signally peopled by actual victims of the Holocaust and Stalinist terrors, by people in exile because of imposed terror—Russians, Poles, Jews, Jews above all (like Willie Kost, the exiled Propertius scholar in *The Nice and the Good*, who was in Dachau, and Levquist, the classical scholar in *The Book and the Brotherhood*, whose father and sister died in Auschwitz, and Marcus Vallar in *The Message to the Planet*, demented by the Holo-

---

[23] Thomas Mann, 'Bruder Hitler' (Mar. 1939), *Politische Schriften und Reden*, vol. iii (Frankfurt am Main: Fischer Bücherei, 1968), 53–8; also in Thomas Koebner (ed.), *Autoren des Exils und des Widerstands sehen den 'Fuhrer' des Dritten Reichs* (Munich: Wilhelm Heyne, 1989).

caust)—people for whom evil is being turned back at the border, and is, precisely, the death-camps. 'All the world's a camp', as old Pleshkov says in *The Time of the Angels*, with all the glum force Murdoch can muster. And, quite arrestingly, it is often the case that it is these victims of European oppression who are themselves oppressive.

Elsa Levkin in *The Italian Girl* and the Lusiewicz brothers in *Flight from the Enchanter* are wicked exiles, behaving now as badly as their oppressors did. Many of the intellectual gurus, the master philosophers, the great scholars, so looked up to by their disciples and pupils and apprentices—that repeated relationship of respect and love in these novels—are masterful in, essentially, deplorable ways. Max Lejour (in *The Unicorn*), Levquist, Vallar, Rozanov, David Crimond, Lucas Graffe (*The Green Knight*)— all based on intellectual masters from Murdoch's own life, the novelist Elias Canetti, the Latinist Edvard Fraenkel, the moral philosopher Donald McKinnon—are intolerably masterful and dictatorial. They hector, they preach, they sermonize, they demand agreement, with a loud force that stands out even in a fiction going in for loud preachifiers in such an abundant fashion. They spurn even their acolytes. And, interestingly, many of them are Jews, refugees, victims in one way or another of power. Compellingly, it is one of these powerful philosopher kings, Max Lejour of *The Unicorn*, who, discussing the difficulty for victims of forgiving their oppressors, recalls the figure of Ate, that ancient Greek personification of the sort of blind folly which prevents people distinguishing right from wrong: 'Power is a form of Ate. The victims of power, and any power has its victims, are themselves infected. They have then to pass it on, to use power on others. This is evil' (ch. 12). Returning evil for evil, wanting an eye for an eye and a tooth for a tooth, using evil means as a weapon against evil, thinking that 'only darkness could cast out darkness' (Rosa's idea about the Lusiewiczes in *The Flight from the Enchanter*, ch. 22) is a grave moral mistake. This is to go 'beyond good and evil' in Murdoch's reckoning, to become precisely Nietzschean. Mir in *The Green Knight* is just one of Murdoch's victims (Lucas Graffe 'killed' him by mistaking him for his brother) who learns a better way than seeking such revenge. But the awful and compelling thing is that vengeance is presented as the temptation of good people, of the victimized, and of Murdoch's admired class of teachers not least. The way the good person can so easily go wrong is one of her most persisting concerns.

This corruption of the good person is offered in fact as the too ready possibility with every case, almost, of what she believes to be the uttermost exemplification of the good, namely love and the lover. Love relations, the main trade of her novels, the main stage so to say on which she conducts her morality plays, her many inspections of moral beings in action, these are precisely where slavery, oppression, mastery reign on the one hand, and enslavement or subjugation flourish on the other. Love, the essence of the good, keeps going terribly wrong. Men imprison the women they desire. Lovers turn rapists. There's a very great deal of sexual violence around. Men can't help it. Some women, we're told, like it. 'I'd let him walk on me', says Millie of Pat (in *The Red and the Green*, ch. 20). 'I'll live in that dog kennel if you like', says Gilbert Opian, offering himself to his beloved Charles Arrowby as a sort of Russian 'house-serf' (*The Sea, The Sea*, 'History', sect. 4). Love easily turns sado-masochistic in Murdoch's plottings. The *coup de foudre*, which is never far away, and will sometimes afflict the same lover several times in the course of a single novel, is a power rarely to be resisted. Love, the lover, hold utter sway, and never mind any ethical consideration that might stand in their way.

Which does, of course, bring nicely into focus some of the real problems with Iris Murdoch's translation of her theory into her novels, the contents of her forms, the forms of her contents. She is extreme, an extremist. Everything is extreme in these pages, and damagingly so; just as love taken to extreme becomes evil. Taking to extreme the good programme, the programme for goodness, for goodness in the form, the characters, the plot, simply undermines that programme. In the worthy name of scope and amplitude, for example, the novels tend to bloat. Some of them simply will not end. The perennial accusation that Murdoch damaged her work by not letting it be edited (the large plastic bags of stuff deposited with her editor must not be tampered with) holds force. Critics often warm to novels as 'hard to put down'. *The Book and the Brotherhood*, I'd say, is a novel increasingly, as you persevere with it, hard to pick up. It goes on and on. In the admirable name of human multiplicity what we tend to get is great repetition—across the œuvre as in individual novels.[24] These big fictional boxes become boxes of utterly familiar tricks—all those sadists and masochists and serial adulterers, all those struck-dumb lovers, all those unhappy families mechanistically multiplied into pairs, twins, doubles, reverse mirror-images, into threes and threesomes and place-changing quartets. These many repetitions, these existences in multiples, make an ironic kind of place for a theory of individualism, a resistance to allegory and to human typing, to have ended up. That curious passage in 'The Idea of Perfection' lecture of 1962, meant to illustrate how repentance can be imagined ('A mother, whom I shall call M, feels hostility to her daughter-in-law, whom I shall call D. M finds D quite a good-hearted girl.... D is inclined to be pert and familiar, insufficiently ceremonious', and so on)[25] clearly reveals how Iris Murdoch thought through her moral-philosophical examples, and probably her plots as well. Whatever particular name they might be travelling under on a particular fictional occasion, here come M and D once again. These houses of fiction keep being inhabited by human tokens, human chess pieces, by D and M.

---

[24] Repetitiveness, of all sorts, is a well-aired charge against Murdoch. See for instance Christopher Ricks's scathing review of *Nuns and Soldiers* in the *Sunday Times* (7 Sept. 1980), discussed by Elizabeth Dipple, in *Iris Murdoch: Work for the Spirit* (London: Methuen, 1982), 82.

[25] In *The Sovereignty of Good*, 17ff; also *Existentialists and Mystics*, 312 ff.

It's small surprise that readers keep reporting that they can't distinguish the characters in *this* novel from those in that other one.

Vain repetition. It's like the *coup de foudre*, which can work very nicely as a mark of love's prevailing force, but loses credibility with so many examples of it. Murdoch's Eros is a jokey manager of human relations who keeps overplaying his hand. Like the principled devotion to contingency and mess that keeps resorting to extreme violence as its illustration—to destruction, explosion, the bloody fight, the car-crash, the smash-up (of bodies, relationships, fish bowls, bibelots), to the grotesque accident and the very nasty death. And Murdoch's novels not only end with large catastrophic climaxes, they tend to open with them, and to fill their middles with them as well. Accidents, bad luck, unexpected death, threaten us all, and are indeed the age-old stuff of tragedy, but they threaten Murdoch's people to an extraordinary degree. Only in a Murdoch novel (*The Book and the Brotherhood*) might two old friends not only fight a duel, but do it Russian-roulette style, taking turns to fire with only a single bullet in each of their weapons. The duel ends with one of them killing another friend who just happens to open the door and step into the path of the killing shot. To lose your lover, your colleague's wife, in a car smash as you speed down the motorway from Oxford to London is an unhappy accident; to lose your next one, the same colleague's second wife, this time in the muddy waters of the Thames, is an Iris Murdoch novel (it's *A Word Child*, of course).

Under the banner of ordinariness, nothing much is actually ordinary in a full-revs Murdoch plot—and the social unordinariness, the kept-up dottiness on bourgeois subjects, with everyone, as it were, a civil servant and his wife with a First in moral philosophy from Balliol, a magical daughter or two, a brainy dog, one brother who's an antiques dealer specializing in Plato on the side, the other an unfrocked archdeacon turned psychiatrist, is the least of the specializings. Here is overheated plotting, steamed-up imagining, with selfhood and gender and thought and sexual behaviour all ricocheting zanily about. Here is French farcicality, over-operatic plotting, Shakespearian comedy running wild, the baroque, the rococo, all turning into the gothic.

Gothic is, of course, a well-established, even venerable way for novels to write evil, but it is one whose extremities of wickedness, their excess, are in constant danger of degenerating into ethical dysfunctionality, even into farce. Putting too much gloss on moral blackness shifts a serious ethical concern over into the arms of the parodic. Mary Shelley's *Frankenstein* is always on the edge of parody (and like Iris Murdoch has been mercilessly parodied). And this precarious balance between the serious and the comic erodes gothic's claims to moral seriousness. Those girls and their mother, weaving and being vegetarian and following Jesus in the house called Seegard with a mad dad in the attic (*The Good Apprentice*) are almost ludicrous. The house, with its elastic labyrinthine structure, a masterpiece of creepy gothic, is certainly ludicrous. Mischa Fox with his bad German memories, and the Lusiewicz brothers, and all that blasphemy and sadism going on in the labyrinthine basements of the government building in *Flight from the Enchanter*, are close to being too bad to be true. The banality of evil, in Hannah Arendt's memorable phrase describing Hitler's henchman Adolf Eichmann, evil precisely in ordinariness, in an ordinary-seeming person, is not only more menacing and a lot more challenging to moral thought, it also seems truer to what we know of the rise of the dictators and to Nazism's ordinary supporters and agents. And Murdoch's plots, Murdoch's people, have little time or place for banality.

A main thing which marks this absence of the ordinary is Murdoch's intense leaning—for all her repudiation in the theory of myth—towards the mythic. In practice she is one of modern fiction's extremest dippers into what Philip Larkin dismissed as the myth-kitty. She is intertextual to a fault. She can't do a pair of brothers without their being Cain and Abel. Errant sons are, of course, Prodigal Sons. *The Green Knight* not only replays the medieval poem of that title, but the biblical raising of Lazarus from the dead, and Tolstoy's novel *Resurrection*. Samaritans, good and bad, throng *An Accidental Man*. *The Nice and the Good* has Circe and the Three Graces and a Virgilian journey to the underworld in it. Nick, in *The Bell*, living on the other side of a ferry crossing with his dog, is, of course, an echo of Charon, Virgil's boatman of the underworld, with his dog, Cerberus. *Hamlet* and *Der Rosenkavalier* and Oedipus inflect *The Black Prince*. *The Philosopher's Pupil* is a kind of *Midsummer Night's Dream*. *The Sea, The Sea* is the story of a modern Prospero giving up his theatrical magics. The story of Apollo flaying Marsyas haunts *The Good Apprentice*. Much of the plot of *Nuns and Soldiers* does variants on Homer's Penelope surrounded by suitors and the fleece-an-heiress-with-a-marriage scam of Henry James's *The Wings of the Dove*. Jane Austen, Shakespeare, James, Dostoevsky, Samuel Beckett, are a kind of larder from which Iris Murdoch freely takes her fictional ingredients. 'I feel so strange, as if I were living in a myth,' says the glorious girl Sefton in *The Green Knight* to Harvey, just after they've done their sexual initiations together ('I worship you, I am in heaven'). 'Myths are dangerous places' is his sensible reply (pt. IV, 'Eros'). It's sensible because, for a start, myths are destructive of reality. And not least by generating plots and characters which are simply formulaic. As the old psychiatrist Thomas (*The Good Apprentice*), one more Prospero wanting to give up his magic, is shown thinking: 'Of course Theseus must leave Ariadne, and Aeneas must abandon Dido, Athens must be saved, Rome must be founded, Prospero drowns his book and frees Ariel and the Duke marries Isabella. And Apollo tames the Furies.' He pondered for a while, 'and then added half aloud, "And flays Marsyas"' (pt. III, 'Life after Death'). Being in a reproduction of a given mythic story naturally does away with any contingency of plot. This constant mythicizing of the real in Murdoch's novels quite spoils or, to say the least, and more neutrally, immensely transmogrifies it.

And this metamorphosing effect, in which this philosopher is Prospero, that widow is Penelope, this boy is Dostoevsky's Holy Fool Prince Myshkin, is all one, I suppose, with the greatest challenge to Murdoch's spirited campaigning on behalf of the untranscendent transcendence of the real, and for the important religio-ethical residualism in ordinary language and thought and experience: namely, the way her miraculously ordinary tends to turn into what is suggested might be the miraculous itself. The return of the lost dog Anax in *The Green Knight* is a 'miracle', 'miraculous', but only in the common or garden sense. People talk of the raising of the old bell in *The Bell* as a miracle, but actually it's done by Dora and Toby using ordinary engineering tackle. Talk of a miracle in such cases (impotent Willie Kost managing coitus in *The Nice and the Good*, for example) is not just the way of ordinary language, nostalgic as it might be for an age of miracle gone by, but a linguistic recollection marking a real absence of what was once denoted by such words. And there are lots of startling things in Murdoch which are indeed only pseudo-miraculous: Levkin's leapings in *The Italian Girl*, Hartley's in *The Good Apprentice*, which only resemble levitation; Mary and Jesse seeming to walk on water (*The Nice and the Good* and *The Good Apprentice*) but actually walking on matted ivy and stepping stones. But it is also the case that Ducane is saved from drowning (*The Nice and the Good*) by a vision of the Virgin Mary, as well as by human agency. And James might actually have walked on water to save Charles from drowning (*The Sea, The Sea*)—even though Charles's record of the event breaks off indeterminately, and he might just have been hallucinating once again. And the ex-nun Anna Cavidge (*Nuns and Soldiers*) meets Christ in her kitchen and her fingers, burnt from touching Him, stay burnt just like real stigmata. And Moy in *The Green Knight* does actually have the power of telekinesis and does move stones by thought. And the mythic man Jackson in Murdoch's last novel, *Jackson's Dilemma* (1994)—a novel shaky, thinned perhaps by its author's failing mental powers—

does travel through time and space, like Jesus in the Gospels. And the healing hands of Marcus Vallar do, it seems, bring the dying Irish poet Pat Penman back from death's door (*The Message to the Planet*). And Peter Mir, the apparently dead murderee of *The Green Knight*, comes back from the dead. And he has healing hands too (he heals Harvey's injured and incurable foot). On these many occasions, clearly, the devoted tracings of transcendence in ordinary language, the recognitions of the wonder of the world, are surpassing themselves. It's as if the nostalgia for real transcendence is getting out of hand, as if the ontological proof were being given something of its old free rein. As if Iris Murdoch, the occasional churchgoer and religious retreat-attender, the nostalgic reciter of the Book of Common Prayer, were reaching back indeed to the orthodoxly baptized imaginings of Sunday School, and turning her fiction, in effect, into what she had seemed so loudly to reject. Into something which William Golding, the Golding at least of *The Double Tongue* (that last, unfinished novel of 1995 about a faking-it Greek prophetess, the oracle of Delphi, finally intruded on, perhaps, by a real divine spirit) might recognize as in his vicinity. Turning it into a kind of magicking which, in their various ways, too, Salman Rushdie and Angela Carter might feel rather close to—even if these novelists would not, as the last two certainly would not, have time for Murdoch's apparent nostalgia for a revived Anglican, High Anglican, Christianity. On such occasions, Iris Murdoch, the cannily realistic George Eliot admirer, seems driven, rather unexpectedly, into a version of magical realism.

11

The Politics of Narrative in the Post-war Scottish Novel

LIAM MCILVANNEY

An upturned boat
—a watershed.[1]

For Edwin Muir, writing in the 1930s, the predicament of the Scottish novelist was easily stated. That predicament was Scotland. How could one write an important modern novel in a country which no longer existed? Not even Walter Scott, the giant of the Scottish tradition, could rise to such a challenge. The failure of Scott, according to Muir, was a failure not so much of lexis as of locus: 'he spent most of his days in a hiatus, in a country, that is to say, which was neither a nation nor a province, and had, instead of a centre, a blank, an Edinburgh, in the middle of it'.[2] Muir's vision of a void at the heart of Scottish life—indeed, of Scottish life itself as a terminal, drear abeyance—became something of a topos in the post-war Scottish novel. In Archie Hind's *The Dear Green Place* (1966), the

[1] Kathleen Jamie, 'On the Design Chosen for the New Scottish Parliament Building by Architect Enric Miralles', *Jizzen* (London: Picador, 1999), 48.

[2] Edwin Muir, *Scott and Scotland: The Predicament of the Scottish Writer* (London: Routledge, 1936), 11–12.

hero, Mat Craig, a failed novelist, blames the failure of his art on the poverty of his environment:

All the background against which a novelist might set his scene, the aberrant attempts of human beings and societies to respond to circumstances, all that was bizarre, grotesque and extravagant in human life, all that whole background of violence, activity, intellectual and imaginative ardour, political daring. All that was somehow missing from Scottish life . . . in Scottish life there was only a null blot, a cessation of life, a dull absence, a blankness . . . [3]

The very rhythm of this passage registers the failure: like a frenetic juggling act, the opening sentence overstrains itself, and the batons strike the pavement one by one: 'blot', 'cessation', 'absence', 'blankness'. In George Friel's *Mr Alfred M.A.* (1972), the eponymous hero, a schoolteacher and a failed poet, shares Mat Craig's perception of Scotland's dismal vacancy:

He was an exile in his native land. Not that he had any love for his native land. He rated it as a cipher, of no value until a figure was put before it. But it had no figures. It existed only as terra incognita to the north of England. Hence formerly known simply as N.B. Note well. A footnote. Whereas England was where they spoke the language he taught, the language he once thought he knew. But he had been refused an immigrant's visa there many years ago when nine publishers rejected his thirty-two poems.[4]

Inert, intractable, cut off from history, Scotland lacks the vitality that might nourish worthwhile art. The figure of the failed artist haunts Scottish fiction of the 1960s and 1970s: Foley in Elspeth Davie's *Creating a Scene* (1971), Pagan in John Herdman's *Pagan's Pilgrimage* (1978), Graham Cameron in Gordon Williams's *Walk Don't Walk* (1972), a novel whose prefatory poem is a wry admission of Scottish third-rateness:

> We knew our country was a smalltime dump
> Where nothing ever happened and

---

[3] Archie Hind, *The Dear Green Place* (1966; repr. London: Corgi, 1985), 87.
[4] George Friel, *Mr Alfred M.A.* (London: Calder and Boyars, 1972), 78.

there was nothing to do.
And nobody had a name like Jelly Roll Morton.[5]

From Scenes Like These, Williams's 1968 novel, is a kind of *Künstlerroman* in reverse. Its hero, Dunky Logan, labourer on a decaying farm at the edge of a lowland industrial town, is the kind of sensitive adolescent who, in another society, might develop into an artist. Here, he learns to hate Catholics and snobs, to broaden his accent so as not to sound like 'some English nancy boy on the wireless', and to lose his 'daft notions' about education and reading. In the course of the novel, Dunky shrivels before our eyes, his aspirations dwindling into nullity like 'the disappearing language and history and literature of Scotland'.[6]

On 1 July 1999, the first Scottish Parliament in nearly 300 years opened its doors on the Mound. Muir's blank had been filled in. Edinburgh was once more a capital of sorts, and national life had a political focus. So what did this mean for the Scottish novel? Well, in one sense, not much. The point about the Parliament, from a cultural perspective, was how little it now seemed to matter. Its coming was welcome, certainly, but hardly seemed critical to the nation's cultural health. Above all, it was belated: by the time the Parliament arrived, a revival in Scottish fiction had been long underway; '[i]n terms of the novel, no period in Scottish culture has, perhaps, been as rich as the period between the 1960s and 1990s'.[7] Without waiting for the politicians, Scottish novelists had written themselves out of despair, had worked up a renaissance. It began in the 1960s and 1970s, with a loose group of working-class West of Scotland realists: George Friel, Archie Hind, Alan Sharp, William McIlvanney, Gordon Williams, Alan Spence, and Carl

---

[5] Gordon Williams, 'A Scots Burgh Boy's Dream of America', *Walk Don't Walk* (1972; repr. Glasgow: Richard Drew, 1988), 8.

[6] Gordon Williams, *From Scenes Like These* (1968; repr. London: Allison and Busby, 1980), 12, 22, 88.

[7] Cairns Craig, *The Modern Scottish Novel: Narrative and the National Imagination* (Edinburgh: Edinburgh University Press, 1999), 36.

MacDougall.[8] By the late 1970s, novels lamenting the absence of a viable tradition had themselves become a tradition of sorts.[9] But the watershed came in the early 1980s, with the so-called 'Glasgow Renaissance' and the emergence of two extraordinary talents.

James Kelman's demotic narratives of Glaswegian working-class life announced a new era in vernacular fiction. In novels like *The Busconductor Hines* (1984), *A Chancer* (1985), and *A Disaffection* (1989), Kelman broke down the traditional barrier between standard English narration and demotic Scots dialogue, developing a free indirect style in which Scots pervaded both. This technique itself bespoke and begot a new confidence: no longer stuck in quotation marks, Scots was tackling narrative, 'the place where the psychological drama occurred'.[10] For an emerging generation of Scottish writers—Janice Galloway, Duncan McLean, Irvine Welsh, Alan Warner, Gordon Legge— Kelman's linguistic daring was exemplary. He showed how to write without condescension about people whom literature habitually ignores.

The achievement of Alasdair Gray was in some ways more significant still. With *Lanark: A Life in 4 Books* (1981), Gray seemed to have found the philosopher's stone: he had made great art out of Glasgow. In its scope and ambition, its prodigious invention and its formal daring, *Lanark* was unprecedented: a realist *Bildungsroman* enclosed within a sci-fi political allegory, the whole thing written in a style of childish ingenuousness that brought astonishing results. Best of all, Gray had achieved all this without, as it were, becoming Muriel Spark, without at least *seeming* to write as an English novelist. He had rooted

---

[8] A useful anthology of the period, featuring these writers and others, is *Identities: An Anthology of West of Scotland Poetry, Prose and Drama*, ed. Geddes Thomson (London: Heinemann, 1981).

[9] Douglas Gifford, *The Dear Green Place? The Novel in the West of Scotland* (Glasgow: Third Eye Centre, 1985), 14.

[10] From the title essay in James Kelman, *'And the Judges said...': Essays* (London: Secker and Warburg, 2002), 40.

the whole thing—sci-fi to boot—in the 'magnificent city'[11] of Glasgow. *Lanark*'s vigorous 'blend of realism and fantasy' (p. 155) anticipates the mixed modes of novelists like Iain Banks, Emma Tennant, Irvine Welsh, and A. L. Kennedy. The short poem which ends the novel observes that 'EVENTS DRIFT CON-TINUALLY DOWN, | EFFACING LANDMARKS' (p. 560). The events of the past two decades have tended rather to elevate Gray's novel, which stands out ever more clearly as a monumental Scottish text, the massy herald of a new dispensation. In *The Picador Book of Contemporary Scottish Fiction* (1997), 'contemporary' means 'post-*Lanark*'.[12]

The literary revival of the past four decades has lifted the spell of Muir's gloomy prognostic. And yet Muir's analysis, lamenting Scotland's missing 'centre', has in part been vindicated, with the novel itself becoming a centre of sorts, taking up the political slack, filling the space where Scottish politics ought to have been. When devolution was stymied in 1979, it was 'as though the energy that had failed to be harnessed by the politicians flowed into other channels'.[13] For much of the post-war period, Scotland's unacknowledged legislators have outpaced the political ones. 'It's this land of the regal brits!' exclaims Rab Hines in James Kelman's debut novel, 'its neither here nor there'.[14] The 'post-British' Scotland to which the Edinburgh Parliament was a laggard response had long been taking shape in the pages of Scottish novels. It's as if Gray's famous motto—'Work as if you live in the early days of a better nation'—had been taken as read by his literary contemporaries.

---

[11] Alasdair Gray, *Lanark: A Life in 4 Books* (1981; repr. London: Picador, 1994), 243.

[12] *The Picador Book of Contemporary Scottish Fiction*, ed. Peter Kravitz (London: Picador, 1997), xvi.

[13] Cairns Craig, 'Preface', in Ian Donnachie, Christopher Harvie, and Ian S. Wood (eds.), *Forward! Labour Politics in Scotland 1888–1988* (Edinburgh: Polygon, 1989), vi.

[14] James Kelman, *The Busconductor Hines* (1984; repr. London: Phoenix, 1992), 221.

'POLITICS WILL NOT LET ME ALONE.'[15] The cry of Jock
McLeish in Gray's *1982 Janine* must be echoed by any critic of
the post-war Scottish novel. However, while the political situation has been a spur to post-war novelists, and has given the
Scottish novel a heightened public profile, it would be wrong to
reduce the novelists to the cheerleaders of a resurgent nationalism. We need to be aware, for one thing, that politics has been a
matter of technique as much as explicit content. Precisely because
of the Scottish novel's status as a kind of substitute or virtual
polity, Scottish novelists have been acutely conscious of the politics of *form*. The disposition of the narrative, the relationship of
character to author and narrator, the autonomy or otherwise of
the protagonist, the linguistic profile of the text: these have been
matters of profound symbolic and ultimately political significance. James Kelman's statement that he 'saw the distinction between dialogue and narrative as a summation of the political
system'[16] gives an inkling of what is at stake. If, for Alasdair
Gray, the omniscient narrator is 'A King with a Bad Constitution',[17] much post-war Scottish fiction has sought to construct a
more equable literary polity—often by a method which privileges
the spoken voice and a form of first-person narration.[18] Even
those novelists who uphold the regime of omniscience do so
with a sense of what, politically, is assumed. In what follows I
discuss the politics of narrative in the work of three of the most
significant post-war Scottish novelists: Muriel Spark, Alasdair
Gray, and James Kelman.

'In art', writes Robbe-Grillet, 'nothing is ever known in advance.'[19] In the art of Muriel Spark, imperiously orchestrated,

---

[15] Alasdair Gray, *1982 Janine* (London: Jonathan Cape, 1984), 231–2.

[16] Kelman, '*And the Judges Said . . .*', 40.

[17] Gray, *Lanark*, 480.

[18] The importance of the spoken, first-person voice in Scottish fiction is discussed
in Carl MacDougall, *Painting the Forth Bridge: A Search for Scottish Identity*
(London: Aurum, 2001).

[19] Alain Robbe-Grillet, from *For a New Novel: Essays on Fiction*, trans.
Richard Howard (New York: Grove, 1965), in Michael McKeon (ed.),

so coolly premeditated, everything seems to be known in advance. Her trademark device is prolepsis: a signal that the novelist, like Calvin's God, 'sees the beginning and the end'.[20] If Spark knows her destination from the off, she is also pretty clear about the stops along the way: 'But it is time, now, to take a closer look at Hubert'; 'It is time now to describe what Tom looked like'; 'Her real name, Beate Pappenheim, now comes into this story.'[21] Everything, in Spark's fiction, has its appointed time and place. The unforeseen and out-of-place are proscribed by the very motion of her prose. Her sentences swing with a catwalk gait—elegant, stylized, preordained. Not even the dialogue is permitted to slouch. Lister's injunction in *Not to Disturb* (1971)—'This is not the time for inconsequential talk'—might be pinned on a three-by-five above Spark's writing desk.[22]

Spark's fictions are often praised for their witty intermingling of life and art. It might be truer to say that, in Spark, the world has the finish and fixity of art, not life's unfettered contingency. There is a reason why Spark constructs her novels around sequestered milieux, 'closed and allegorical communities'[23]—a girls' school, a nunnery, a hospital ward, an island, a lonely mansion. Already halfway to art, these little worlds are ordered and stratified, redeemed from the chaos of unfiltered experience. Spark's protagonists, too, are held a little above the fray. Even within their fictional worlds, her characters are characters. They stride to the footlights, purged of redundancy. Like Robinson they are 'near-mythical'; they move, like the Abbess of Crewe, in the

---

Theory of the Novel: A Historical Approach (Baltimore: Johns Hopkins, 2000), 824.

[20] Muriel Spark, *The Prime of Miss Jean Brodie* (1961; repr. Harmondsworth: Penguin, 1965), 120.

[21] Muriel Spark, *The Takeover* (1976; repr. Harmondsworth: Penguin, 1978), 19; *Reality and Dreams* (1996; repr. Harmondsworth: Penguin, 1997), 71; *Aiding and Abetting* (Harmondsworth: Viking, 2000), 20.

[22] Muriel Spark, *Not to Disturb* (1971; repr. Harmondsworth: Penguin, 1974), 5.

[23] Patrick Parrinder, 'Muriel Spark and Her Critics', in Joseph Hynes (ed.), *Critical Essays on Muriel Spark* (New York: G. K. Hall, 1992), 79 (first pub. in *Critical Quarterly*, 25 (Summer 1983), 23–31).

'sphere... of mythology'.[24] If minor characters they are 'one-dimensional types',[25] apparently drawn from a lumber room of literature: Marigold Richards in *Reality and Dreams* (1996) is 'worthy as any woman or man in the works of George Eliot' (p. 34); Rose Stanley in *The Prime of Miss Jean Brodie* (1961) is 'like a heroine from a novel by D. H. Lawrence' (p. 110).

Often, you want to protest at the foreclosing of Spark's characters, the way they stamp into view with the burden of their souls laid out across their arms. Making her appearance at the start of *The Abbess of Crewe* (1974), Sister Winifrede emits a 'whine of bewilderment, that voice of the very stupid, the mind where no dawn breaks' (p. 7). There is no possibility that a character might recover from such a description. Winifrede will neither develop nor reveal anything more of her personality. She is known, exhaustively and definitively, from her first appearance in the novel, like the Anglican nuns in *Symposium*:

It is sad to observe that of those nine nuns of St Pancras only three were of vital interest, and that those three were fairly unprincipled. The remaining six were devout and dutiful, and two of them very sweet and trusting, but all those six were as dreary as hell.[26]

What does become 'dreary as hell' is this mania for judgement, and it is sad to observe that, of all Spark's characters, only Jean Brodie is of vital interest, because only Jean Brodie has a vivid human surplus, suggesting a life beyond the requirements of plot. For the most part, Spark writes novels about 'Characters in a novel'.[27]

The reflexive quality of Spark's fiction has been linked to her involvement with the *nouveau roman*.[28] But it may also relate to

---

[24] Muriel Spark, *Robinson* (1958; repr. Harmondsworth: Penguin, 1964), 130; *The Abbess of Crewe* (1974; repr. Harmondsworth: Penguin, 1975), 16.

[25] Craig, *The Modern Scottish Novel*, 179.

[26] Muriel Spark, *Symposium* (1990; repr. Harmondsworth: Penguin, 1991), 103.

[27] Muriel Spark, *The Comforters* (1957; repr. Harmondsworth: Penguin, 1963), 202.

[28] See, for instance, Ruth Whittaker, *The Faith and Fiction of Muriel Spark* (London: Macmillan, 1982).

something more conventional: a penchant for exerting strict authorial control. In an avowedly fictive realm, where no mimetic purpose is claimed, the writ of the author runs uncontested. As readers, we have no competence here, no comeback, no grounds for demurral. Faced with Spark's tart, complacent narrators, our job is to follow in their wake, like tourists after a gallery guide. Awkward questions are not invited. You want to know *why* it is now time to describe what Tom looked like? It just is. At times, too, the narrator's omniscience rather oversteps its mark. There may be a saving irony in the suggestion that, in 1945, 'all the nice people in England were poor', but what do we do with the contention that 'generally speaking, Scotswomen who do not dye their hair have a homogenous island-born look . . . which does not apply in the south'?[29] This is to treat the world like the world of a novel. Through the conventions of fiction, we are obliged to assent when told that Mary Macgregor 'was too stupid ever to tell a lie' or that Jean Brodie 'was by temperament suited only to the Roman Catholic Church':[30] but we cannot be asked to believe that all Scotswomen look the same.

It may be, of course, that Spark is polemically exaggerating her narrative omniscience, that she wants to point up the contentiousness of all fictional narratives. The Sparkian novel, we are assured, 'convicts itself as a medium which can never tell the truth, and must therefore advertise the dangers of its lies'.[31] Now, it is true that Spark's baddies—her plotters and forgers, her quacks and sharpers, her concocters of scenarios—generally have the cut of novelists. It is also true that Charmian Piper in *Memento Mori* compares 'the art of fiction' with 'the practice of deception'.[32] Still, the image of Spark as an anguished Calvinist,

---

[29] Muriel Spark, *The Girls of Slender Means* (1963; repr. Harmondsworth: Penguin, 1966), 7; *Aiding and Abetting*, 39.

[30] Spark, *The Prime of Miss Jean Brodie*, 11, 85.

[31] Cairns Craig, 'Doubtful Imaginings: The Sceptical Art of Muriel Spark', *Études Ecossaises*, 2 (1993), 71.

[32] Muriel Spark, *Memento Mori* (1959; repr. Harmondsworth: Penguin, 1961), 187.

impugning her own duplicitous craft, seems a trifle overdone. It fails to explain, for one thing, why a writer who views the novel as an impious rival to God's creation, should be so unabashedly godlike in her own artistic practice. Not all novelists wield the sceptre with the cold aplomb of Spark. And then, to avail oneself of the most intrusive authorial techniques over the course of twenty-one novels suggests a writer who is less perturbed than 'somewhat arrogant about the extent of the novelist's power'.[33]

Particularly in the later books, Spark revels in her sovereign power, extols the artist's unaccountability. 'How does one explain an act of art?' is the question in *Reality and Dreams* (1996), and the artist as God seems a bright and brilliant trope. Tom Richards, the film director hero of the novel, is recuperating after a fall from a crane. No one uses cranes on set anymore, but Tom does and he tells us why: 'Yes, I did feel like God up on that crane. It was wonderful to shout orders through the amplifier and like God watch the team down there group and re-group as bidden' (p. 14). Tom's exhilaration is shared by Spark, for whom he embodies the ruthlessness of art, its necessary monomania and predatory detachment. His vindication comes in a spat with one of his stars. An actress called Jeanne is demanding greater prominence in the movie—more close-ups and lingering shots. What she ignores is that the film requires her character to be a minor presence, 'a throw-away item seen always at an angle' (p. 78). Cheered on by his author (who kills Jeanne off in another crane accident), Tom asserts his authority and disregards Jeanne's pleas. As an artist, after all, Tom rules by divine right: 'What do they think a film set is? A democracy or something?' (p. 14)

Like Tom, Spark isn't slow to let us know who's in control. At one point in *Reality and Dreams* an old boyfriend of the protagonist's daughter is referred to as 'the boy, whose name for the present purpose is irrelevant' (p. 122). Instead of silently omit-

---

[33] Frank Kermode, 'The Novel as Jerusalem: Muriel Spark's *Mandelbaum Gate*', in Hynes (ed.), *Critical Essays on Muriel Spark*, 179 (first pub. in *Atlantic*, 216 (Oct. 1965), 92–8).

ting the name, the narrator ostentatiously withholds it. This is classic Spark. Like the Mexican ranch in *Aiding and Abetting*, Spark's fictions are 'constituted on hierarchical lincs' (p. 128), and it is no coincidence that the most apposite description of Spark's novels is Jean Brodie's verdict on fascist Germany: 'magnificently organized' (p. 122). There is a politics at work here—a politics of form, not just of content—and it comes to the fore in Spark's treatment of class.

There is a sense in which Spark's narrative focus on the rich and the very rich should attract no comment at all. A novelist must be free to explore a particular milieu, and need not be comprehensive in her social coverage. The problem is that Spark herself makes an issue of class. It is not that she overlooks the poor: Spark turns from their plight with a meaningful flourish. What *Aiding and Abetting* calls 'people like them' (p. 46) are, she wants us to appreciate, no part of her subject. This, surely, is what we take from the second chapter of *Brodie*, in which the girls are led on a walking trip round Edinburgh's Old Town, that 'reeking network of slums' (p. 32). These few pages take us to a realm seldom visited in Spark, a squalid underworld of random violence and shouted obscenities, a 'misty region of crime and desperation' (p. 32). For Sandy Stranger, the Old Town seems like a 'foreign country' peopled by improbably dirty, inscrutable aliens. She comes across a long queue of dole-men, hawking and coughing, smoking stubby cigarettes:

The laughter of the girls met that of the men opposite, who had now begun to file slowly by fits and starts into the labour bureau. Sandy's fear returned as soon as she had stopped laughing. She saw the slow jerkily moving file tremble with life, she saw it all of a piece like one dragon's body which had no right to be in the city and...was unslayable... [T]he snaky creature opposite started to shiver in the cold and made Sandy tremble again. (p. 40)

The correspondences here—the laughter and the trembling— merely underscore the massive gulf between the groups. The monstrous 'dragon' inhabits an alternative dimension to that of the Brodie girls. It occupies a world in which motives are obscure—'A man sat on the icy-cold pavement; he just sat' (p. 32)—and language is inscrutable: a crop-haired woman tells a street bully 'I'll be your man' (p. 33). It is a world in which not even the consumption of food can be predicted: sometimes the fathers drink their dole-money 'and their children starve' (p. 39). Spark can do nothing with this world: its fractured, menaced lives are not amenable to her method, and it remains a foreign country. Like the Brodie set, the narrative crosses the street, passes by on the other side. And yet Spark makes us pause for a moment, to take a bewildered glance at these ravaged, voiceless men. There they stand, outcast and other, beyond the scope of the novelist's interest, beyond the reach of her art: 'They are the Idle' (p. 39).

Spark's image of the unemployed men as a sinister organism, a lumbering 'dragon', points forward to the brief crowd scenes in *The Girls of Slender Means*. On VE day and VJ day, the 'huge organic murmur of the crowd' (p. 17) ripples through London. Again, there is unexplained violence and menacing sexuality. Again, Spark's characters—once more a group of genteel young ladies—are defined in opposition to this roiling scrum of beery humanity. This crowd, this vulgar urban swell, is what Spark's aesthetic vision habitually screens out. We are compelled to acknowledge that 'artistic apprehension',[34] defined as the process of privileging certain data and excluding others, is connected—in the work of Spark—with *class* privilege and *social* exclusion. In Spark's eyes it is always 'people like them' who are surplus to requirements, 'irrelevant' or—that word which tolls through *Reality and Dreams*—'redundant'. Spark's aesthetic lexicon—privilege, exclusion, economy, redundancy—has a social application which is not entirely fortuitous.

---

[34] Muriel Spark, *Loitering with Intent* (1981; repr. Harmondsworth: Penguin, 1995), 13.

In a significant essay of 1970, 'The Desegregation of Art', Spark registers her distaste for socially 'concerned' writing, for that 'art which condemns violence and suffering by pathetic depiction'.[35] The 'cult of the victim' is, for Spark, a dangerous heresy, one which threatens to cloud the cold, satirical eye of the genuine artist. Throughout her novels, blubbing do-gooders and friends of the wretched always turn out to be nasty little schemers: Letizia in *The Takeover*, Effie in *The Only Problem*, Marigold in *Reality and Dreams*. In the Old Town section of *Brodie*, Spark sets up a scenario which seems to cry out for 'pathetic depiction'. But while Sandy Stranger (another lachrymose schemer) gives way to compassion—'She wanted to cry as she always did when she saw a street singer or a beggar' (p. 40)—Spark herself remains unmoved. In the economy of Spark's novel, these men have a function: they are Damned Souls to the Brodie girls' Elect. Beyond this function they have no claim on Spark's attention, and so she goes about her business. That in so doing she replicates society's marginalization of these men is not her concern. The novel is not a democracy.

A contempt for the wretched, a relished indifference to suffering, is indeed an unsettling aspect of Spark's artistic personality. It emerges—in fact, it is paraded—once again in *Aiding and Abetting*, Spark's fabular version of the Lucan affair, in which Sandra Rivett, the murdered, working-class nanny, fills the same sort of role as the dole-men in *Brodie*. For Spark, who appears to regard the Lucan affair as a matter of great and ongoing public resonance, evolving attitudes to Lucan reflect the changing mores of British society. At the time of the murder, the sheer panache of Lucan's arrogant self-image, his aristocratic hauteur, overawed his acquaintances and hampered the police. Now, in a brasher, less deferential age, his contempt for

---

[35] Muriel Spark, 'The Desegregation of Art' , in Hynes (ed.), *Critical Essays on Muriel Spark*, 36 (first pub. in *Proceedings of the American Academy of Arts and Letters*, 21 (1971), 21–7).

the nanny strikes us as shocking. This notion is voiced by Maria Twickenham, one of Lucan's erstwhile abettors:

But what was the difference, Maria wondered, between then and now? More than a quarter of a century was the difference.... There was something in the air one breathed. Habits change. States of mind change. Collective moods change. The likeable, working-class murdered young nanny was now the main factor. At the time the centre of the affair was Lucan. (pp. 62–3)

Now, what is significant about this passage is the manner in which Spark signposts a potential new direction—the story of the Lucan affair as told from the nanny's perspective—only to turn off down the old familiar route. Popular perceptions of the Lucan affair may now place Sandra Rivett at its centre; Spark's novel doesn't. *Aiding and Abetting* flaunts its indifference to the murdered nanny: the 'main factor', so far as Spark is concerned, remains Lucky Lucan.

What are we to make of this? As in *Brodie*, it seems, Spark is taking her stand against 'the art and literature of sentiment and emotion'.[36] There may be compelling emotional, moral, or political reasons for making Sandra Rivett the focus of attention: but for Spark there are no valid *artistic* reasons. The 'English story' (p. 1) told by the novel is Lucan's, not Sandra Rivett's. And so Sandra remains a cipher, like Jeanne in *Reality and Dreams*, 'whose part in the story was by definition that of a nobody' (p. 110). We begin to grasp that, for Spark, 'sentimental' is a synonym for 'left wing'. When a character in *The Takeover* is described as having 'sentimental sympathies towards the political left wing' (p. 102), this is, in Spark's terms, a tautology. Like Hildegard Wolf in *Aiding and Abetting*, Spark feels she cannot afford such sentimentality, which is why her narrators share Tom Richards's craving for altitude. They occupy a zone of frosty elevation, beyond a moral tree-line where sympathy cannot flourish.

---

[36] Spark, 'The Desegregation of Art', 35.

It may be significant that Spark's freest, most rewarding writing is the most closely autobiographical, whether in *Brodie*, the first-person novels of 1950s London (*Loitering with Intent*, *A Far Cry from Kensington*) or the memoir *Curriculum Vitae* (1992). It is here that Spark's baleful puritan economy, in which everything must be working to an orchestrated purpose, is relaxed, and the writing follows only the random pull of memory. Those opening pages of *Curriculum Vitae*—with their reveries of oatcakes and soda scones ('small, sharp-tasting lumps, thirsty for butter'), their vignettes of the young Spark learning to brew tea and making landscapes on her dinner plate—are among the best things she has written.[37] There is a concentration on the thing itself, and a fluent, provisional quality not often seen in Spark. The prose is being shaped before our eyes, it seems, like the butter-blocks slapped and patted by the girl from the Buttercup Dairy. It is here, if anywhere, that Spark's writing fulfils her 'attempt to redeem the time'[38] of her early life. In its freedom and plenitude, in its joyous attention to 'redundant' detail, *Curriculum Vitae* slips the net of Spark's 'totalitarian imagination'.[39] But then, as Spark herself concedes in *Loitering with Intent*, the politics of the *biographical* narrative are haphazardly democratic: 'The story of a life is a very informal party; there are no rules of precedence and hospitality, no invitation' (p. 43).

If Spark relishes the despotism of authorship, Alasdair Gray seems merely embarrassed by it. He is like the monarch who arranges his own feast of fools, exposing at every turn his own regrettable frailty. Determined strategies of self-effacement are pursued throughout his œuvre, beginning with the 'Index of Plagiarisms' which occupies the margins of the epilogue to *Lanark*. Even the designation 'author' or 'artist' sits too grandly

[37] Muriel Spark, *Curriculum Vitae* (1992; repr. Harmondsworth: Penguin, 1993), 18.
[38] Frank Kermode, 'The House of Fiction: Interviews with Seven English Novelists', *Partisan Review*, 30 (Spring 1963), p. 80.
[39] Craig, 'Doubtful Imaginings', 78.

for Gray's liking: he describes himself in artisanal terms as 'a maker of imagined objects'.[40] His autobiographical notes have a dead-pan baldness, as if ignorant of the very possibility that the artist be thought someone special: 'Alasdair Gray is a stout, elderly, married Glaswegian who lives by painting and writing things'.[41] His *Saltire Self-Portrait* has barely begun before we're being assured that its author has small genitals and a bulging paunch.[42] When Gray makes an appearance in *Lanark* it's as 'Nastler', the shifty and cowardly 'king' of the novel, who lords it over his characters while scribbling in a dirty bed. Not content with including hostile reviews on his dust-jackets, Gray himself weighs in with self-directed barbs. In *McGrotty and Ludmilla* (1990), he mocks himself as 'Our Bigheaded Author'.[43] In his recent survey of the Scottish literary tradition, Gray dispatches *Lanark* as 'a grossly over-rated novel'.[44] Authorship, for Gray, is not a vocation so much as a tainted, encumbering office he hankers to resign. From time to time, indeed, he has handed in his badge, declaring that he has run out of ideas and that his current book will be his last.[45]

Even if he can't stop writing books, however, Gray can always share the blame. Wherever possible he credits friends and collaborators with the ideas, insights, and suggestions for his novels. He thanks 'a close friend for a money loan' which allowed him to finish *Poor Things*.[46] He acknowledges the technicians of his novels, the typists and compositors, the proofreaders and designers. It is no surprise that Gray's most positive

---

[40] *Saltire Self-Portraits 4: Alasdair Gray* (Edinburgh: Saltire Society, 1988), 4.

[41] Alasdair Gray, *A History Maker* (1994; repr. London: Penguin, 1995), p. i.

[42] *Saltire Self-Portraits 4: Alasdair Gray*, 1.

[43] Alasdair Gray, *McGrotty and Ludmilla, or, The Harbinger Report* (Glasgow: Dog and Bone, 1990), p. vii.

[44] Alasdair Gray, *A Short Survey of Classic Scottish Writing* (Edinburgh: Canongate, 2001), p. xiii.

[45] See, for instance, Alasdair Gray, *Something Leather* (1990; repr. London: Picador, 1991), p. i; *The Book of Prefaces* (London: Bloomsbury, 2000), 'Author's Blurb' on flyleaf.

[46] Alasdair Gray, *Poor Things* (London: Bloomsbury, 1992), p. iv.

treatment of creative endeavour comes in the account of Jock McLeish's job as a theatrical electrician—one who spotlights the achievements of others. Gray's obsessive self-effacement reaches its culmination in *The Book of Prefaces* (2000). Here, Gray has all but made his escape through the door marked 'EMERGENCY EXIT'.[47] With a team of thirty collaborators (including James Kelman, Janice Galloway, and A. L. Kennedy) he has compiled a collection of other writers' words. It is as if the format of *Lanark*'s epilogue has been reversed. The writers in the 'Index of Plagiarisms' have now taken over the body of the text, while Gray's commentary runs redly and in smaller font down the margins of the page. Still, though his own words have been marginalized, there is no mistaking Gray's position as animator and orchestrator of this heterogeneous assembly. It is worth recalling that, in the 'Ministry of Voices' section of *1982 Janine*, the smallest typeface is employed to render the voice of God.

In the frontispiece to Book 1 of *Lanark*, Gray revises the Glasgow city motto. 'Let Glasgow Flourish by the Preaching of the Word' becomes 'Let Glasgow Flourish by Telling the Truth' (p. 119). Though no one is doing much flourishing in the full-page illustration—it depicts a Glasgow drowning in apocalyptic floods—Gray's amendment holds the key to his art. Throughout his fiction, the truth at which Gray worries is the old one—of exploitation, class brutality, man's inhumanity to man. 'Man is the pie that bakes and eats himself and the recipe is separation', as Monsignor Noakes puts it in *Lanark* (p. 101). In *1982 Janine*, Jock McLeish is less enigmatic: 'The winners shaft the losers, the strong shaft the weak, the rich shaft the poor' (p. 121). This is the truth which seeks out Gray's protagonists and shatters their complacency. This is the hell which underlies all life, and what obscures this truth is 'Preaching'—the lies of ministers, of politicians, of schoolteachers and, naturally, of novelists, whom

[47] Gray, *Lanark*, 376.

Gray classes among the 'policemen and functionaries who keep society as it is'.[48]

In Book 3 of *Lanark*, the eponymous hero descends to the Institute beneath the city of Unthank. Here, a class of doctors and bureaucrats derive fuel and food from the processed bodies of the incurable poor. When served up in the staff dining clubs, this human meat is billed as 'Enigma de Filets Congalés' (p. 77). It is this pernicious glossing, this ability of language to mask unpleasant facts, that Gray seeks to challenge through a style of militant plainness. Where other writers use Latinate diction as a form of syntactic suspension, its syllabic plenitude cushioning the bumps, Gray wants us to feel every jolt, to register the force of each earthy Saxon word. He refers to 'folk', not 'populace'; 'bossing', not 'government'. A section of *The Book of Prefaces* is headed 'The Wasting of Old English Speech and How a New Was Got' (p. 59). A whole linguistic philosophy is embodied in that participle. Not 'established'. Not 'developed'. *Got*. The word stands foursquare in its squat sufficiency. Why would we replace it, if not because we prefer to use words which seem 'politer, grander, the result of dearer educations' (p. 65)?

When Lanark reads over the manuscript of his memoir, he realizes that much of the prose is redundant: 'he noticed half the words had no definite meanings, having been added to make the sentences sound better than they were' (p. 15). For Gray, this is the function of all rhetoric: to make things sound better than they are. Gray's crusade is to show the painful truth. For Jock McLeish, Scotland has not been tactlessly governed or insensitively administered or discomfited by the ineluctable vicissitudes of globalized capital: 'Scotland has been fucked' (p. 136). In some ways, the logical extension of Gray's prose is the childish phonetic script of Bella Baxter in *Poor Things*, that innocently inflammatory medium which wrong-foots euphemism: 'I thot evray wun I met woz part ov the saym frendlay family, eeven

---

[48] Gray, *Poor Things*, 176.

when a hurt wun acted lic owr snapish bitch. Whi did yoo not teech mee politics God?' (p. 145).

Bella Baxter is the child who notices connections that adults have been trained not to see: for Jock McLeish, 'Thinking is a pain because it joins everything together' (p. 66). Like Don DeLillo, Gray's concern is to expose these relationships, to make connections. His 'blend of realism and fantasy' has a political motive: his fantasy worlds bring out the 'true' relationships obscured in reality. In *Lanark*, global capitalism's lapsed metaphors of 'consuming' and 'making a killing' are rendered literal in the Institute, where 'the connection between feeding and killing folk' (p. 101) is made gruesomely explicit. In *1982 Janine*, Jock McLeish's sadistic sexual fantasies are—as he begins to realize—allegories of his own exploited state and that of his 'fucked nation' (p. ix).

For the Gray who feels a 'longing to return to the political and moral values of a previous age',[49] fantasy offers a means of critiquing a monstrous present. It is crucial to appreciate that the motto emblazoned on the boards of Gray's books—'Work as if you live in the early days of a better nation'—points backwards as well as forwards. It not only anticipates a resurgent, presumably independent Scotland: it commemorates the 'better nation' of 1950s Britain in the 'early days' of the Welfare State. Throughout Gray's fiction, 'forties-fifties Britain'[50] functions as the model of a well-ordered state—not utopia, just 'an unusually decent country'. Gray's great theme is the long transition between 'DECENT BRITAIN' and 'INDECENT BRITAIN', between the Britain of full employment and free school milk and the Britain of Thatcher and Polaris.[51] For all his formal innovation, Gray's project is quite straightforward. His novels undertake an impressionistic social history of post-war Britain from a Clydeside perspective. What makes this project intriguing is that

[49] MacDougall, *Painting the Forth Bridge*, 59.
[50] Gray, *1982 Janine*, 230.
[51] Gray, *McGrotty and Ludmilla*, 128, 129.

the more recent period is rendered as fantasy. The Britain Gray admired has mutated into a place as perplexingly alien as a Wellsian dystopia. There is, then, nothing whimsical or escapist in Gray's surreal cityscapes: as Jock McLeish observes, 'nowadays Britain is OF NECESSITY organized like a bad adolescent fantasy' (p. 139).

What troubles Gray is the perception that his novels are organized along much the same lines. 'How can I forget politics when your fantasy has such a convincing political structure?'[52] Sontag's query to Jock McLeish applies with equal force to Alasdair Gray. *His* fantasies—in which real people are turned into characters and manipulated by a despotic authority—are working models of the world they seek to condemn. As much as Jock McLeish, Alasdair Gray works with 'security installations'. This is why Gray is so uncomfortable in the role of novelist and why he stages symbolic confrontations between character and author. On his mission to plead for Unthank's survival in front of the general assembly of council states, Lanark enters a door marked 'EPILOGUE' to discover his author, 'Nastler', lying scribbling in bed. Here he learns that considerations of realism, popularity, and generic convention have persuaded Nastler to make Lanark's mission a failure. Nastler's judgement admits of no appeal. Like Thaw's enraged rants against a 'criminal' (p. 321) God, Lanark's dispute with Nastler cannot alter his fate. And yet, constraint is what makes knowable Lanark's limited scope for freedom, the 'One *if* to five *ise*s!' (p. 482) which the voice of God permits him. One cannot break the fabric of the 'bad adolescent fantasy', but small-scale victories remain possible—like those of Jock McLeish, who successfully faces down 'Mad Hislop', his sadistic schoolteacher, and who later resigns from his job after realizing that for twenty-five years he has been a 'character in a script written by National Security' (p. 333). Lanark's mission to save Unthank and to bring down

---

[52] Gray, *1982 Janine*, 67.

the military-industrial complex by the force of his impassioned eloquence is a schoolboy daydream. His real victory is to retain a commonplace humanity in the face of the degradation among which he moves. In this respect, our final glimpse of Lanark is a vision of triumph: 'He was a slightly worried, ordinary old man but glad to see the light in the sky' (p. 560).

James Kelman's Booker-winning novel, *How Late it Was, How Late* (1994), doesn't drag its feet: 'Alasdair Gray, Tom Leonard, Agnes Owens and Jeff Torrington are still around, thank christ'.[53] We have yet to reach the Acknowledgements, and already the voice is full-on Kelman: assured, indignant, bristling with belligerence. All the key elements are here. There is the disregard for convention and protocol, like a head-butt during a pre-match handshake. There is the sense of embattled integrity, in this band of Glasgow writers fighting the good fight, holding it together in the teeth of a hostile Establishment. There is the hard-edged demotic voice—'thank christ'—and the implicit warning: proprieties will not be observed, the reader's ease will not be consulted. As a gesture, it's not far away from Tom Leonard's V-sign in the opening lines of 'Good Style':

> helluva hard tay read theez init
> stull
> if yi canny unnirston thim jiss clear aff then
> gawn
> get tay fuck ootma road.

Like Leonard, Kelman writes with a reckless outcast swagger which comes from a sense of literary homelessness. This dissident pose might appear somewhat strained from one who has been unrelentingly lionized by Scottish and English critics, who has bagged a Booker Prize and who (along with Tom Leonard and Alasdair Gray) holds a professorship in creative writing at

---

[53] James Kelman, *How Late it Was, How Late* (London: Secker and Warburg, 1994), p. iii.

the University of Glasgow. Nevertheless, Kelman's road to this kind of acceptance has been a long one. On their appearance, Kelman's stories of bus conductors and factory workers, drifters, tramps, and jailbirds were anything but conventionally Scottish. When, in one of the early stories, a Scottish tramp in London is berated by an irate compatriot—'You're a bloody disgrace... giving us a showing up in front of the English'[54]—the resonance is clear. And then there is the language question. Largely thanks to the work of Kelman and Leonard, urban vernacular has become a legitimate—some might say an oppressively dominant—Scottish literary register. When Kelman was starting out, most of the Scottish literati viewed it as a broken-down, vulgar patois.[55]

From the beginning, then, Kelman had been writing not so much out of a literary tradition as against one. Specifically, his target has been the tradition of working-class fiction in which a conventionally 'articulate' narrative voice *explains* the working-class characters to the reader. For Kelman, this approach—the one which dominates Scottish fiction of the 1960s and 1970s—is a sell-out, a travesty, a betrayal of the kind identified by Francis Russell Hart in 1978:

If local realities and affiliations matter, then authentic local speech matters. If local speech is seen as a test of cultural fidelity, then the faithful narrator may seem insular and the distanced narrator is hard pressed to seem anything but an accomplice of the betrayers.[56]

In recent years, Scottish fiction has been exercised less by the fear of insularity than by the awareness that, especially when dealing with Scots-speaking working-class characters, a 'distanced' third-person narrator presents certain problems. In *Lanark*, Duncan Thaw's story is narrated by the disembodied voice of

---

[54] James Kelman, 'The Glenchecked Effort', *Lean Tales* (with Agnes Owens and Alasdair Gray) (London: Jonathan Cape, 1985), 20.

[55] A. J. Aitken, 'Bad Scots: Some Superstitions about Scots Speech', *Scottish Language*, 1 (1982), 30–44.

[56] Francis Russell Hart, *The Scottish Novel: A Critical Survey* (London: John Murray, 1978), 407.

the 'oracle'. As the story begins, Lanark interrupts to ask—'how do you know this? Who are you anyway? . . . What bits will you leave out?'—before the oracle drones on in a 'male, pompous elderly voice' (p. 105). It is this establishment voice that Kelman sets out to explode. The problem with most British novelists, he argues, is that 'none of them seems to have bothered working out that this "third party voice" they use to tell their stories is totally biased and elitist, economically secure, eats good food and plenty of it, is upper middle class paternalist'.[57]

For Kelman, the rejection of this voice is an urgent, political act: 'Getting rid of that standard third-party narrative voice is getting rid of a whole value-system'.[58] Kelman's narrative technique—in which there is no linguistic distinction between narrative voice and dialogue—is an attempt to keep faith with his characters. For Kelman the imperative is always the same: to avoid talking to the reader over the heads of the characters. This is why his third-person narrators abstain from omniscience, proffering nothing in excess of the characters' knowledge. Pointedly, indeed, we are often told less: in *A Chancer*, we learn that Tammas has been having a dream, but not what the dream was about, or that he has written a note to his girlfriend, Vi, but not what the note contains. In effect, Kelman's novels are first-person narratives told in the third person. It is a narrative perspective like that obtained from the bed recess in Rab Hines's kitchen: 'while being inside the subject is also outside' (p. 162).

In some quarters, the voice with which Kelman replaces 'that standard third-party narrative voice' has itself been an object of scorn. There are those who see nothing in Kelman's prose but a surrender to inarticulacy, to the obscenity-driven rants of the indifferently educated. To a large extent, however, complaints about 'inarticulacy' in Kelman's work are beside the point—the point being what Tom Leonard, in one of his poems, has called

[57] Kirsty McNeill, 'Interview with James Kelman', *Chapman*, 57 (1989), 5.
[58] Ibid. 4.

'the extra-semantic kinetics | uv thi fuckin poor'.[59] Expletives, hesitation, repetition, aposiopesis: much of the dynamism of Kelman's prose derives from elements of communication which have no definable semantic content:

Hines covered his face with both hands. Too bad to be true, too fucking bad, no kidding ye man bad, too fucking bad, really fucking bad man I'm no kidding ye.[60]

This is the syncopation of despair, the mind stuttering through a realization it can hardly bear to contemplate: 'Jesus Christ. It was unbelievable. Fucking unbelievable man really, it was unbelievable, ye just'.[61] Kelman refuses to clean up and 'improve' the voices of his characters. He leaves in the fucks and cunts, the repetitions, the broken syntax. His language doesn't describe so much as *register* the pressures confronting his protagonists.

Often, it is the failure to find the right word that is precisely what matters. In *How Late it Was, How Late*, for instance, Kelman uses the paragraph break to capture the moment when the mind, fumbling for a word, gives up the search and moves on: 'That isnay a misunderstanding it's a total | whatever' (p. 17); 'He had just been | who knows, who knows; his brains were all ower the place' (p. 18). Again, for the author to step in and supply the missing word would be beside the point. Similarly, Kelman resists the temptation to paraphrase gestures. His fiction is full of starkly narrated body language: 'Hines nodded', 'Patrick looked at him', 'Tammas sniffed', 'Sammy cleared his throat'. Sometimes verbs are abandoned altogether and we get a two-word paragraph like 'Reilly's frown'. Kelman never interprets these gestures; he never supplies a determining adverb or a helpful 'as much as to say'. The gestures speak for themselves. Their meaning is allowed to emerge—or not—from the context.

---

[59] Tom Leonard, 'ah knew a linguist wance', in *Intimate Voices: Selected Work 1965–1983* (1984; repr. London: Vintage, 1995), 113.
[60] Kelman, *The Busconductor Hines*, 64.
[61] *How Late it Was, How Late*, 261.

It is as if there is a kind of eco-system here, an economy of gesture with which Kelman will not meddle.

Kelman's narratives follow the rhythms of the protagonist's life. He never forces his characters into 'dramatic' situations to titillate the reader: 'I think the most ordinary person's life is fairly dramatic.... The whole idea of the big dramatic event, of what constitutes "plot", only assumes that economic security exists'.[62] There are no sensational set pieces in Kelman. His fiction drops the economic baseline to reveal a world of 'everyday routine horrors': the father trying to put his toddler down for a nap while a neighbour's stereo shakes the thin walls; the factory worker at the tea-break card school, who squanders his wages trying to make up his losses; the unemployed bachelor surviving the 48 hours until his giro cheque arrives. 'Wee horrors': the title of an early short story signals the intimate, small-scale nightmares on which Kelman's fiction battens.[63]

As Cairns Craig has pointed out, Kelman grants his characters an autonomy denied them in real life.[64] By allowing his working-class protagonists to control the narrative he empowers a class of people who are usually treated as characters in someone else's fiction. In *How Late it Was, How Late*, Sammy Samuels effectively narrates the novel, but he constantly has to struggle against being incorporated into the hostile narratives of others. He spends the novel being written about by the powers-that-be—the police, the doctor, DSS bureaucrats. In each case, Sammy's experience is altered, distorted, doctored. The police use existing narratives—Sammy's 'form-book' (p. 24) or police record—to write up his current statement. The DSS clerk decides what is 'material' and what isn't in Sammy's testimony. His 'colloquialisms' are altered. His language is censored:

[62] McNeill, 'Interview with James Kelman', 9.

[63] James Kelman, 'Wee horrors', *Not not while the Giro, and Other Stories* (Edinburgh: Polygon, 1983).

[64] Cairns Craig, 'Resisting Arrest: James Kelman', in *The Scottish Novel Since the Seventies: New Visions, Old Dreams*, ed. Gavin Wallace and Randall Stevenson (Edinburgh: Edinburgh University Press, 1993), 103–4.

'Don't use the word "cunts" again, it doesnay fit in the computer' (p. 160). Sammy is like Caroline Rose in Spark's *The Comforters*: 'Then it began again. Tap-tappity-tap; the typewriter'.[65] Just as Caroline overhears the Writing Ghost, so the sounds of his would-be authors are forever in Sammy's ears: 'And always... the sound of a computer keyboard tap tapping away' (p. 14).

Perhaps the most insidious of Sammy's enemies is the well-meaning Ally, the working-class wideboy who acts as Sammy's 'rep'. Ally wants to fight Sammy's claim for compensation and benefits, taking $33\frac{1}{3}$ per cent if he's successful. He will speak on Sammy's behalf in the language of the authorities. He knows the system: 'ye have to play the game. It's them that make the rules' (p. 239). To play his role effectively Ally must become a kind of double-agent: 'See what ye have to understand about repping; I need to think the way they do' (p. 238). In fact, Ally has become almost indistinguishable from the authorities: 'The closer I get to courts and tribunals the more like them I get. . . . If ye listen to us ye wouldnay know the difference!' (p. 240)

Ally, of course, is more than a 'rep'. He is Kelman's metaphor for a kind of naive working-class novelist, one who aims to 'represent' the lower classes to a middle-class audience and perhaps win redress for their sufferings. For Kelman, such attempts to speak for the working class are pointless, naive, condescending. They always end up censoring and patronizing those they purport to help—at one point Ally warns Sammy to watch his language. In this context, Sammy's refusal to rely on a rep—'There's a difference between repping somebody and fucking being somebody; know what I'm talking about, being somebody?' (p. 241)—signals Kelman's rejection of this tradition of working-class fiction. Sammy's initial response to Ally— 'I thought ye were a spook' (p. 231)—carries a wider resonance. From Kelman's perspective, Ally *is* a spook—a snooper, a nark,

---

[65] Spark, *The Comforters*, 43.

'an accomplice of the betrayers'. The political import of Kelman's fiction lies in rejecting this approach. He will not interpose
an authoritative 'rep' between Sammy and the reader. If there is
any redress on offer, it happens within the novel itself. It consists
in letting Sammy Samuels speak for himself: 'And the book
reports nothing but his experience, limited and uncertain as it
is. It is a man here, now, who is his own narrator, finally.'[66]

Scotland and the novel: for much of the twentieth century it has
seemed almost reckless to mention them in the same breath;
their incompatibility, their stubborn incongruence has been
such a rooted feature of cultural analysis. For the most part,
blame has been laid with Scotland, with its attenuated public life
and its impoverished literary heritage. There is, however, another possibility: that the problem lies less with Scotland than
the novel. For many post-war Scottish writers, the novel has
been a suspect device, a form whose narrative traditions, linguistic conventions, and 'ontological assumptions' have worked
to marginalize the kind of working-class experience which has
most pressingly engaged these writers' attention.[67] For those
seeking to root their fiction in working-class culture, the novel
has figured as an instrument of subjection, a malign polity, a bad
constitution. The problem for working-class novelists has been
that, as ultimate rulers of these polities, they cannot abdicate.
They can seek to mitigate or expose their absolutism, but they
cannot destroy it. As a result, the novel can envisage freedom, it
can lead a character to the point of freedom, but it cannot
narrate that freedom. As in the epics discussed by Nastler in
Lanark, 'success is left outside the scope of the book' (p. 487). In
the post-war Scottish novel, true freedom lies beyond the text,
beyond the 'GOODBYE' on Gray's final pages, in the narrative
void after Jock McLeish's 'All right', in the 'Hyper-Utopian
Euphoria' of the unwritten chapters of *Lanark*. From Kelman's

---

[66] Robbe-Grillet, in McKeon (ed.), *Theory of the Novel*, 823.
[67] Craig, *The Modern Scottish Novel*, 213.

A Chancer (1985) to Irvine Welsh's *Trainspotting* (1993) to Andrew O' Hagan's *Our Fathers* (1999), the Scottish novel likes to end with the hero poised on the cusp of a new life, heading off to an uncharted elsewhere. When they cut loose on the novel's final page, these protagonists are escaping, not merely from Scotland, but from the novel itself, from the purview of writer and reader, moving, like Sammy Samuels, 'out of sight'.

12

The Ruined Futures of British Science Fiction

Patrick Parrinder

Can Britain Take It? The 1950s Disaster Novel

Marooned on the top floor of an Oxford Street department store overlooking the flooded London Basin, a radio journalist forlornly searches the wavebands. The BBC and its rival, the English Broadcasting Company, have gone off the air. The British Government, when last heard of, had moved to a spa town in Yorkshire. The world's coastal cities have been submerged by the rise in sea levels engineered by a group of hostile aliens who have melted the polar ice caps. Occasional broadcast enquiries are picked up from North America, Australia, and East Africa, but in general the rest of the world is preoccupied with its own troubles. On one occasion the narrator overhears 'a voice speaking with historical dispassion of "l'écroulement de l'Angleterre."' 'The word *écroulement* was not very familiar to me,' our narrator adds, 'but it had a horribly final sound.'[1]

---

[1] John Wyndham, *The Kraken Wakes* (Harmondsworth: Penguin, 1955), 227. Subsequent page references in text.

In John Wyndham's *The Kraken Wakes* (1953; US title *Out of the Deeps*), as in his other disaster novels, the integrity of British life is at stake but the narrative voice bears witness to its continuation and eventual triumph. The hero and his wife—Wyndham's characters are remarkably uxorious—will manage to survive in a world in which the BBC and the Continent have been cut off, there are no more newspapers and nothing in the shops, and the French are—well, just a little premature in announcing the demise of the English.

Wyndham's critical stock has fallen sharply since his death in 1969, though his novels are still widely read. For some years after 1950 he was Britain's most prominent science-fiction writer, and his tweed-jacketed photo adorned countless Penguin back covers. He was born in the same year as George Orwell, and like Orwell he wrote under a pseudonym—several pseudonyms, in fact. (His full name was John Wyndham Parkes Lucas Beynon Harris.) The brief biographical note put out by Penguin Books brings out his difference from such predecessors in British science fiction as H. G. Wells, David Lindsay, Olaf Stapledon, Aldous Huxley, C. S. Lewis, and Orwell himself: 'From 1930–9 he wrote stories of various kinds under different names almost exclusively for American publications. He has also written detective novels.... In 1946 he went back to writing stories for publication in the U.S.A.' Wyndham was a professional writer of genre fiction, not a satirist, pundit, or visionary who turned to science fiction as and when it suited him. Moreover, he was nearly 50 before he found a regular British readership. Like his younger contemporary Arthur C. Clarke, he was one of the first British writers in any genre to have served his literary apprenticeship writing for the popular American market.

Wyndham's choice of themes clearly shows his indebtedness to Wells, most of whose science fiction from *The Island of Doctor Moreau* (1896) to *The War in the Air* (1908) falls into the category of the disaster novel. A younger writer once called Wyndham the 'master of the cosy catastrophe', an epithet that still rankles.[2] His catastrophes are not, in fact, cosy—*The Day of the Triffids* (1951) opens with a scene of Beckettian horror set in a hospital where everyone has been suddenly blinded—but his heroes succeed in facing the worst with a combination of good luck, prudent foresight, and austere belt-tightening. Wyndham's novels reflect his experience as a non-combatant on the Home Front in the Second World War, whereas—to take his two severest critics in the next generation—Brian Aldiss fought in Burma and J. G. Ballard was interned by the Japanese. It is, perhaps, the combination of sentimentality and Puritanism in Wyndham's moral fables that they find irksome. A rigorous self-discipline helps his marooned protagonists to hold out until a helicopter or other unlooked-for deus ex machina comes to the rescue.

The basic narrative premiss of the 1950s catastrophe adventure story is seen most clearly in a novel by one of Wyndham's contemporaries, *The Death of Grass* (1956; US title *No Blade of Grass*) by 'John Christopher' (C. S. Youd). Here a virus attacking all forms of grass, including corn and rice, causes worldwide starvation, beginning in China and ultimately spreading to Great Britain. The government, faced by rioting mobs, prepares to drop hydrogen bombs on the major cities. (In all the 1950s disaster novels there is a remarkably unrestrained use of nuclear weapons.) As the country collapses into anarchy the hero, John Custance, briefly wonders when the Americans will arrive, 'handing out canned ham and cigars, and scattering . . . immune grass seed on their way,' but, he decides, there can no longer be any 'last-minute reprieve for mankind'.[3] Instead, the novel turns into a Buchanesque thriller tracing the adventures of a small armed gang heading for Blind Gill, the supposedly secure Cumbrian outpost farmed by Custance's brother David. The theme of

---

[2] Brian W. Aldiss, *Billion Year Spree: The History of Science Fiction* (London: Weidenfeld, 1973), 293.

[3] John Christopher, *The Death of Grass* (Harmondsworth: Penguin, 1958), 124. Subsequent page references in text.

the rural sanctuary, a fortified island or valley serving as a last redoubt of 'Britishness', is common to almost all the British disaster novels written in the post-war period of imperial withdrawal. The retreat to such an immemorial stronghold as Blind Gill—an archaeological site and possibly an Iron Age fort—involves a return to a mythical bedrock of British identity, but it can only be accomplished at a price. John Custance, his wife, and two children leave London on what feels at first like an innocent family picnic, but by the time they reach Cumbria they have been morally coarsened and have fallen in with a thuggish, cold-blooded killer. Meanwhile David Custance, the owner of Blind Gill, has failed to maintain his authority there and is held as a virtual hostage inside the redoubt. John and his party mount a commando-style assault, and David is killed in the thick of the fighting, possibly by a shot from his brother. Firm leadership has won the day, but we are left with a final, shocking metaphor for Britain's plight.

John Christopher, born in Lancashire, sets his rural *imperium in imperio* in the Northern Pennines. Wyndham spent most of his life in southern England, and *The Day of the Triffids* ends in a militaristic, triffid-free sanctuary on the Isle of Wight. Here a group of scientists are preparing for the time when 'we, or our children, or their children, will cross the narrow straits on the great crusade to drive the triffids back and back with ceaseless destruction until we have wiped the last one of them from the face of the land that they have usurped'.[4] This sounds like one of Winston Churchill's speeches before D-Day. The triffids (giant mobile vegetables capable of blinding and maiming their human victims) come once again from the East, though from a laboratory in the Soviet Union rather than from Berlin. Their war parallels Hitler's war (in which the narrator's father has fought) in various respects. They win a second Battle of Britain by stealth (after all, they are only plants) and mount a successful invasion,

---

[4] John Wyndham, *The Day of the Triffids* (Harmondsworth: Penguin, 1954), 272. Subsequent page references in text.

leaving London abandoned and in ruins. Huge numbers of people are killed, although—fortunately for the narrator and his fellow resistors—motor vehicles are triffid-proof and, while petrol supplies last, the remaining sighted people can move around in cars. The arrival of the Americans is constantly expected, but does not take place. The narrator, a biologist, holes up in rural Sussex until the resistors on the Isle of Wight (who need his scientific expertise) send up a helicopter to comb the countryside for him. Britain stands alone (or so it seems) against the triffids, but the remaining British survivors are divided against themselves. To get away from the mainland, the narrator has to evade an emergent reactionary Fascist regime which is equally hostile to the triffids and to the scientific research needed to overcome them. In style and plot, *The Day of the Triffids* (especially in its second half) is cruder than Wyndham's later novels, written when he had finally gained public recognition and a measure of financial independence. Despite its Anglocentric focus, the novel was first published as 'The Revolt of the Triffids' in the American 'slick' magazine *Collier's Weekly*. 'Triffid' soon became a proverbial name for any sort of gardening menace, and in Britain, at least, it remains so.

If Wyndham's novels can be regarded as a displaced form of Second World War fiction, they are also variations on themes first broached by Wells half a century earlier. Ideologically speaking, the ending of *The Day of the Triffids*, with the scientific researchers ranged against a bunch of mindless Fascists, is pure Wells.[5] Moreover, one of Wells's earliest short stories had contained a murderous orchid, and in 'The Sea Raiders' he had shown vicious marine creatures attacking bathers and pleasure-boaters off the

---

[5] See particularly the Wells/Alexander Korda film *Things to Come* (1936), *passim*. Modern audiences find young Harding's earnest question (as war is on the point of breaking out) irresistibly funny:

  CABAL: Those fools are capable of ... anything.
  HARDING: In that case what happens to medical research?

'"Things to Come"; The Release Script', in Leon Stover, *The Prophetic Soul: A Reading of H. G. Wells's 'Things to Come'* (Jefferson, NC: McFarland, 1987), 186.

English south coast. In a third story, 'In the Abyss', Wells imagined a highly advanced civilization glimpsed by deep-sea divers on the ocean bed. To such beings, Wells wrote, we should be known as strange, meteoric creatures wont to fall catastrophically out of the 'sky'. 'The Sea Raiders' and 'In the Abyss' provide the germ of *The Kraken Wakes*, which begins with an apparent meteor shower at sea. The Earth is being invaded by extraterrestrial creatures accustomed to life at very high pressures, for whom the deep-sea bed is the only environment in which they can survive unprotected. The novel's locations are more far-flung than in *The Day of the Triffids*. The first signs of the invasion are observed from a cruise-ship in mid-Atlantic south of the Azores. Later, on the Caribbean island of Escondida, the aliens are seen coming ashore in 'sea-tanks' armed with whiplash-like tentacles. Traumatized by the resulting massacre, Wyndham's narrator, Mike Watson, retreats to a Yorkshire manor-house while his wife Phyllis quietly lays in emergency food supplies at their hilltop cottage in Cornwall. The aliens survive underwater atomic bombing, and the world's 'boffins' and 'backroom boys' (as the narrator insistently calls them) are manifestly 'stumped' for a solution (p.205). Finally the boffins may have come up with something—but not before the invaders have melted the ice caps, drowning London and turning the Watsons' Cornish hilltop redoubt into yet another island off the south coast. Four-fifths of the British population have died from starvation and plague, and, as Phyllis remarks, the changes undergone by the Earth in a few years are reminiscent of the great changes in prehistory:

'I was just thinking ... Nothing is really new, is it, Mike? Once upon a time there was a great plain, covered with forests and full of wild animals. I expect our ancestors hunted there. Then one day the water came in and drowned it all—and there was the North Sea ...'

'I think we've been here before, Mike ... And we got through last time...' (p. 240)

Wyndham's optimism is undoubtedly facile, though it does still raise a smile. The statement that 'we got through last time' is meaningless insofar as our remote evolutionary ancestors arc referred to as 'we'. The emotional resonance of the idea comes, once again, from the British wartime experience of Dunkirk and after.

The Kraken Wakes illustrates Wyndham's mastery of popular fiction but, curiously, his major theme was yet to emerge. Children play very insignificant roles in the two novels already considered; in both *The Chrysalids* (1955; US title *Re-Birth*) and *The Midwich Cuckoos* (1957; US title *Village of the Damned*) the plot centres on the 'Different Child' and the idea of genetic mutation leading to a further evolution of the human species. Here the stark Darwinian morality that was implied in the earlier novels is explicitly stated, for Wyndham is no humanitarian in the usual sense of the term, despite his weakness for sentimental endings.[6] In *The Chrysalids* the narrator, David, is a boy with mild telepathic powers growing up in an isolated community in Labrador several centuries after global civilization has been destroyed in a nuclear holocaust. David's telepathic ability is a fallout-induced 'deviation' from the supposed biological human norm which his defensive and hypocritical Puritan community rigorously upholds. Once his powers have become common knowledge, his life is in danger. His younger sister, Petra, a far more gifted telepath, makes contact with a group of New Zealanders who set out across the world on a rescue mission. But their interest is only in saving Petra and the small group of children to whom she extends her protection. The children survive thanks to the New Zealanders who come in by

---

[6] Rowland Wymer uses *The Chrysalids* to undermine the alleged cosiness of Wyndham's catastrophes: 'How "Safe" is John Wyndham?', *Foundation*, 55 (Summer 1992), 25–36. David Ketterer examines the 'Different Child' theme in *The Midwich Cuckoos* in '"A part of the … family[?]": John Wyndham's *The Midwich Cuckoos* as Estranged Autobiography', in Patrick Parrinder (ed.), *Learning from Other Worlds: Estrangement, Cognition and the Politics of Science Fiction and Utopia* (Liverpool: Liverpool University Press, 2000), 127–45.

helicopter and slaughter the non-mutant population. The strict and dour Labradorians have played their part in ensuring the continuation of the species, but their end is swift and brutal. David finds the ruthlessness and ingratitude of the 'New People' hard to accept, but to wonky, superhuman Petra (representing the next stage in human evolution) it all seems quite natural. The book's Darwinian monologues give it a moral earnestness that is largely absent from Wyndham's earlier catastrophe novels. The New Zealanders' mission is 'to preserve our species against other species that wish to destroy it—or else fail in our trust' (p.195), and this gives them a licence to kill other, less advanced human beings. The argument leaves a disturbing taste. Its tough-minded post-holocaust evolutionary logic speaks for a scientific anti-humanism which had already come under powerful attack from neo-Christian novelists such as C. S. Lewis and William Golding. Lewis's *Cosmic Trilogy* (1938–45) and Golding's *The Inheritors* (1955) dramatize a growing realization that modern scientific materialism had taken on the dimensions of a religious faith and that (like most religions) it had a sinister, dark underside. *The Chrysalids* is a novel of ideas but it is not, unfortunately, a dialogue novel since David's reservations about the New People's mission are left undeveloped. The book ends in a mood of self-congratulatory euphoria and David never seems to realize that his rescuers have acted out of simple, cold-blooded expediency. In the future he himself will very likely become as expendable as his parents obviously were. As in most religious wars, the New People are driven by a kind of fanatical rationalism that is not at all unlike the simple Puritan faith of the Labrador community who are their enemies. In Wyndham's Wellsian perspective the Puritan tyranny of Labrador represents one necessary stage in humanity's re-emergence after the nuclear holocaust; the New Zealand tyranny is the next stage; and the need for such tyrannies will only disappear in a society where abundance has at last replaced deprivation and scarcity.

Post-Wyndham: The 'Darkening Island'

John Wyndham in his heyday was one of the best-selling authors in science fiction's history. Yet for later British writers he is maligned and half-forgotten, even though his apocalyptic scenarios have been revisited again and again. Wyndham's shadow still lies over anyone who attempts to write the 'memoirs of a survivor' (to quote the title of Doris Lessing's 1974 novel) in a supposedly realistic, near-future English setting. Thus *The Kraken Wakes* was quickly followed by the watery topography of J. G. Ballard's *The Drowned World* (1962) and Brian Aldiss's *Greybeard* (1964). The retreat to an island off the south coast recurs in Christopher Priest's *A Dream of Wessex* (1977; US title *The Perfect Lover*) and Julian Barnes's *England, England* (1998). The development of telepathic powers during the dark age following a nuclear holocaust is shown in Sheila Sullivan's *Summer Rising* (1975) and (in the form of communication with dogs) in Russell Hoban's *Riddley Walker* (1980). Examples could be multiplied.

Perhaps the most striking instance of anti-Wyndham reaction is to be found in a remarkably prescient early work by Christopher Priest, a novelist forty years younger than Wyndham. In *Fugue for a Darkening Island* (1972; US title *Darkening Island*) the author portrays a breakdown of civil order leading to a degree of savagery unknown in Europe between the end of the Second World War and the collapse of federal Yugoslavia in the 1990s. In Priest's southern England, as in the wars in Bosnia and Kosovo, there are barricaded towns and villages, lawless army and police detachments, internment and rape camps, ethnic cleansing, and repeated massacres unhindered by a toothless and passive UN presence. The novel portrays a relapse into barbarism without any suggestion that self-discipline is the answer or that we can take comfort from having 'got through last time'. In place of Wyndham's uxorious narrators, Priest's protagonist Alan Whitman recounts the breakdown of his marriage (both before and during the wider social crisis) in pitiless detail. Whitman's drab, disjointed, paranoid narrative constantly resorts to bureaucratic euphemisms to disguise his own emotional inadequacies. He is, by the time he comes to write his story, a lone killer and thorough-going psychopath whose confession could be designed to fore-stall a war-crimes tribunal. Moreover, *Fugue for a Darkening Island* has disturbing racial overtones.

Written shortly after the Conservative politician Enoch Powell's 1968 speech describing unrestricted Commonwealth immigration as the policy of a country 'busily engaged in heating up its own funeral pyre', Priest's novel envisages the arrival on Britain's shores of huge numbers of starving refugees following a nuclear war in Africa. The narrator, who starts out as an apa-thetic white liberal, eventually joins a nomadic band led by a man called Lateef, of unspecified race. His wife and child are then seized by armed 'Afrims' (African immigrants), and he himself at one point visits a field brothel or rape camp, pausing only during his copulation with a black woman to nudge out of sight (and later steal) a rifle he finds by her bedside. The novel ends with the image of an effective apartheid regime on the south coast of England. On the one hand, there is the heavily guarded, all-white 'respectable town' where the inhabitants pretend to be living a normal life and the xenophobic *Daily Mail* (now printed and published in France) is delivered every morning. A few miles away, in an Afrim garrison town, Whitman comes across the naked, blackened bodies of his wife and young daughter dumped on the beach, the refuse of another soldiers' brothel. At first he feels no reaction; later he is overcome by terror and hatred, and murders a young African in cold blood. Priest's narrator is undoubtedly a survivor—how else could he have told his story?—but there is no rescue helicopter waiting in the wings. Nevertheless, the grimness and drabness of his confession surely echoes Wyndham's puritanical sense of catastrophe as an event requiring gritted teeth and the abandonment of com-fortable humanitarian assumptions in the face of unpleasant duties.

Disaster as Desire: J. G. Ballard

A broad look at the British disaster novel since 1950 would include not only the specialist genre writers from Wyndham to Priest, but a set of novels by such 'mainstream' figures as Kingsley Amis, Martin Amis, Julian Barnes, Anthony Burgess, Angela Carter, Michael Frayn, William Golding, Russell Hoban, Doris Lessing, Ian McEwan, Naomi Mitchison, and Angus Wilson. Given the pervasive fear of a nuclear holocaust to which many of these writers refer, we might suppose that disaster was a theme of special fictional importance in the later twentieth century; but, as a precautionary move, some disentangling of literary history from sociology should be attempted. In the present context, Anthony Burgess may be confronted with J. G. Ballard.

Burgess, whose eclectic output includes such futuristic fantasies as *A Clockwork Orange* (1962), believed that 'only very minor literature dares to aim at apocalypse.'[7] Visions of disaster were not a speciality of the nuclear age. During his Catholic childhood, Burgess wrote (he was born in 1917), he too had been obsessed by the idea of apocalypse: 'At school, with the nuns, the end of the world was in Christ's promise to the disciples—... Without benefit of Biblical prophecy, much popular culture dealt with the end. The *Boy's Magazine* had a serial about it that excited me so much that my father burned it.' When, later in life, Burgess condemned disaster fiction as belonging to the 'lowest order of literature', it was his turn to play the heavy father. Surveying the tradition of apocalyptic fiction in a 1983 *Times Literary Supplement* review, he alludes to J. G. Ballard's pronouncement (repeated in his Penguin blurbs throughout the 1960s) that 'science fiction is the apocalyptic literature of the twentieth century, the authentic language of Auschwitz, Eniwetok, and Aldermaston'.[8] Clearly, Burgess felt that such juvenile

---

[7] Anthony Burgess, 'The Apocalypse and After', *Times Literary Supplement*, 18 Mar. 1983, p. 256. All subsequent quotations from Burgess are from this source.

[8] Aldermaston and Eniwetok were the places where the British 'nuclear deterrent' was manufactured and tested.

glibness had to be put in its place. To do so, he appealed to the shadow not of H. G. Wells but of Wells's antagonist Henry James:

If Henry James had written a story about a group of people awaiting the end in an English country-house, his concern with personal relations would have rendered the final catastrophe highly irrelevant, the mere blank part of the page after the end not of time but of the story.... Fiction is not about what happens to the world but what happens to a select group of human souls, with crisis or catastrophe as the mere pretext for an exquisitely painful probing ... of personal agonies and elations.

Part of the agony and ecstasy of personal relations is, of course, that all such relations are inherently temporary. Nevertheless, Burgess is remarkably cavalier in assuming that the causes of such transience are irrelevant and that it makes no difference if a group of characters are about to be separated by the end of a weekend house-party, or by nuclear war. In fact, the sense of impending separation affects emotional relations in precise, and precisely differing, ways. At some level, the separation is desired as well as feared; but such a desire may be entirely innocent, or it may be an enormity. It has been alleged that John Wyndham's disasters are secretly longed for, though this may be said of any extraordinary and harrowing event that becomes the subject of a fictional plot. In Ballard's novels disaster is openly longed for. This longing dominates the emotional lives of the protagonists and determines their actions. By the time that he published his autobiographical novel *Empire of the Sun* (1984) it had become clear that his fiction, like Wyndham's, was fuelled by memories of the Second World War, when, as an adolescent interned in Shanghai, he saw the overturning of British imperial power at first hand. His position among the Europeans in the Lunghua internment camp was that of a bored, frequently indulged but emotionally deprived schoolboy among careworn, responsible adults. Throughout his novels, Ballard's protagonists tend to be outwardly orthodox British professional or service types known only by their surnames. Through a process of disaster that is itself therapeutic, they overcome their repressions and set out on a pilgrimage leading equally to self-fulfilment and self-destruction. In these novels catastrophe becomes carnival, a charmed but temporary upside-down state in which the ordinary constraints of civilized life have been miraculously lifted. Whatever the cause of the disaster—ecocide, global warming, the end of the Space Age, or the collapse of law and order in a city apartment block or a luxury beach resort—it provides an experience as thrilling and transgressive as some adolescent initiation rite. Lacking the moral earnestness of a Wyndham or a Priest, Ballard's novels are far more addictive.

Above all, his fiction demonstrates the absurdity of Burgess's pronouncement in the *TLS* review cited above that there is 'not one SF writer whom we would read for his style'. Ballard's prose is instantly recognizable, and—if a limiting judgement were required—it might be argued that style is exactly what we read him for. Like a boy playing endlessly with a Meccano set, his hard-edged sentences with their thrusting present participles and obsessive similes seem to come ready-made from some personal lexical tool kit. His affection for the surrealist painters is well known, and his long sequence of novels and stories with their repetitive landscapes and almost interchangeable plots suggests a painter's œuvre rather than a conventional novelist's. Early in his career Ballard pronounced that the traditional novel was 'as glorious and as out of date as the steam locomotive', and he at least has remained true to that insight.[9] Martin Amis, reviewing *The Day of Creation* (1987), invented the following dialogue between two Ballard fans:

'I've read the new Ballard.'
'And?'

---

[9] J. G. Ballard interviewed by Frank Kermode in 'Is an élite necessary?', *Listener*, 29 Oct. 1970, p. 574.

'It's like the early stuff.'
'Really? What's the element?'
'Water.'
'Lagoons?'
'Some. Mainly a river.'
'What's the hero's name? Maitland? Melville?'
'Mallory.'[10]

As with many modern paintings, the most distinctive feature of these works is their author's rhetorical signature. Even the names Maitland, Melville, and Mallory are recognizable as variations on his own name, and in *Crash* (1973) the narrator is, indeed, called Ballard.

After his release from Lunghua, the real J. G. Ballard read medicine at Cambridge and worked as a copywriter and an RAF pilot. His experiences as a medical student and a pilot have been much remarked upon, since a sizeable proportion of his characters are doctors, pilots, or astronauts. Copywriting also seems to have left its mark, especially on the early Ballard: there is a certain intellectual glibness in his stories, and he likes to advertise his familiarity with the world's disaster zones. As his hero Kerans reflects in *The Drowned World*, 'Just as the distinction between the latent and manifest contents of the dream had ceased to be valid, so had any division between the real and the super-real in the external world. Phantoms slid imperceptibly from nightmare to reality and back again, the terrestrial landscapes were now indistinguishable, as they had been at Hiroshima and Auschwitz, Golgotha and Gomorrah.'[11]

In *The Drowned World*, the landscapes are so 'indistinguishable' that Kerans, a Londoner by birth, has difficulty in recog-

---

[10] Quoted by Roger Luckhurst, '*The Angle between Two Walls': The Fiction of J. G. Ballard* (Liverpool: Liverpool University Press, 1997), 179. Luckhurst devotes a whole chapter to 'The Signature of J. G. Ballard'.

[11] J. G. Ballard, *The Drowned World* (Harmondsworth: Penguin, 1965), 72. Subsequent page references in text.

nizing the partially submerged tropical city to which he has been sent on a biological expedition. It is only when a lagoon is drained to reveal the mud-coated remains of Leicester Square that the novel's geographical location becomes unmistakable. The drainer of the lagoon is Strangman, a white-suited playboy and leader of a gang of drunken pirates, who mocks at Kerans and his fellow-scientists, and is given to quoting from Eliot's *The Waste Land*.[12] The scientists are investigating the psychic impact of global warming, which, it is claimed, revives unconscious species memories of the Triassic Age. Strangman on the other hand is 'fascinated by the immediate past', since 'the treasures of the Triassic compare pretty unfavourably with those of the closing years of the Second Millennium' (p. 91). Under his direction the 'unreal city', now a necropolis, becomes the setting for an elaborate orgy. Kerans, however, is only temporarily diverted by his rich friend's nostalgia for a vanished world of power-boats, cocktail parties, and drunken nights out in Piccadilly. Refusing to return to the biological expedition's Arctic base, Ballard's protagonist is last seen heading southwards among the tropical swamps, 'a second Adam searching for the forgotten paradises of the reborn sun' (p. 171). The image of the reborn sun is overdetermined and can be read on several levels, including that of Ballard's boyhood fascination with the victorious Japanese empire. Kerans's search for mystical self-transcendence makes him— like so many of Ballard's heroes—a kind of belated kamikaze pilot.

Ballard invokes a more postmodern London landscape in a sequence of later novels: *Crash*, set on the motorways and feeder roads around Heathrow Airport; *Concrete Island* (1974), where a crashed motorist becomes a second Robinson Crusoe marooned in the middle of the A40/M41 interchange at White City; and *High-Rise* (1975), in which a Docklands apartment

---

[12] Strangman's role in the text as jester and parodist is noted by Luckhurst, '*The Angle between Two Walls*', 56, 61.

building reverts to primordial savagery. Other novels and stories inhabit a variety of post-cultural wildernesses, from Pacific islands devastated by atmospheric nuclear testing to the futuristic resort complexes of the French Riviera and Costa del Sol. (The one location his fiction seems determined never to occupy is Wyndham's, and Wells's, rural England.) Some of his finest stories are set on the abandoned coast of Florida in the aftermath of the Space Age, showing wrecked and deserted beach communities and motel strips dominated by the ruins of the NASA installations at Cape Kennedy (now Cape Canaveral). This group, which we may call the Cocoa Beach stories, includes 'Myths of the Near Future', 'Memories of the Space Age', 'The Dead Astronaut', and 'The Cage of Sand'.[13] The protagonists in these stories are middle-class, middle-aged derelicts—traumatized former professionals (typically doctors, architects, and space pilots) who have returned to haunt the Florida littoral. In their prime, like the designer of unbuilt cities on Mars in 'The Cage of Sand', they were the builders of the future; now they try to make sense of their ruined lives by becoming compulsive ruinologists, the survivors of a future that was abandoned before it had even begun. The architect in 'The Cage of Sand' has returned to Cocoa Beach because it is the 'abandoned Mecca of the first heroes of astronautics', a 'corner of earth that is forever Mars'.[14] The failure of the Mars colony has turned Florida into a poisoned, forbidden no-man's-land, haunted by fugitives who are pursued and hunted down by the police and the military. Like all Ballard's doomed characters, the protagonist of 'The Cage of Sand' is a pilgrim following a kind of inner light towards a pyschic breakthrough which is inherently self-destructive. The story ends with a hallucinatory moment of victory which is also abject defeat. The hero's inner world has

---

[13] Luckhurst (ibid. 138) treats the first three stories as a group, but omits 'The Cage of Sand'.

[14] J. G. Ballard, *The Four-Dimensional Nightmare* (Harmondsworth: Penguin, 1965), 135–6, 145.

distorted his understanding of the outer world almost to the pitch of insanity.

Ballard returns to the carnivalesque mood of the middle section of *The Drowned World* in novels such as *The Unlimited Dream Company* (1979) and in a 1976 novella, 'The Ultimate City', set in the ruins of a future New York once the world's fossil fuel reserves have been exhausted. The city's population has moved across Long Island Sound to new settlements like Garden City, an ecologically self-sustaining community in which 'everything was so well made that it lasted for ever'.[15] Bored by this post-technological utopia, Ballard's protagonist Halloway builds a glider, crosses the sound, and returns to the deserted metropolis. His mission is one of urban regeneration and, once the electricity and sound systems are back on, hordes of nomadic children flock to the city. Soon Halloway's efforts have led to the reanimation of a few city blocks. Delighted to see the re-emergence of street crime, narcotics abuse, and even road rage, Halloway takes on the role of police chief patrolling the precinct and watching its feverish after-life on closed-circuit television. His toytown paradise cannot last, but, like Strangman, Halloway makes the point that contemporary New York or London are indeed 'ultimate cities'—chaotic, frightening, wasteful, yet bursting with a youthful energy that the geriatric utopia of Garden City can never hope to match. The best a post-capitalist, post-technological future can hope for is an anarchic and temporary restoration of the past. The vision of a restarted New York is a parody of the past, which Ballard presents in fiction that is also implicitly parodic. His style is not (as is sometimes said) 'inimitable' but he is, in a sense, his own best parodist. Like the 'ultimate city,' the 'ultimate Ballard' is already with us, and has been since his earliest stories. But that has not stopped him from endlessly recycling himself in new and surprising inventions.

[15] J. G. Ballard, *Low-Flying Aircraft and Other Stories* (St Albans: Triad Panther, 1978), 17.

Dream Machines: Angela Carter, Christopher Priest, and Julian Barnes

Although Ballard's external landscapes invariably correspond to inner, psychic landscapes, their ontological status is not really questioned. Ballard's repetitions draw the reader into his fantastic settings in almost hypnotic fashion, suspending our disbelief in the way that earlier writers of 'romance' fiction such as Robert Louis Stevenson had aimed at. This is not the case, however, in such Ballard-influenced works as Angela Carter's *Heroes and Villains* (1969) and Christopher Priest's *A Dream of Wessex*. Here the future setting invokes the conventions of the fantastic romance but we are constantly reminded that it is also a self-conscious mental projection.

Heroes and Villains traces a young girl's sexual initiation (a common Carter theme) in a barbaric future that is itself parodic, a bran-tub of motifs from the literary tradition and contemporary popular culture. This post-nuclear world is divided between the Professors, who live excessively rational lives inside fortified compounds, and the Barbarians and mutants who live outside. The Professors are descendants of the privileged few who were allowed into the deep shelters offering protection against nuclear fallout, and Marianne is a Professor's daughter. But she longs to escape and live among the Barbarians, a dream that comes true when she is abducted and violently raped by Jewel, the handsome young tribal chieftain who eventually marries her. Jewel, the 'ragged king of nowhere', is also 'the sign of an idea of a hero', a cross between a legendary outlaw such as Robin Hood and a twentieth-century hoodlum or rock musician.[16] The union of Marianne and Jewel offers an extreme version of the bodice-ripping kind of literary romance, but it also seems to parallel the much-publicized relationship between two actual 1960s celebrities, Mick Jagger and Marianne Faithfull (who was, in fact, a

[16] Angela Carter, *Heroes and Villains* (Harmondsworth: Penguin, 1981), 53, 71. Subsequent page references in text.

professor's daughter). Jewel and his tribe live in the greenwood familiar from traditional English ballads and historical fiction. Jewel at one point dreams that he is an 'invention of the Professors' (p. 82), and his leadership of what amounts to a warrior band is, in fact, stage-managed by Donally, the renegade Professor who is the tribe's self-appointed witch-doctor. Jewel knows that, were he to be taken alive by the Professors, he would become a laboratory animal or a museum exhibit. As for Marianne, she 'knew in her heart that none of this was real; it was a kind of enchantment' (p. 103). Such knowledge is denied to Ballard's heroes, but it is no help to Carter's protagonists since, try as they may, they cannot escape from the dream. Towards the end of the novel Jewel and Marianne find themselves on a beach close to a submerged city—a 'time-eaten city up to its ears in the sea', in Carter's lushly Romantic idiom—which clearly alludes to one of Ballard's lost worlds. Jewel tries, and fails, to commit suicide by drowning himself. There is a hopeless circularity about this future romance, representing both the downward spiral of a degenerating world and the giddy entrapment of a bad dream. *Heroes and Villains* is an early, perhaps naive work in the Carter canon, but it exemplifies the dandyism, the self-conscious decadence, and the rewriting of earlier structures of romance and fairy tale that are found throughout her writing. Like Ballard, Carter is a poet of dead and dying cultures that are wilfully and theatrically brought back to life.

Christopher Priest's *A Dream of Wessex* is a more orthodox science-fiction novel, in the sense that the dream-future it portrays is the product of a collective scientific experiment. The Wessex Project uses an advanced life-support system to enable a group of volunteers to spend weeks or even months in a state of controlled hypnosis. As hypnotic subjects, they are sent 150 years into the future to experience life in the year 2137, when the English monarchy has collapsed, industry and agriculture have been collectivized, and the nation has been absorbed into the Soviet bloc (a version of near-future England that is very differently portrayed in Kingsley Amis's 1980 novel *Russian Hide-and-Seek*). Only the former county of Dorset, now cut off from the mainland after catastrophic earthquakes, is relatively free from Soviet bureaucratic control. The Wessex Project is based at the ancient fortress of Maiden Castle near Dorchester, which in 2137 has become home to a kind of hippy commune. This composite vision of the future—a mixture of deliberate extrapolation and of the participants' conscious and unconscious desires—is disastrously altered for the worse when an unscrupulous new member joins the Project. The participants know that the future they inhabit in their dream-lives is unreal, yet it comes to dominate their experience since their twenty-second century doubles live more fulfilling lives than they themselves do. The simulacrum replaces reality because it is more addictive than reality. This theme, familiar in science fiction since the 'feelies' and soma-induced happiness of Aldous Huxley's *Brave New World*, has become increasingly pressing at a time when literary fiction itself seems to be engaged in a losing battle with visual and electronic forms of 'virtual reality'. Priest's use in his novel of Maiden Castle (an Iron Age settlement overwhelmed by the Roman legions) and of the former Saxon kingdom of Wessex suggests a concern with national history which looks back to the novels of John Wyndham and John Christopher rather than to J. G. Ballard. At the same time, the novel strongly implies that the remote past symbolized by Maiden Castle is a real past, while the nation's Soviet-dominated future is only a fantasy. But what if our ideas of national history and national identity are also extrapolations, in the sense of being the products of a deliberate backward projection coloured by unconscious wish-fulfilment? A theme park or scale model could then be no less authentic than the supposed archaeological-historical 'reality' of the nation's past.

This is the case in Julian Barnes's *England, England* (1998), a satirical comedy of the twenty-first century in which the British nation is brought to its knees, not by a natural disaster or military defeat, but by the simple act of setting up a rival tourist attraction—an artificial and intensely visitor-friendly England in miniature—on an island off the south coast. (Here, as in *The Day of the Triffids*, the Isle of Wight becomes the England of the future.) The island is bought up, and its local officials bribed or blackmailed into opting for independence from the mainland, by the megalomaniac Sir Jack Pitman, chairman of a multi-national corporation which owns, among other things, much of the British press. Guided by market research into the top fifty characteristics associated with the word 'England' among prospective customers, Sir Jack's design team constructs 'England, England', which soon swallows up virtually all of Old England's tourist trade. The King decamps from Buckingham Palace to Osborne House, where, under contract to Sir Jack, he becomes the toytown ruler of a carnival kingdom of actors, stagehands, and tourist guides.

Sir Jack, the Island Project's inventor, is partly modelled on the British newspaper magnate Robert Maxwell, whose career had ended in apparent suicide and posthumous disgrace a few years before Barnes was writing. Sir Jack is ousted from his position as corporate boss due to the threat of blackmail over a lurid sexual peccadillo—a transparently novelistic device—though it is surely financial failure, rather than sexual embarrassment, that he has most to fear. It does not seem to have occurred to Barnes that the Island Project was a rich man's playground which could never have repaid its initial investors—since Sir Jack does everything on borrowed capital—and could scarcely have covered its running costs. One would like to think that his bankers would have closed down Sir Jack's expensive folly long before Fleet Street had caught up with him *in flagrante delicto*, though, admittedly, Maxwell's story (not to mention the more recent saga of London's Millennium Dome) might suggest otherwise.

Although it brings in the punters, Sir Jack's national show soon gets out of hand. The actors, like the participants in Priest's Wessex Project, become addicted to their roles. 'Dr Johnson' develops an exaggerated melancholy which is offensive to the tourists who have paid to have dinner with him, while 'Robin Hood and his Merrie Men' turn into genuine outlaws. The role of incompetent Sheriff of Nottingham has passed to Sir Jack's temporary successor, Martha Cochrane, who becomes the moral centre of the novel because she has too much integrity to believe in the absurd tourist extravaganza she is trying to run. Once she has been deposed and Sir Jack is back in charge, the Island's success continues unabated. Martha eventually returns to Old England (now known as Anglia), to live out her retirement in a village in Wessex. Anglia, an isolated, impoverished and shrunken republic, has reverted to virtually pre-industrial status. The Asian and Caribbean immigrants have left, the cities have dwindled, and a resurgent Scotland and Wales have bought up most of the border counties. England is a place of 'yokeldom and willed antiquarianism',[17] a closed country which no longer welcomes visitors or possesses a tourist industry. Nevertheless, the rural birds and animals are more numerous than they used to be. For Martha it is a perfect retirement home.

In fact, the Anglia of the novel's bucolic final section is (as the title *England, England* suggests) Barnes's second ideological version of England in miniature. It is just as artificial as the Island Project. In Martha's village the local farrier and rural wiseacre, Jez Harris, was once an American legal expert; the schoolmaster is a retired antiques dealer; and Martha, the former chief executive of a big corporation, is the only one of the local worthies who actually grew up in the countryside. The novel closes with the revival, or perhaps, 'since records were inexact' (p. 246), the institution, of an annual village fête and carnival procession. Once again, a dead or dying culture has been reanimated or, perhaps, simply invented. Both the Island Project and Martha Cochrane's Wessex village represent different kinds of utopia—of utopia as retrotopia, so to speak—and

[17] Julian Barnes, *England, England* (London: Picador, 1999), 254. Subsequent page references in text.

Barnes's attitude towards these upside-down worlds seems deeply ambivalent. By the end of *England, England* his satire has turned into an elegy for something that may never have existed.

Conclusion: Looking Forwards, Looking Backwards

> 'Didn't somebody or other once say: "This is the way the world ends, not with a bang but a whimper?"'
> Phyllis looked shocked. '*Somebody or other!*' she exclaimed. 'That was Mr Eliot!'
>
> (*The Kraken Wakes*, 222)

There is (to use a Tennysonian image) nothing new about an English elegy in which a last battle has been fought, the nation's magical bond has been dissolved, and Sir Bedivere is left wringing his hands by the waterside. Barnes's concern is specifically with national identity, but in most British science fiction a futuristic English setting provides the occasion for an elegy for the whole human world. (Wells's *The Time Machine* is paradigmatic in this respect.) In the late twentieth century the Wellsian genre of the 'scientific romance' itself began to exact retrospective tributes, such as Christopher Priest's *The Space Machine: A Scientific Romance* (1976) and Ronald Wright's *A Scientific Romance* (1997).[18] It should be noted that the science-fictional projections of the future of the 'darkening island' run parallel to a genre of discursive, non-fictional elegies for Englishness and the English nation by Conservative ideologues who take themselves very seriously and expect others to do so. Science fiction, as a much-despised popular genre, may be foolish in its representations of the national future, but at least it acknowledges

---

[18] A related phenomenon is so-called 'steampunk' fiction set partly in an alternative nineteenth century, such as William Gibson and Bruce Sterling's *The Difference Engine* (London: Gollancz, 1990). *Automated Alice* (London: Doubleday, 1996), a 'sequel' to the Lewis Carroll books by the Mancunian writer Jeff Noon, is a particularly interesting example of this.

their speculative and fictional status. Its visions of the 'river Tiber foaming with much blood' are sometimes satirical and sometimes almost nostalgic; but they are cathartic rather than rabble-rousing.[19]

Finally, there is another English science-fiction writer whose career spans the second half of the twentieth century and who specializes in a poetry of ruins and archaeological recovery. This is Wyndham's rival and near-contemporary Arthur C. Clarke. In Clarke's hands, it has been alleged, British science fiction loses whatever individuality and national identity it once had; his novels celebrate a 'globalized culture based on high technology', and their provenance could as well be American as English.[20] I remain unconvinced of this, though at first sight Clarke's sense of the future is untouched by the nostalgia we find in Wyndham, Ballard, Carter, and Priest. The ruins in his novels are not the ruins of the past or the present, but the ruins of the future and, above all, the as yet undiscovered traces of alien or post-human civilizations. The mysterious alien monoliths of *2001: A Space Odyssey* (1968) and its literary sequels suggest that the Search for Extraterrestrial Intelligence (SETI) so generously subsidized by American taxpayers in the late twentieth century is, at best, a search for dead signs in a universe that is unthinkably remote in both space and time.

Clarke's alien monoliths are meant to embody hope for the future and the possibility of unlimited human expansion, but it is a curious kind of hope. At most, our destiny as a species might be to project ourselves far enough and to leave a sufficient impression on the universe for others to one day read the signs we have left behind us. Try as he may to argue that human history is only just beginning, Clarke's novels, like much British science fiction of the later twentieth century, can also be read as

---

[19] This Virgilian image was used in Enoch Powell's 1968 speech referred to above.

[20] Nicholas Ruddick, *Ultimate Island: On the Nature of British Science Fiction* (Westport, Conn.: Greenwood, 1993), 176.

implying that the futures we imagine, however emotionally fulfilling, may be no more than some sort of deluded endgame. The aliens' absence from the monuments they have built prefigures our own. In that case, what counts is perhaps that we should go out with a bang of our own devising, rather than with a whimper. The protagonists of British disaster fiction find ways of asserting their identity even as the old order changes and they confront 'new men' (or, in Wyndham and Clarke, new creatures), 'strange faces', 'other minds'.[21]

[21] Alfred, Lord Tennyson, *Idylls of the King*, ed. J. M. Gray (London: Penguin, 1996), 299.

13

P. D. James and the Distinguished Thing

MARTIN PRIESTMAN

It is a favourite trope of reviewers that the dividing wall between the novel proper and popular detective fiction has been impregnable until breached, just now, by the writer they wish to praise. We hear increasingly often of first-class novels which are, stunningly, first-class thrillers too; or, conversely, of cracking good detective stories which are also profoundly sensitive and insightful novels. It sometimes seems as though combining the virtues of the two is a magical act like squaring the circle or discovering the philosopher's stone, at last bridging the gulf between the two worlds of serious and popular literature. Although few readers nowadays would regard the gulf as impassable in their own reading practice—we're mostly omnivorous—there is still something very comforting in the idea that someone has removed simultaneously both the vestigial guilt of reading thrillers and the prospect of hard work in reading literature. Sometimes the approval bestowed for such achievements can result in a suspension of the critical faculties whereby—partly because of the reviewers' ban on revealing the ending, and hence how the plot really hangs together—the actual relationship between the 'detective' element and the 'literary' element goes unexplored.

No one is more secure in this dual reputation than P. D. James, or Baroness James of Holland Park as she became in 1991. Widely acclaimed as a 'national treasure', she is a fixture on the highbrow interview circuit and her reverently awaited, generously spaced works are reviewed at length in the broadsheets and *Times Literary Supplement*. Her Booker-Prize-nominated *A Taste for Death* (1987) was greeted by reviewers as 'an astonishing novel of range and complexity', a 'major and magisterial book' by 'a wonderful stylist'; and an academic critic argues that 'P. D. James's œuvre is one of tragedy, in the mode of *King Lear*'.[1] To put such claims to the test, I shall try to read two (in particular) of James's works—the early *Cover Her Face* (1962) and the more recent *A Certain Justice* (1997)—as major, possibly great, novels of range and complexity.

As a literary novelist, James offers three things in liberal helpings: carefully described settings, a wide range of generously developed characters, and an impeccable style, replete with high-cultural overtones. The settings normally alternate between London and a sombrely attractive rural area in southern England: sometimes Dorset but usually East Anglia. In one or other location is to be found, almost invariably, a large old house whose architectural minutiae are lovingly inventoried: sometimes still private but more often converted to a workplace for members of the educated professions. Normally, the conversion of the house's function is registered as a desecration: proportions destroyed by splitting rooms in two, soulless light-fittings, and so forth, though with a sighing acknowledgement that things

---

[1] Antonia Fraser and Malcolm Bradbury in *Mail on Sunday*, quoted on the paperback covers of James's *Time to Be in Earnest* (London: Faber and Faber, 1999) and *A Certain Justice* (Harmondsworth: Penguin, 1998; first pub. Faber, 1997); *The Times* and Peter Levi in *Today*, on the cover of *A Taste for Death* (London: Sphere, 1987); Susan Rowland, *From Agatha Christie to Ruth Rendell* (Basingstoke: Palgrave, 2001), 196. Unless otherwise stated, publication dates given in the main text for James's works refer to the initial Faber edition, while note references for quotations are taken from the subsequent Sphere or Penguin paperbacks.

must move on and the new function may well be worthier than the old.[2]

Unlike the lounge lizards of yore, the occupants of these buildings have things to do and places to be, and introducing them first in relation to their work routines and only slowly in relation to their private lives gives us a satisfying sense of travelling some distance with each of them. Another dimension of characterization adding to the general reality-effect is a sometimes rather gruff take on the varieties of human sexuality. More in sorrow than anger, James's novels keep abreast of such controversial behaviours as unmarried motherhood, homosexuality, incest, and exhibitionism. While rarely seen as much fun (but then neither is straightforward heterosexuality), these activities are gravely acknowledged as examples of the need to arrange those 'exchanges of gratification' (in a favourite phrase) to which the human lot condemns us.

The style in which James presents these settings and characters is intensely serious. She more than once appreciatively quotes her namesake Henry's reference to death as 'the distinguished thing', and often seems to evoke this built-in distinction of her subject matter to spread a general atmosphere of reproof over whatever enjoyment we may be deriving from the fact that we think we are reading a mere whodunit.[3] It is a style rife with careful discriminations, negations, and suppressions of foolish ideas. It can already be found, surprisingly fully formed, in *Cover Her Face*, her first novel, which begins with a description of a dinner party as recalled by its hostess, Mrs Maxie:

Memory, selective and perverse, invested what had been a perfectly ordinary dinner party with an aura of foreboding and unease. It became, in retrospect, a ritual gathering under one roof of victim and suspects, a staged preliminary to murder...

---

[2] See *Original Sin* (Harmondsworth: Penguin, 1996), 222; *Shroud for a Nightingale* (London: Sphere, 1973), 58.

[3] See *A Taste for Death* (London: Sphere, 1987), 38; *Death in Holy Orders* (London: Faber and Faber, 2001), 285.

At the time, of course, the party was both ordinary and rather dull.[4]

The 'of course' puts us nicely in our place should we presume to relish this pre-murder repast as the prescribed whodunit ritual it actually is, as against the dull reality which is the only thing serious literature should really recognize.

There is a certain congruence between this negating style and the wrong-footing of assumptions which is the whole basis of the detective form, but negatives also come thick and fast in the presentation of the characters' sex lives, or lack of them. Thus two central characters in *Cover Her Face* find 'advantages in not being lovers', since a love affair or 'irregular union' imposes conventions 'as rigid and compelling as those of marriage', such as going to bed whenever the opportunity offers. The fact that the man has not even asked the woman to sleep with him raises doubts about his sexuality—somewhat bold for 1962—which are then neatly skirted through a further set of negatives: 'most of their friends considered him to be a natural bachelor, eccentric, slightly pedantic and perenially amusing. They might have been unkinder', but for the obvious truth that 'a man cannot be either effeminate or a fool who holds both French and British decorations for his part in the Resistance Movement' (pp. 24–5). The fact that so many negatives would have to be removed to make anything in this situation straightforwardly positive simply seems to reflect the style's valuing of restraint for its own sake.

Cover Her Face anticipates later work in several other ways, although, in allegiance to the Golden Age tradition to which James is apprenticing herself, it is set in an actual country house rather than the converted variety. Somewhat symbolically Simon Maxie, the owner of Martingale House, lies dying up-stairs, tended through his senile dementia by his wife, daughter, and female domestics, among the last of whom signs of class restiveness are starting to display themselves. His son and heir is

---

[4] *Cover Her Face* (London: Sphere, 1974), 5.

presented as heartless and uncaring, chiefly because he prefers working as a doctor in London to anticipating his inheritance at home. In an age which acclaimed Evelyn Waugh's lament for the fall of Brideshead, this could still be accepted as a serious moral dilemma if not the chief Condition of England Question itself. The source of disquiet in the lower orders is the housemaid Sally Jupp, whose unmarried-mother status is the main subject of debate at the opening dinner party. Sally's irreverence towards the sanctities of Martingale is contrasted with the devotion of the biblically named housekeeper Martha, living proof that Marthas as a species are not 'complicated people', being 'concerned with the comfort of the body, the cooking of food, the unending menial tasks which someone must carry out before the life of the mind can have any true validity. Their own undemanding emotional needs found fulfilment in service' (p. 86). The crossover here between the well-being of the upper classes and 'the life of the mind' is symptomatic: in James's subsequent books, the latter easily substitutes for the former in a modified Toryism where artistic sensibility and intellect constitute the kind of deference-demanding moral absolute that used to be represented by 'breeding'.

If we removed the murderer and detective but retained its often sharp depictions of its characters' perceptions and suppressed passions—a good many are allotted 'point of view' status, insofar as the need to conceal the culprit permits—*Cover Her Face* could for long stretches be read as a solid British country-house novel in the 'two inches of ivory' tradition of James's beloved Jane Austen, and it also manages to confront what for 1962 were some relatively hot contemporary issues. These include the recognition that men do sleep with women (and sometimes even each other) outside wedlock, and that when this results in children the old semi-criminalizing approach—as represented by the Victorian 'St Mary's Refuge', from which Sally is rescued by the Maxies—is open to question. The book also acknowledges the existence of other worlds through glimpses of Sally's lower-middle-class upbringing with her uncle and aunt. The gulf is, however, established somewhat parodically, as when a Maxie daughter catches the uncle acting suspiciously at the garden fête, and he explains he is looking for the toilet. ' "If you mean the lavatory," said Deborah shortly, "there's one in the garden. It seemed adequately sign-posted to me" ' (p. 39). The non-U status of 'toilet' had indeed been well signposted five years earlier, in Nancy Mitford's *Noblesse Oblige*.[5] Later, a sympathetic character has to remind himself sternly that the uncle and aunt's suburb has 'an enviable record of good public services and that not everyone wanted to live in a quiet Georgian house in Greenwich' (p. 130).

Such well-bred responses are not merely those of the Martingale social circle. Many of them are shared by James's detective hero Adam Dalgleish, whom we first encounter ignoring a subordinate's banal assessment of Martingale as a 'nice-looking place':

Detective Chief-Inspector Adam Dalgleish did not reply but swung himself out of the car and stood back for a moment to look at the house. It was a typical Elizabethan manor house, simple but strongly formalized in design. The large, two-storeyed bays with their mullioned and transomed windows stood symmetrically on each side of the square central porch. Above the dripstone was a heavy carved coat of arms. (p. 48)

Similar moments are repeated throughout the novels: we are shown the activities of the big house's occupiers in considerable detail, but have to wait for Dalgleish's arrival to receive authoritative, Pevsnerian guidance as to its architectural merit. He is, however, careful not to confuse aesthetic with professional judgements, pointing out that the local *parvenu* squire who lives in a Victorian monstrosity 'is a philistine, no doubt, but not, I think, a murderer' (p. 152).

5 See *Noblesse Oblige*, ed. Nancy Mitford (London: Hamish Hamilton, 1956), 43.

Dalgleish's identification of one of the house's paintings, which makes a suspect exclaim that he thought 'cultured cops' were 'peculiar to detective novels', is a reminder that such suavities as recognizing Stubbs would be *de rigueur* in the work of Margery Allingham, Dorothy L. Sayers, and Ngaio Marsh, the three Queens of Crime to whom James has confessed her greatest debt.[6] But the widely accepted claim of one critic that 'Adam Dalgleish is a more interesting person than Albert Campion, Lord Peter Wimsey or Roderick Alleyn' is, I think, worth re-examining.[7]

Dalgleish's emotional life, though often dangled before us, is a mainly offstage affair. His wife died before his first appearance and a subdued flame for *Cover Her Face*'s toilet-deriding Deborah Briscoe flickers out after two books, to be replaced by a similar arms-length tendresse for the Cambridge literature don Emma Lavenham in *Death in Holy Orders* (2001). More strikingly character-defining is the fact that he is an acclaimed poet, possession or knowledge of one of whose volumes is generally proof enough that a character is *simpático*. Thus Dalgleish experiences 'a sense of waste, of personal, irrational loss' on noting that one innocent victim's bookshelves include such favourites as 'Greene, Waugh, Compton-Burnett, Hartley, Powell, Cary' as well as a complete set of Jane Austen and some 'modern poetry, his own last volume included'; and an educated police sidekick looks forward to a case in London's Inns of Court because the setting might well 'inspire a new slim volume of verse. It's time he gave us one.'[8]

But making a key fictional character a major poet has certain drawbacks unless the author also happens to be one. Whereas other qualities can be described physically or evoked in action,

[6] See *Cover Her Face*, 82; *Time to be in Earnest*, 12.

[7] Robin W. Winks, 'The Sordid Truth: Four Cases', in R. W. Winks (ed.), *Detective Fiction: A Collection of Critical Essays* (Englewood Cliffs, NJ: Prentice-Hall, 1980), 215.

[8] *Shroud for a Nightingale* (London: Sphere, 1973), 55–6; and *A Certain Justice* (Harmondsworth: Penguin, 1998), 143.

literary ability demands to be demonstrated on the page itself, as with Boris Pasternak's obliging selection from his hero's work at the end of *Dr Zhivago*; and so far the demonstrable works of Adam Dalgleish add up to 'The Bereaved', four lines of juvenilia which we are invited to find 'remarkable for a fourteen-year-old' but for which he can hardly still be held responsible.[9] Nonetheless, taken with the titles of his two slim volumes—*Invisible Scars* and *A Case to Answer and Other Poems*[10]—its sombre content and neat versification suggest a tight-lipped aesthetic of loss and pain faced up to and contained. Without further evidence, however, his status as a poet demands to be read chiefly as a marker of a certain cultural distinction which other policemen lack.

Occasionally, it is true, James hints at a deeper connection between poetry and detection, more than once by way of Graham Greene's remark about 'the creative artist's splinter of ice in the heart'.[11] In line with this remark, Dalgleish often observes his own responses to blood-splattered corpses with an 'artist's' detachment, about which he also feels guilty. Somewhere here there is perhaps a signalling of the author's anxiety about her exploitation of these corpses to fuel her own literary creativity; but cold dispassion is the occupational hazard of police work and nowhere are we convincingly shown that Dalgleish solves cases particularly well because of the fine-tuned artistic awareness which renders his own icy splinter uniquely necessary. An exception is perhaps *Shroud for a Nightingale*, whose solution rests on the rather shaky if poetically licensed *aperçu* that in contrast to the 'essentially stupid and dull' Suspect A, only Suspect B (with whom Dalgleish is himself smitten) has 'a face so beautiful and so individual' that it could still be

---

[9] See *Death in Holy Orders*, 68 (see too p. 266 for three impromptu heroic couplets on the current murder victim).
[10] See *The Black Tower* (London: Faber and Faber, 1975), and *Devices and Desires* (London: Faber and Faber, 1989).
[11] See *A Certain Justice*, 477; *Time to Be in Earnest*, 66–7.

recognized after thirty years and thus lay her open to the black-mail which prompted the murder.[12]

In the contemporary whodunit, the reader's sheer wonder-ment at scientific and deductive methods *per se* no longer consti-tutes the detective as literary hero; today, our interest is mostly focused on the mystery rather than its solver, unless he or she pulls some dazzling new technique out of the hat, or begins to bend the rules in some striking way such as breaking the law or getting too involved with the suspects. Dalgleish does none of these: he largely puts two and two together before our eyes (haring ahead of us just a bit towards the end), adheres firmly to the law and its procedures, and only hints his feelings to Deborah and Emma when they have ceased to be suspects. Leaving aside the fine perceptions and high-cultural reference points, Dalgleish is basically just a Plod: a necessity of his genre, who has nothing very distinctive to do except follow in the culprit's footsteps a few pages before the rest of us.

To base an assessment of James on her first novel would be unfair: she has moved from the private country house into other worlds, darker, more deeply researched and sometimes more egalitarian. Her novels have also grown massively: the recent *A Certain Justice* is nearly 500 pages, two-and-a-half times the length of *Cover Her Face*. But some aspects have remained remarkably constant. In terms of style, for instance, we can compare the earlier opening ('Memory, selective and per-verse . . .') with this one from *A Certain Justice*:

Murderers do not usually give their victims notice. This is one death which, however terrible that last second of appalled realization, comes mercifully unburdened with anticipatory terror.[13]

From these sentences we can deduce that, unlike victims of sudden traffic accidents or instantaneous heart attacks, the victim of repeated abusive violence which one day goes too far

---

[12] *Shroud for a Nightingale*, 281.
[13] *A Certain Justice*, 3.

has no inkling of what is about to happen. Nothing in this opening is, or even could be, good: murder clearly isn't, nor is the idea that murderers might give notice, nor even (note 'usually') is the idea that we might make some sort of comforting rule out of their not doing so. After her death, 'the few who had liked' the murdered barrister Venetia Aldridge 'found themselves muttering' that it would have pleased her that her last murder case was tried at her favourite courtroom in the Old Bailey. Lest we think that James herself wants us to accept these mutterings without question, we are abruptly met with the one-sentence paragraph: 'But there was truth in the inanity.' The inanity is, of course, of James's own careful devising, and actually the whole purpose of the introduction, but somehow a world is evoked where we all rise above such things, though in this case we would—aha!—be wrong to do so.

The point about Venetia's favourite courtroom leads us into her own view of it. Though, like any James character worth his or her salt, she 'had always tried to discipline that part of her mind which she suspected could be seduced by tradition or history', she responds to the room with 'an aesthetic satisfaction and a lifting of the spirit' thanks to 'a rightness about the size and proportions, an appropriate dignity' in its seventeenth-century decor. The liberal use of indefinite article plus abstract noun, which also appears in *A Certain Justice*'s title, itself denotes a passion for delimiting whatever positives slip past the censoring net: it is not that the size and proportions are simply right, but that only one of many possible types of rightness has survived the author's scrutiny. However, 'Like all places perfectly designed for their purpose with nothing wanting, nothing superfluous' the courtroom induces 'a sense of timeless calm, even the illusion that the passions of men were susceptible to order and control'. As in many novels, this early description drops a subliminal hint as to how we are to read the book itself. James's novels, too, offer readers what she admits is the illusion that 'we can cope with violent death...and show that even the most intractable mystery is capable of solution'.[14] And, like her style, the detective novel's illusory sense of control comes from a series of negations, in which suspect after suspect is dangled in front of us until a 'certain' solution is declared to be correct, and accepted by the reader out of exhaustion.

Unlike her first novel, after this poised opening *A Certain Justice* loses no time in plunging us into the Lower Depths. One of James's most dramatic acknowledgements that not everyone chooses to live in 'a quiet Georgian house in Greenwich' appears in her presentation of the young psychopath Garry Ashe, whom Venetia successfully defends on a charge of murdering his aunt in their squalid home in a condemned backstreet. An alcoholic prostitute, the aunt has insisted on Ashe having sex with her as well as photographing her doing so with clients. James's creation of these two characters is a testimony to her earnestness, her clear determination to tackle, without blinking, some of the nastier things one reads about in the papers. One of the most unpleasantly dwelt-on sights in all her work is the aunt's corpse, as represented in Ashe's last snapshot:

She was lying on her back, naked except for a thin négligée which had fallen open to reveal the black smudge of pubic hair and breasts white and heavy like giant jellyfish. . . . The knife wounds in the chest and belly gaped like mouths from which the blood was oozing like black sputum. There was a single gash across the throat. (p. 89)

Asked why he photographed the body he still claims not to have killed, he replies, 'Because I always photographed Auntie on that couch. That's what she liked' (p. 90).

Though such kinky fusions of violence with sex are the stock-in-trade of some recent thriller writers, this is strong stuff for James and seems at first to testify to a wish to say something very urgent about a society where such things can go on. Instead, Ashe becomes more and more of a special case, fighting against the light of a high-cultural world of which he is aware but which

[14] *Time to Be in Earnest*, 17.

is somehow obscurely castigated for its inability to save him. He thus joins a long literary line of such social scourings as Pinky in Graham Greene's *Brighton Rock* and Jack Havoc in Margery Allingham's *The Tiger in the Smoke*, as well as—from more distant genres—Steerpike in Mervyn Peake's *Gormenghast* trilogy and Alex in Anthony Burgess's *A Clockwork Orange*. High intelligence and a nascent aesthetic awareness constitute these youths as existential Hamlets who somehow represent all 'we' fear about their class; that they themselves are corroded with a disgust for their world also makes them our exceptional, charismatic representative within it. In Pinky's and Ashe's case, this disgust emerges particularly in a puritanical sex-hatred which makes them classic Freudian cases for treatment, while adding to their monstrosity through the contempt they show for the hapless Ophelias who fall under their sway. As with Pinky's devotion to the Catholic litany and Alex's to Beethoven, Ashe's social alienation does not prevent him from constructing self-revealing collages which juxtapose naked breasts and buttocks with faces from reproductions of great paintings. These faces regard 'the jumble of crude sexual images with distaste or patrician disdain' (p. 83). A common murderer like Ashe might be hard for us to understand, if he did not survey his degraded life with our own, more patrician eyes.

Even so, it is impossible to imagine Ashe's sordid crime as the main one in the book: as in several James novels, an initial common-or-garden murder is used to establish the normal workings of a group professionally concerned with crime—forensic scientists, local police, lawyers—before the main murder strikes in the middle-class heartland. It is the circumstances of this murder that make these novels whodunits rather than—ultimately—anything else. (Rather than the American 'mystery' or the broader 'detective fiction', the jocular old term 'whodunit' is most appropriate to novels devoted to identifying a single culprit from a range of suspects rather than, for instance, identifying several diverse criminals or a generally bad state of affairs.) James's novels observe a great many whodunit rules, which push them away from the sombre realism, psychological analysis, or profound symbolism they often seem to lay claim to.

As W. H. Auden explained, the whodunit genre exerts a particular pressure on our emotional (or 'aesthetic') responses to its characters. Before the murder, everyone can be of equal emotional interest: rounded, characterful, etc., as well as apparently 'ethical'. After the murder, this interest is put on hold, to be replaced by a new aesthetic purely dependent on each character's potential to be the murderer. 'The suspects must be guilty of something, because, now that the aesthetic and the ethical are in opposition, if they are completely innocent (obedient to the ethical) they lose their aesthetic interest and the reader will ignore them.'[15] The kinds of peccadillo through which the suspects can retain our interest range from illicit amours to unfulfilled murderous impulses to covering up for loved ones. These minor sins tend to lead to much coincidental rushing around at the time of the crime as well as to much stonewalling, but once uncovered those guilty of them drop virtually out of sight as far as our feelings are concerned. Only after the exposure of the murderer can they briefly return to an ethical/aesthetic dimension in which we can care about them for their own sake, but by this point there is no room for more than a rapid tying up of loose ends.

This is what is really going on beneath the apparently 'novelistic' interest in James's characters as developing beings. Apart from the beginning and end of the book, they remain frozen in the postures in which the moment of the murder arrested them. Development is not really their point any more—except in the sense that a photograph of a single instant is slowly developed in the darkroom—and they have to eke out a precarious emotional existence on the outer fringes of the plot. At the same time, the

---

[15] W. H. Auden, 'The Guilty Vicarage', originally in *The Dyer's Hand and Other Essays* (London: Faber and Faber, 1948); reprinted in Winks (ed.), *Detective Fiction*, 20.

genre also demands that we keep watching them one by one, either in formal interviews or in the narrations where their 'point of view' is cleverly arranged to conceal more than it reveals about the only thing we are interested in. Though the Golden Age British-style whodunit can be often justly described as elitist in overall class terms, once it has established its cast of characters it is its crushing democracy which can make it so deadly: the endless obligation to visit and revisit everyone in turn, once of course you have defined, via the snapshot moment of the murder, who 'everyone' is. With James, the democracy of detection, as practised by the bureaucratic Dalgleish, is matched with a democracy of narrative point of view, or as nearly so as will allow the murderer's identity to lurk undetected behind the shrubbery of his or her passing thoughts and impressions.

When the final revelation comes, very little is discernible in terms of a critique of particular social pressures. It is of course an essential part of the whodunit tradition that there should not be any obvious social pattern to who is guilty (though there are exclusions, such as the much-maligned butler); nonetheless, it is possible to read the choice of murderer in Conan Doyle, Christie, and others as constructing critiques of particular kinds of money obsession or status insecurity. The brief but intense moment when the culprit's real identity has all our attention can also be the moment when the other strands somehow come together to make a new kind of sense. Generally speaking they do not with James: although the culprits usually explain their personal motives at length and then the loose ends all get tied up in a thoroughly professional manner, we learn little new about the endemic pressures of the particular social milieu to which we have been so painstakingly introduced.

To generalize that James's solutions do not usually shed much new light beyond themselves does not mean that there are no patterns across her work as to the kinds of people who are usually the killers and the killed. To quote Auden again, the ideal victim 'has to involve everyone in suspicion, which requires that he be a bad character'; but also 'has to make everyone feel guilty, which requires that he be a good character'.[16] Auden's Freudian conclusion that 'the best victim is the negative Father or Mother Image' applies well to James's male victims. In five novels, powerful and authoritative men are killed by resentful male subordinates, but there is no real feeling that they should not have had their power in the first place.[17] When the victims are women, however (in another five cases including Sally Jupp, Venetia Aldridge, and two would-be blackmailers), they are generally killed for being too pushy and usually by or at the instigation of older, more authoritative, and often maternal women. If the classic Oedipal resentment pattern works well for the male figures, for the women the classic roles of Electra and Clytemnestra are reversed.[18]

This pattern of an older woman murdering a younger is well exemplified in *Cover Her Face*, which is arguably an exception to my strictures on James's failure to use her conclusions to make us rethink the worlds she has shown us. Sally's murder is a puzzle because as well as being strangled she has been drugged and her door has been locked—all of which is assumed to be the work of one person but turns out to be that of three. These are all people to whom Sally owes some dutiful respect which she has flouted: the uncle she is blackmailing, the housekeeper she openly insults, and the employer to whose son she has just announced her engagement. She was strangled by the last of these, Mrs Maxie, whose giveaway statement that 'there must be a limit to what these people expect' could be taken to express a wider view (p. 77). Though it turns out that Sally was married and simply playing games with the family's feelings, *Cover Her Face* could be

---

[16] Auden, 'The Guilty Vicarage', 19.

[17] See *Unnatural Causes, Death of an Expert Witness, A Taste for Death, Original Sin*, and *Death in Holy Orders*. In the first case, admittedly, the male subordinate plays second fiddle to a woman murderer.

[18] Apart from *Cover Her Face*, see *Shroud for a Nightingale* and *Devices and Desires*. The woman victim in *A Mind to Murder* is killed for different reasons.

read as a study of the clash between the old order and the 'people'—young, sexually predatory class-gatecrashers—currently being celebrated in the Angry Young Man (and occasionally Woman) plays and novels of the time. But the fact that the murderess apparently epitomizes patrician tolerance, and that her thoughts have been the first we encountered, produce a satisfying sense of shock, along with the realization that the book's continuous concern with class difference and family values has been thematically central rather than mere local colouring.

Though James soon dropped the naked class orientation of her first novel, the theme of the too-assertive female victim has continued up to *A Certain Justice*, where the ambitious barrister Venetia Aldridge has also pushed a certain amount of success too far. This time, the array of ill-wishers who have left a confusing embarrassment of clues in the body's vicinity all find something particularly offensive in a woman who sacrifices her marriage to defend murderers she knows to be guilty, and who shows no tolerance for the peccadilloes of her male peers. Once again, the book leaves us with a strong feeling that such a widely shared view must be right, but this time the murderer is—quite unguessably—the uncle of the wife of the colleague whose malpractice Venetia was about to expose. Despite sharing with Ashe's aunt whatever 'philia' it might be that covers excessive love of one's sibling's offspring, there is little that makes this particular suspect more (or satisfyingly less) likely than any of the others. A far more powerfully drawn ill-wisher, who vents her hatred on Venetia both before and after death, is an older woman whose young female relative has been killed by someone Venetia has successfully defended in court. The implication of the novel's clear sympathy with this matriarchal avenger is a deep distrust, not only of ambitious professional women but also of the 'innocent until proved guilty' assumption on which the law is based— a theme which recurs when Dalgleish has to let the actual murderer go for lack of hard evidence.

There are, then, certain recurrent social concerns in James's work, generally of a very conservative—certainly pre-feminist—nature. But even when they happen to chime in with feelings held by others, the killers' motives are always presented as purely personal. Perhaps surprisingly, the majority kill for the sake of someone else, most often a blood relative: to keep the children of a broken marriage, to save a brother from blackmail, to avenge a wife and children killed in the Holocaust, to secure an inheritance for a recently discovered son. Where the villains are more evilly self-interested, there is often a whiff of something sexually 'wrong' at the root of it: a wheelchair-bound woman frustratedly infatuated with her victim; a homosexual drug-runner; an illegitimate son besotted with his half-sister. The implication here is that the evil kink is purely individual rather than shared across a larger section of society. Most murderers have their moment in the sun when (often before or after a dramatic life-and-death tussle with Dalgleish) they explain their motives with enormous articulacy. But they always express their feelings as isolated, autonomous individuals, often with intense family attachments but not as members of groups or classes responding to the shared social ills of the given milieu.

Thus in four novels—*A Mind to Murder* (1963), *Shroud for a Nightingale* (1971), *The Black Tower* (1975), and *Death of an Expert Witness* (1977)—we are presented with meticulously detailed pictures of a range of medical establishments which we might expect to add up to some kind of thesis about the pressures and problems of the National Health Service, for which James worked for nineteen years.[19] But, despite some incidental mockery of psychiatry in *A Mind to Murder* (where some of English fiction's earliest LSD experiments take place, with dubious but not pivotal results), and a general sense that such institutions force people into unhealthy proximity, the murders turn out to revolve round such matters as money and

[19] See *Time to Be in Earnest*, 109–14.

sexual rivalry which have nothing to do with these social arrangements. To quote Auden yet again, the classic whodunit setting is 'The Great Good Place', the static, immobilized Eden to which society can return once the Fall of the crime has been reversed.[20] For James, the Great Good Place is still the English stately home, or the bastion of cultural or welfarist power which has been superimposed on it, as endorsed by Dalgleish's masterly appraisal of its venerable architecture. Any critical thoughts he may have are those of an insider, deploring a falling-off from ideals he profoundly endorses.

To clarify this point about milieux further, it is useful to contrast the whodunit with another form with which James has briefly flirted: the private eye story. In this form—which for Auden failed to qualify in whodunit terms because it described the Great Wrong Place, and was thus dangerously close to becoming art—the detective is privately hired to investigate something well short of murder, but soon finds himself or herself wading ever deeper into a world, or interlocked series of worlds, featuring several crimes at once.[21] The real case, insofar as there is only one, consists of uncovering the interconnections between these various crimes and milieux, and the view is very much from the bottom up rather than, as with Dalgleish, from the top down. The drawback of the form is that the answer is usually the same, i.e. that the corruption goes all the way to the top, generally by way of the client. Its advantage as a form is that it is critical of power rather than impressed by it, and hence can be used to question large-scale social structures rather than simply the torments of individual souls. In *An Unsuitable Job for a Woman* (1972), James's gumshoe Cordelia Gray was one of the very first of the wave of female private eyes which became tidal some years later. Repeatedly threatened, coshed, and thrown down wells, Cordelia observes hardboiled precedent by following a circular trail (admittedly through the not very

[20] See Auden, 'The Guilty Vicarage', 19.
[21] Ibid.

mean streets of Cambridge) which leads right back to her fat-cat client. She also covers up a subsequent crime, in line with the private eye's traditional distrust of legal niceties. As the title suggests, the novel uses the private eye's built-in Jack-the-Giant-Killer vulnerability to make significant points about the male domination of women although—after the gothic romance *The Skull Beneath the Skin* (1982), which holed Cordelia up on an island with the traditional circle of well-heeled suspects—James seems to have concluded that private detection *is* an unsuitable job for a woman by dropping Cordelia altogether.

Rather more diffusely, James has also made approaches to another form of crime fiction capable of looking at a variety of locations with a critical eye: the Police Procedural. Here the point of focus is on a police team wrestling with a number of cases simultaneously, and with a realistic awareness that not all cases will be satisfactorily solved. This form unites some of the thrill of the private eye's odyssey through a range of geographical and social locations with the reassurance that our centre of sympathy will remain within the law and that what we are reading feels authentic in ways that the traditional tale of the lone genius—public or private—clearly is not. In *Death of an Expert Witness* and *Devices and Desires*, the early discovery of a murdered body acquaints us with teams of law enforcers and their techniques in a convincingly 'procedural' way before the main mystery kicks in, while from *A Taste for Death* on, Dalgleish's own retinue has expanded from the standard dim sidekick to include a working-class female officer and at least one firmly characterized male one, whose endowment with substantial 'point of view' status removes some of the burdens of omnipercipience from their boss's increasingly distinguished shoulders. Perhaps only the fact that she fits into an unbroken line of sidekicks whose surnames begin with 'M'—Martin, Masterson, and Massingham—subliminally signals that the Inspector Kate Miskin who comes near to starring in *A Taste for Death* will soon lapse back into an essentially handmaidenly role in later novels. For a brief period, the pressures of living with her gran in a working-class high-rise and various personality conflicts with her male opposite numbers make Kate a satisfactorily grainy alternative centre of interest from Dalgleish and even the suspects.[22] But once again, while not exactly unsuitable, a policewoman's job has proved insufficiently absorbing to keep James's sustained attention. Miskin now seems permanently affixed to a Dalgleish who, once in the saddle, continues to project our approach to the bastions of institutional power as one of insiderly equality.

Referring to her friend and fellow peer Ruth Rendell, James has written 'Neither Ruth nor I are didactic writers'; however, she makes the distinction that while 'I never set out to point a moral or to deal specifically with a social problem,' Rendell increasingly uses detective fiction 'to deal with social affairs about which she feels concern'.[23] The same could be said of other successful crime writers such as Reginald Hill and Ian Rankin, who, with Rendell, have opened out the procedural form into an effective vehicle of social inquiry. Their police heroes—Rendell's Wexford, Hill's Dalziel and Pascoe, and Rankin's Rebus—are all fixed within coherent police teams at (more or less) inspector level, rather than being summoned from Scotland Yard or somewhere loftier, like Dalgleish. Their beats are firmly located, as is a whole network of relationships bedding them into their communities. They are also, typically, involved in several cases at once, the discovery of links or parallels between which often gives the kind of closing frisson which I am complaining is missing in James. It happens that these writers share a broadly leftist perspective in exploring issues such as present-day slavery, environmental protest, and domestic abuse

---

[22] The fact that Kate's first male sparring-partner is the class-and-sex-prejudiced Chief Inspector (the Hon.) John Massingham may well have given the initial hint for Elizabeth George's even less probable pairing up of the rough-edged Sergeant (and upwards) Barbara Havers with Inspector Thomas Lynley, eighth Earl of Asherton, in her popular series beginning with *A Great Deliverance* (London: Bantam, 1989).

[23] *Time to Be in Earnest*, 58.

(Rendell), the Profumo scandal and industrial corruption (Hill), or refugee-smuggling and property speculation (Rankin).

Where James does focus on social issues, it tends to be from the opposite side of the fence from these writers. An example is her handling of race, where anti-racism rather than its reverse is taken to represent the corruptions of the system. Thus, after herself struggling free of the class prejudice which greeted her first appearance, Kate Miskin, in *Death in Holy Orders*, finds herself on the verge of quitting after the Macpherson Report has accused the police of 'institutional racism': 'I perceive this report as racist—racist against me as a white officer' (p. 201). Though we are assured many of Kate's friends are black, we never meet them or indeed any other non-white person in James's pages. Though James has sometimes been praised for confronting the legacy of Nazi atrocities, which is pivotal in two novels, the main thrust in both is that others are too quick to judge those involved in them: an ex-Death Camp nurse is driven to murder to conceal her secret from a Nazi-obsessed superior, and the avenger of a family sent to its death by a Vichy collaborator kills the wrong people.[24] (In the latter case, it also becomes clear that a promising Jewish detective has become too emotionally involved to be viable police material.)

My argument is not that such views detract in themselves from James's status as a serious novelist. It is that the classic-whodunit structure she has chosen does not allow her to open out these or any other issues in the body of the book, since they must either be held in reserve for the big surprise ending or presented as incidental background to it. By contrast, both the procedural and private-eye forms pose society itself as a problem, with the various cases explored as symptoms or examples into which we slowly work our way from start to finish. This sense of movement from A to B, rather than from a single question to the cul-de-sac of a single answer, allows for a real

[24] See Rowland, *From Agatha Christie to Ruth Rendell*, 196; and *Shroud for a Nightingale* and *Original Sin*.

interplay with the aims of the serious novel. This is not to claim greater realism for these forms, or that they are any less rule-bound than the classic form; simply that alongside the enjoyment of suspense they also give us a sense of following some kind of argument.

One index of the difference is that James's beginnings tend to be better than her ends; her setting of the murder scene more striking and dramatic than its final explanation. She has often described how she can only start a new novel when she has visualized the discovery of the body.[25] As well as the place, this often includes bizarrely picturesque postmortem additions or subtractions, which constitute something of a Jamesian signature: missing hands; a primitive statue clutched to the breast; a toy snake in the mouth; a bloodstained judge's wig on the head; a scrawled arrow pointing at the corpse from a nearby medieval mural of the *Last Judgement*. The last three cases in particular read like free-floating messages from the author (or perhaps God) about the vanity of earthly ambition, especially given that the victims are all powerful figures whose addenda seem to comment specifically on their pretensions: a powerful publisher, a star barrister, and a hard-hearted archdeacon. The problem with such graphic symbols is that, generally, they are insufficiently motivated once we find out who put them there. The snake just happened to be lying around; the bloody wig is added on the spur of the moment by a vengeful character who stumbles on the body; and the mural grafitto has been used to lure the victim to the scene when anything else would have done. (In the last case the symbolism is well deserved because the archdeacon is a murderer, but his killer—a committed atheist—was completely ignorant of this.)

Such anomalies between picturesque murder and final explanation need not matter in the traditional whodunit, existing on the same prankish level as the bedroom-farce-like proliferation

---

[25] See *Time to Be in Earnest*, 89–90.

of suspects round the crime scene at which James also excels. The sense of simply having fun with the form—demanding a certain heartlessness of plotting by both culprit and author—can indeed be found in some of her earlier (and shorter) novels, such as *Unnatural Causes* (1967), where the handless state of the corpse found adrift in a boat at sea has a gleefully tasteless explanation which matches both the initial shocking image and the warped mind of the perpetrator. But in most later novels, the high-serious demand that we understand the killer emotionally leads to a deliberate muting of ingenuity, whereby the complications of the initial mystery have arisen either by accident or by fairly straightforward attempts to confuse the trail.

James is right to say, 'I never set out to point a moral or to deal specifically with a social problem.'[26] This refusal may sound convincing in high-art terms (even Samuel Johnson's highly moralizing *Vanity of Human Wishes*, from which 'to point a moral' comes, uses the phrase to denote something crass and superficial), and her position above the fray may well contribute to the quasi-constitutional 'Queen of Crime' status often claimed for her. But as we have seen, other successful crime writers have condescended to point morals, including social ones. By contrast, Lady James is fond of quoting her namesake Henry's remark 'never believe that you know the last word about any human heart' as her own last word on the mystery of murder.[27] To leave the answer here is perhaps a deeper kind of conservatism than the incidental kinds one encounters throughout her work. It postulates that we are all one kind of (articulate middle-class) person, who make our free choices prompted only by the mysterious workings of the heart. Lately, perhaps, this cul-de-sac in social terms has allowed glimpses of another type of explanation in religious ones, as suggested in titles such as *Original Sin* and *Death in Holy Orders*. In the latter the atheist

---

[26] See n. 23 above.
[27] See *The Skull beneath the Skin* (London: Sphere, 1982), 311; *A Certain Justice*, 61.

murderer explains his deed in terms of his despair at the decline of civilization, including 'the death of beauty, of scholarship, of art, of intellectual integrity', which has led him to 'join the barbarians' and offer the son for whom the murder was committed the choice between God and Mammon, in hopes that the latter will win (p. 380).

Why is James still so particularly revered today? I would argue that her presiding status as Queen of Crime offers the literary world a useful way of apparently bridging the split between high and low culture which is still felt necessary, although embarrassing to mention too directly. No one now speaks of crime fiction with outright contempt, and virtually everyone enjoys it at times. It would be nice if its pleasures and those of a literature which takes us onto a higher level of understanding the human condition could turn out to be the same thing. It seems to me that such fusions actually can take place within the forms of crime fiction that take us on some kind of social journey, however crude, from A to B. But despite many enjoyable and gripping scenes, James's conformity to the model in which our interest in most of the characters remains provisional until a closing encounter with the sorry state of Colonel Mustard's soul, leads to a finally frustrating experience not always sufficiently alleviated by the sense that it was fun while it lasted.

14

The Novel Adapted for Television

Elizabeth Jane Howard

Adaptations from one art form to another have always been subject to adverse criticism. The puritan or elitist view is that if a work is created in one form it will be lessened by translation to another. It will, at the least, certainly not be the same (as good). There can only be two answers: far more people have heard and seen *La Traviata* than have read *La Dame aux Camélias*, but there is nothing to stop them from reading Dumas's novel—in French, or any of the languages into which it has been translated. Secondly, the novel is still *there*, in spite of having to compete with Verdi. From novel to opera is a considerable leap; from novel to play less startling. There is nothing between a novel and its readers but their imagination, perceptions, and their sense of the writer's intention. When a novel is translated to drama there are other peoples' perceptions to take into account, and when the drama is for film or television the other people become a positive army. The scriptwriter has to choose what to use and what to leave out of the novel, the producer has to battle with budgets (a whole lot of other people come into it here), with weather and time, with finding the right director and with casting. Then there are designers, location hunters, and a host of other technicians who determine how the production will look. You have only to look at the list of credits at the end of any film or television play to see that an army is hardly an exaggeration. All these people, however good they are in their field, will change and affect the original work, and, although they need not render it unrecognizable, it must become different, although, in theory, at least, it does not have to be inferior.

But if the television version of a novel will inevitably be different and in most cases fail to give the original a faithful translation, why do it at all? This argument could—did—apply to the theatre versus cinema when the latter was taking over from the former, when instead of repertory theatres, music hall, cabaret, stand-up comedians—live performances of one kind or another—there was film, work that when rehearsed, shot again and again, edited and honed, ended with a single performance that was the same for its audience everywhere.

Cinema was part of an evolution in technology that will no doubt continue: sound with film and vision with sound in the sitting room have marked major changes, but as art forms, when they can be considered as such, it is necessary to recognize that they are comparatively young: they have not, except indirectly, evolved simply from thousands of years of storytelling, like the novel, and thence to the enactment of stories, like live drama. In other fields they can provide us with information that most of us would not get in any other way (programmes about natural history is an obvious case in point), but when it comes to drama, the technology can and often does obstruct the likelihood of excellence. Actors, for example, have no opportunity to build a performance as they would in rehearsal for a theatre production, since the order of scenes is determined entirely by practical considerations and their job is to do the best they can with the fractured moments—often only a few seconds—presented each day on the shooting schedule.

Added to that, producers of television drama have to contend with an audience who have not had to make the slightest effort to see any programme—since it comes with the set, as it were—and with the video, people can watch whatever it is whenever they like. This is true, of course, of reading a book, with one essential difference. When they choose to read a novel, say, there it all *is*, they are presented with all or none of it, it is up to them. But the lack of effort required of a TV audience has all too often come to mean that the programme-makers treat them like slightly irritable convalescent children: their attention span is dangerously short, their comprehension poor, they are hardly fit to make any kind of intellectual or emotional effort to understand what is going on, and should not be expected to try.

In spite of these low expectations, there have been some interesting, worthy, and even very good dramatizations of novels. Perhaps it is worth saying here that works of excellence are always perched on top of a mass of mediocrity—you have to have a lot of something to get anything good, and below great the cultural climate shifts with time. For every nineteenth-century novel that is now a classic, there are hundreds that have sunk into oblivion, many of which were immensely popular in their day. But in regard to contemporary work there is also the tiresome intellectually snobbish theory prevalent that something popular is probably no good—that the *seriously* good can only be appreciated by an intellectual elite. This is as silly as thinking that if something is popular it must be good.

Television, in its ubiquity, has problems here. It aims—perhaps it has to aim—at audiences of millions rather than a few hundred or thousand. In the case, let us say, of adapting an Austen novel this means that the producers have to contend with the cognoscenti who will always be able to find omission, distortion, and uncalled-for additions to the work they know and love, and also with the far larger quantity of people who have never heard of Jane Austen and whose reception of her will rest entirely upon what they are shown. But my point is that they *are* shown and that there are consequences in that they have at least been introduced to something that otherwise they might never have experienced. Book sales of almost any novel dramatized for television prove this: of all the extra thousands of copies sold, some must surely get read. This can't be bad.

There are other consequences. When Richardson was writing *Clarissa*, which appeared in seven volumes over the space of a year, the danger to which she was exposed and the uncertainty about her fate excited readers throughout England and a large part of Europe as well. People wrote, not only to Richardson, but to each other, and there is something beguiling in the thought that a novel, albeit a great one, could command such interest and concern. Something of the sort happened with *The Forsyte Saga* and *I, Claudius*: people were made aware of and became fascinated by Galsworthy's family saga and Graves's Roman epic. The audiences may not have reached the proportions that quiz shows and interviews with 'celebrities' command now, but they were a respectable number, and commanded a devoted and enthusiastic following. Since then, we have had many adaptations of varying length and quality, but all, or perhaps most, of them have drawn attention to the original novel.

I have an interest here, and not simply because I am a novelist. I do believe that novels cannot only be a subject of art, but of moral politics since they may deal with matters both dear and significant to everyone who takes the trouble to experience them. They can provide, to some degree or other, unique chances for insights and opportunities to see both ourselves and other people in a more informed and kindly light; points of view and temperaments which are of universal interest can be illumined; all the aspirations, the fantasies, the *unsteadiness* of human nature can be explored—in rehearsal as it were. And as we continue to enslave, or eliminate, any other species we deem of commercial value or threatening, at the same time as we mistreat, torture, and murder our own, any sort of education—a little less ignorance about what it feels like to be someone else— might be seen as some short of shaky start towards civilization. (I am not writing here about the downside of television, but only want to point out that potentials cut both ways, and usually as deeply in one direction as another.)

If it is good to dramatize novels either for film or television, what goes wrong? Why aren't they all faithful masterpieces? There are two main reasons why we get presented with so many shoddy failures (as well as fewer good ones); one I have already touched on. Both films and television are now made in committee. Gone are the days when Chaplin or Keaton shot a film in three weeks on a few hundred pounds. This is roughly what it is like now. It all starts innocently enough. Somebody, somewhere, reads a novel and thinks it would make a good film or TV play. They then have to persuade others to think likewise. Often this isn't too difficult either. At this point everybody is quite keen on the author who is often invited to write the script (serious money cannot be raised without a script). But even while this is being done, people are meeting, discussing the book, arguing about the audience it is to be aimed at—in the case of films often how it can be made into a suitable vehicle for a contemporary star. A script arrives. The committee read it and their collective and disparate views are discussed. Naturally they do not agree, but if they are to continue working together they have to find some consensus. This usually involves cutting a good deal of the plot. When the script comes back a second time with these cuts there still seems to be something wrong with it, and they then realize that the cuts have removed the main character's motive for his behaviour. Never mind; they didn't much care for his behaviour anyway, he can easily be turned into some prototype more readily acceptable—the sort of hero that Mr Star is known for playing. Film moguls are very like Miss Prism about fiction: 'the good ended happily, and the bad unhappily etc.' The script goes back to the poor old writer. This goes on and on and on until the committee has a script that is much like scripts they have known for years. None of this stops them from advertising the movie as 'Henry James's best-selling novel about love and revenge, now an action-packed movie'.

This is the worst scenario, but we can all think of films like that. The prevailing committee mentality does not stop some wonderful films being made, but for every single exception there will have been one or two dedicated people prepared to fight to the death for their original conception of the piece.

The other hazard—and this particularly applies to television—is the terrible fear that companies have of things going on for *too long*. Many subjects have been ruined by this timorous attitude. Examples: Rosamond Lehmann's *Invitation to the Waltz* and *The Weather in the Streets*—her two best novels compressed into one play, which ruined the magic of the first novel and made trite the heroine's plight in the second; recently the same treatment was accorded to Nancy Mitford—two novels rendered nearly incomprehensible by compression. On the other hand, a while back *Brideshead Revisited* was allowed thirteen episodes, and with John Mortimer's admirable script came completely alive while remaining true to the novel. It is a mystery why this desire to telescope everything is so persistent. *Brideshead* was a resounding success, as was *The Jewel in the Crown*, Paul Scott's tetralogy. Why do people get so devoted to series and serials? Because they get to know the characters—and once they do, they want more of them. They loved *Middlemarch* and Mrs Gaskell's wonderful novel *Wives and Daughters*, both of which were given enough room to succeed. On the other hand, the plays done of Anthony Powell's enormous set of novels were reduced to farce, and made no impact. You would think that someone in the BBC or ITV companies would have noticed this.

The trouble, I think, is that the programme planners and executive pundits have become obsessed by numbers, by ratings, by how many million people respond to whatever they put on, and since any artistic venture involves an element of risk, it is safer to spend as little as possible on drama, which in any case is more expensive than far more popular programmes, many of which pay for themselves. *Who Wants to be a Millionaire?* is funded by the expensive telephone calls people make trying to get onto it. In Britain, all television companies, by their charters, have an obligation to produce some programmes of an uplifting or educational nature. Drama sometimes slips through the net here, because entertainment and education are not commonly supposed to go together. We are also up against what all but the most educated executives—most of whom are still male—think of the novel. Back, in fact, to Jane Austen's famous remark about 'only a novel', a remark as true today as ever it was in Austen's time. Like me, many novelists have endured the following dinner-party duologue.

> He: And what do you do?
> Me: I write novels.
> He: Oh. Ought I to have heard of you?
> Me: I don't think it need be regarded as a duty.
> He: (after a pause) I'm afraid I don't have time to read novels.

One never has the heart to pursue the implications of that remark: that he reads philosophy, poetry, history, economics, etc. What it usually means is that he read one James Bond (or John Grisham or Nick Hornby) on holiday and has for some months had a political biography lying about that his mother-in-law gave him for Christmas. The novel is up against a good deal of that kind of thing, in this country, at least.

And yet reading is like food, and a balanced diet does nourish the mind. It is not what you know that makes you interesting; it is what you know that you *don't* know that does that.

And so I am in favour of dramatizing novels—particularly for television—since they might expose some elements of the human condition that reach beyond the dreary spectacle of people killing one another, bonking, and wanting more money.

15

Against Dryness

MARTIN AMIS

'Like being chained to a corpse, isn't it?' This remark was offered to John Bayley by a fellow-sufferer in an Alzheimer marriage. He found himself 'repelled' by the simile, and didn't care to give it the demolition it deserved. A corpse, we may reflect, has several modest virtues: it is silent, stationary, and, above all, utterly predictable. A corpse, so to speak, has done its worst. In addition, a corpse is not loved, and a corpse will not die.

Moreover, the corpse John Bayley was allegedly chained to was Iris Murdoch: the pre-eminent female English novelist of her generation, and some would say (Updike is one of them) the pre-eminent English novelist of her generation *period*. There can be no argument about the depth, the complexity, and indeed the beauty of Murdoch's mind: the novels effusively attest to this. And so the terror and pity evoked by Alzheimer's are in her case much sharpened. Bayley gave us that tragedy in three leisurely acts, namely *Iris* (1998), *Iris and the Friends* (1999), and the more tangential and novelistic *Widower's House* (2001). The recent movie, *Iris* (2002), unfolds the story before our eyes in one hundred minutes.[1]

---

[1] Subsequent references to these works are cited in the text, with page numbers from the paperback editions of *Iris* and *Iris and the Friends* (London: Abacus, 1999, 2000) and from the hardback of *Widower's House* (London: Duckworth, 2001). The opening remark about being 'chained to a corpse' is from *Iris*, 53–4.

Very broadly, literature concerns itself with the internal, cinema with the external. In Bayley's meditative trilogy, the agony is partly eased by the consolations of philosophy, by the elegant and entirely natural detours into Proust, Hardy, Tolstoy, James. Richard Eyre's movie, on the other hand, for all its subtlety and tenderness, is excruciatingly raw. As you collect yourself while the credits roll, you find you have developed a lively admiration for cancer.

The Bayleys were eccentric—'out of centre'—in their complementary brilliance (he is a novelist, a quondam poet, a literary critic of effortless fluidity). But they were also famously eccentric in their temperament and habits; and if you're an American, you *don't* know the type. They're the kind of people who like being ill and like getting old, who prefer winter to summer and autumn to spring (yearning, as Bayley puts it in *Widower's House*, for 'grey days without sun', 98). They want rain, gloom, isolation, silence. 'We had no TV of course,' writes Bayley, commalessly (*Iris*, 203), and the reluctant acquisition of a radio feels like a surrender to the brashest modernity. The Bayleys were further cocooned and united, it has to be said, by their commitment to extreme squalor.

At their place, even the soap is filthy (*Widower's House*, 102). 'Single shoes [and single socks] lie about the house as if deposited by a flash flood . . . Dried-out capless plastic pens crunch underfoot' (*Iris*, 286). An infestation of rats is found to be 'congenial, even stimulating' (*Iris*, 166). Everywhere they go they have to hurdle great heaps of books, unwashed clothes, old newspapers, dusty winebottles. The plates are stained, the glasses 'smeary' (*Widower's House*, 58). The bath, so seldom used, is now unusable; the mattress is 'soggy' (*Iris*, 169); the sheets are never changed. And we shall draw a veil over their underwear. On one occasion a large, recently purchased meat pie 'disappeared' in their kitchen (*Iris and the Friends*, 14–15). It was never found. The kitchen ate it.

One of the unforeseen benefits of having children is that it delivers you from your own childishness: there's no going back. John and Iris, naturally, did not toy long with the idea of becoming parents; it was *themselves* they wished to nurture ('two quaint children' and 'co-child' are typical Bayleyisms).[2] This is intimately connected to their embrace of dirt and clutter, a clear example of *nostalgie de la boue*—literally, homesickness for the mud, for the stickiness and ooziness of childhood, babyhood, wombhood. The plan seems to work. Professor Bayley and Dame Iris are crustily cruising into a triumphant old age. And then a 3-year-old comes to stay, to live, to die. It is Iris Murdoch.

Richard Eyre's movie is devotedly faithful to the main lines of Bayley's narrative. Yet there is also an undertow of creative defiance. He has taken a highly unusual story about two very singular people—a story saturated with oddity, quiddity, exceptionality—and he has imbued it with the universal. How?

In the Iris books Bayley glides around in time and space, indulging his 'intellectual being', in Milton's phrase, 'those thoughts that wander through eternity'.[3] Eyre, characteristically, is direct and rigorous, almost geometrical in his approach. He constructs a double time-scheme of present and past, and lays down a reciprocal rhythm of back and forth, of ebb and flow. Throughout, the film tremulously oscillates between the 1950s, when the two principals are just entering each other's force fields, to the 1990s, and the protracted visit from 'the dark doctor': Doctor A.

Thus, in the opening scenes, we watch the young Iris riding her bicycle (comfortably outspeeding the more timorous John), her head thrown back in exhilaration, appetite, dynamism; she is rushing forward to meet the fabulous profusion of her talent. Then we fade to the elderly Iris, in the chaos of her study,

---

[2] The former comes from *Iris*, 171; the latter is reprinted in Peter J. Conradi's *Iris Murdoch: A Life* (London: Harper Collins, 2001), as in the title to ch. 14: 'An Ideal Co-Child'.

[3] The phrase is from *Paradise Lost*, bk. 2, 147–8.

working on what will be her final fiction. In the margin she writes out, again and again, the word 'puzzled'. 'Puzzled' puzzles her; she is puzzled by 'puzzled'. 'All words do that when you take them by surprise,' says her husband, comfortingly. Iris puzzles on; and in her eyes we see an infinity of fear. 'It will win' is the pathologist's prognosis. It will win: age will win. Eyre's emphasis is very marked. *Iris* becomes a tale of everyman and everywoman; it is about the tragedy of time.

What scenarists would call the 'back story' is a comedy of courtship. A vital symmetry establishes itself here, because young John is younger than young Iris (31 to her 37) and most decidedly the junior partner. He is a lovestruck provincial virgin with a bad stammer. She is a robust bohemian and free spirit; and he soon learns 'how fearfully, how almost diabolically attractive' she is to all men (and most women). Her numerous lovers are artists and scholars, big brains, dominators. And her greatest resource is the private universe of her imagination. This, though, turns out to be John's *entrée*. In at least two senses, Iris settles for him, however lovingly. She intuits that domesticity— and the scruffier the better—will liberate her art.

The 'front story', the age story, begins with the onset of the disease, and spans the five years between diagnosis and death. Soon, 'the most intelligent woman in England' (Bayley's plausible evaluation, at the end of *Iris and the Friends*, 28) is watching the Teletubbies with a look of awed concentration on her face. This is now Iris at her best. A clinging, smothering dependence is punctuated by spells of terrifying agitation; she rattles the latch; she bolts, she flees. Alzheimer's is symmetrical, too, in its way: each new impoverishment reduces the awareness of loss. It is John's sufferings that multiply; and we are not spared his surges of rage, bitterness, and contempt. He had always wanted to possess her mind and its secrets. Now, as total master, he does possess it. And there's nothing there. Murdoch-readers won't mind (because they already know), but the movie never quite gives a sense of the intellectual height from which she fell.

Certain cerebrovascular disasters are called 'insults to the brain'. As already noted, the more prodigious the brain, the more studious (and in this case protracted) the insult. Iris's brain was indeed prodigious. Returning to her novels, with hindsight, we get a disquieting sense of their wild generosity, their extreme innocence and skittishness, their worrying unpredictability. Her world is ignited by belief. She believes in *everything*: true love, veridical visions, magic, monsters, pagan spirits. She doesn't tell you how the household cat is looking, or even feeling: she tells you what it is *thinking*. Her novels constitute an extraordinarily vigorous imperium. But beneath their painterly opulence runs the light fever of fragility, like an omen.

Maritimers talk of a turn in the tide as the moment when the waves 'reconsider'. Over and above its piercing juxtapositions of youth and age, *Iris* has an oceanic feel, and this provides a further symmetry. Although she never cared for George Eliot (or, relevantly, for bathwater), as Bayley notes, Iris's 'wholly different plots and beings remind me of Maggie Tulliver in *The Mill on the Floss* saying, "I am in love with moistness"' (*Iris*, 127). And 'Against Dryness' was one of the more famous of her philosophical essays.[4] The imagery of Eyre's film is against dryness: the lakes and rivers in which John and Iris habitually immersed themselves; the sea, of course (Iris's key novel was *The Sea, The Sea*); and the rain, the rain, that seemed to hide them from the world.

---

[4] The essay was published in *Encounter*, 16 (Jan. 1961), 16–20.

16

Commissioning and Editing
Modern Fiction

DAN FRANKLIN

Last year I went to stay with friends in Wales. With me I took two new novels in manuscript. I hoped to read at least one of them and part of the other. I am the publishing director of Jonathan Cape, one of the imprints owned by the Random House group and a literary publishing house with one of the best fiction lists in Britain. Both the manuscripts in question were, I had reason to believe, prime contenders for the Cape list.

The story of how those manuscripts got into my hands and what happened afterwards will I hope illustrate something of what happens at the 'sharp end' of the literary business, where the stakes in the roulette game of contemporary literary publishing get alarmingly high.

Novel A was a first novel by a young Australian woman, a recent graduate of a well-known creative writing course in the United States taught by a prominent American novelist whose books are on the Cape list. It was being sold by one of the very best literary agents in New York, who had told me about it six months earlier at the Frankfurt Book Fair. He had also described the method he intended to use in order to sell the book. It was novel but might just be very effective in securing the highest possible advance for his client. Because the author was Austra- lian he intended to sell the English language rights in three separate territories: the USA, Australia and New Zealand, and the UK and British Commonwealth. (Normally, Australia and New Zealand would be sold to the British publisher as part of his traditional territory.) Author and agent would travel the world meeting interested publishers, and the book would be sold in New York on Monday, in Sydney on Wednesday, and in London on Friday.

As it turned out I think their trip took a little longer than a week, but only a few days more. The submission letter that came with the manuscript read as follows: 'If you are interested in publishing, we would ask you to submit your offer . . . by the end of the day on Tuesday, February 27. On Wednesday 28 and Thursday 1 March [the author] will meet with the publishers who have presented the four best offers; and we'll make a deci- sion on Friday 2 March.'

Having created an expectation at Frankfurt, the agent now intended to capitalize on it. In a normal book auction, the agent will send the manuscript to a number of publishers, invite offers, and conduct the auction through a series of 'rounds', the number of publishers diminishing as the price gets higher. In the first round the publisher can therefore make a low bid, just in case it turns out that all his rivals have decided not to offer at all. In the case of Novel A, however, a low bid was not an option. Assum- ing that the book was good and one wanted to publish it, the personality of the author would be crucial to its success. If one wanted to be in with even a chance, it was vital to be amongst the four best offers.

That weekend in Wales I read Novel A first. I enjoyed it enormously, but felt that it needed a little more work on the part of the author. Elements of the book still read as though they were in first draft, and there were various parts of the plot that could be sharpened. Much would depend on how the author responded to editorial criticism; it was therefore doubly important that one's offer was high enough to achieve that crucial meeting.

Novel B,[1] the other manuscript I had taken away for the weekend, was very different, as were the circumstances under which I was reading it. It was also a first novel, a 'literary thriller' written by an American law professor. He too was represented by a major New York agent. The manuscript was nearly 1,000 pages long, four times the length of Novel A.

I had first heard about Novel B a week earlier. US rights had been auctioned in New York, and the bidding had been frantic. It had eventually been sold to Knopf for millions of dollars, according to the New York press the highest price ever paid for a first novel. Alfred A. Knopf is also part of the Random House group and we enjoy close contact. In London we were therefore aware of Novel B even before the New York auction was over. But so too, of course, were our rivals in the other major London publishing houses, most of whom have sister companies in America.

When I started to read Novel B on the Sunday it had not been officially submitted to Jonathan Cape. The manuscript had been couriered to London from New York by someone at Knopf, and that weekend it was being read by several people at Random House UK, including the Chairman of the General Books Division and the publisher at Vintage, our literary paperback imprint. Given what had happened in America, this was a book to take very seriously indeed.

And so it proved. Novel B was beautifully written with a ferociously clever plot, strong characters, and a setting that had never before been treated so skilfully in fiction. It was set in the world of academic lawyers and Washington politics, and the protagonist was a member of the black upper middle class.

By the time I set off back to London I had read 250 pages of Novel B and was very excited indeed. Here, it seemed, was the

---

[1] Actually, Novels B & C, for this was a two-book package, of which only one was written. For convenience I shall refer only to Novel B.

work for which all publishers are searching, a novel that is at once literary and commercial, a book with big ambitions that will appeal to a very wide audience. Umberto Eco's *The Name of the Rose* is such a book, as is Tom Wolfe's *Bonfire of the Vanities*. Both were huge best-sellers and they have gone on selling long after their first publication.

At the office on Monday morning I discovered that although neither of my colleagues had read the entire manuscript of Novel B, both were as excited as I was.

Unfortunately, another publisher shared our enthusiasm. He, to his credit, had also managed to finish the manuscript over the weekend. When offices opened in New York that afternoon we learned that he had made a pre-emptive bid of $500,000 for a two-book contract. (A 'pre-empt', as they are normally known, is a bid of such a size that it is intended to persuade the agent to withdraw the book from sale. As in this case, they are usually made before the book is put up officially for sale. This is one of the reasons why major British publishers employ 'scouts' in New York. A scout's job is to notify his or her client publishers of important or exciting books and, better still, to obtain a copy of the manuscript *before* it is officially submitted.)

We heard a rumour that our rival had been given until the end of business in London to improve his offer to $1 million. If he did so, his pre-empt would be accepted. To prevent this, we would effectively have to persuade the agent that it would not be in her and her author's interest to accept the pre-empt, in other words that we would offer more.

Although none of us had actually finished Novel B, we were all agreed that, on the basis of what we had read, it was one of those 'miracle books', the Holy Grail itself. We also knew that this was the strong opinion of our colleagues in America. Nevertheless, it is not a common experience to bid $1 million for a first novel one has not yet read in its entirety. Suppose it 'fell to bits at the end', as do so many books that begin promisingly? And while one could see that Novel B's plot and setting would have huge appeal in America, where there is a large market for books of black interest, the same did not apply in Britain. Should we try to intervene, and would we succeed?

By ten days later we had acquired both books. We did succeed in matching our rival's pre-empt and keeping Novel B in play. A day later Novel B was finally submitted officially to us and other publishers. By then we had finished reading it and the bids were already escalating between us and our rival. At this point a third publisher joined the bidding. Round followed round for over a week and still no one dropped out. It was a period of considerable excitement and not a little anxiety. Eventually, with all the fighters panting on the ropes, the agent asked for 'best bids' together with a marketing plan describing how each publisher intended to publish and promote the book. I believe that there was very little to choose between the 'best bids' and that our success was due to our marketing plan.

For Novel A, my bid was at a more normal level, though unquestionably higher than would have been the case in a conventional auction. It was enough to win me the right to meet the author or—as publishers are known to put it—to enter the 'beauty contest'. A 'beauty contest' consists of the agent bringing the author to meet his or her prospective publisher. Each can size up the other, the author can impress the publisher with plans for future books, and the publisher can show what brilliant stratagems he or she has for making a best-seller out of this one. On a more human level, the author/publisher relationship is an important one that might last for years and years. It is vital that you like each other.

I did like the author of Novel A, very much. And I was impressed by the way she saw her own book. She knew it needed more work and was happy, indeed eager, to do it. She had also worked out a very clever approach to the novel's design. She, presumably, liked us, for at the end of the meeting the agent, about to leave for the airport and the final, homeward stage of his round-the-world journey, informed us that we were the chosen publisher. I have no idea whether ours had been the highest offer: only the agent and author know that.

The two cases I have outlined above are exceptional in almost every particular, but they illustrate something of the mechanics and psychology of the market place for modern fiction in manuscript—i.e. how an editor acquires it initially before he goes on to earn back his advance in royalties from sales of the book itself in its final form.

At the time of writing such exceptional cases are becoming more common. Good fiction—whether 'literary' or 'commercial'—is selling faster and more expensively than ever before, for reasons that are not entirely clear. Hence the huge advances that the press delight to write about.[2] Of course publishers have never not believed this to be the case, and delight in mocking their rivals' absurd overpayments, but it is important to remember that publishers are gamblers. They have their instincts, their experience, their crack sales force, their brilliant publicity and marketing departments, but they are still taking a gamble every time they acquire a book.

The everyday reality of acquiring fiction is very much more prosaic than the cases mentioned above. These days very few books indeed are bought 'off the slush pile'—i.e. are sent in unsolicited by the author, read by a junior member of staff, and then passed up to a commissioning editor, who makes the author an offer. Most submissions come from literary agents, and most authors are sophisticated enough to realize that it is worth 10 or 15 per cent commission in order to have an agent submitting your book and negotiating your deal. An agent will know which editors in which publishing houses will be most likely to appreciate the book and publish it well. They will know editors' tastes and foibles, and their propensity to be mean or generous in their offers.

---

[2] A word of caution. The deals for both Novels A and B were reported in the British press. The sums mentioned were wrong by at least 25% in every story.

Agents will not normally auction a first novel. They would have to be certain that what they were selling was really exceptional and that there would be genuine competition for it. Usually they will submit the book to four or five editors, hope that they all like it enough to offer, and that the submission will turn into an auction of its own accord, and if that doesn't work they'll pray that *one* of those editors will offer even a modest advance.

Make no mistake, most first novels are not sold at all. Most of those that are go for very modest advances. (Five thousand pounds is currently the least you can get away with as a publisher without looking mean, though I doubt whether even half of the books bought for that sum eventually earn their advance.)

As an editor, I am having to weigh a number of considerations. First, of course, I must like the book. Second, I must think that my company can sell enough copies to make it worth our trouble. Third—and this probably applies more to 'literary' publishers than to 'commercial' ones—I must decide whether, even if I can't really convince myself that we'll sell more than 800 copies in hardback or 1,000 in trade paperback, I *am* convinced that this novel is exceptional, that it might win a prize or be bought by a film producer, and that its author has a very considerable career ahead of him or her. Fourth, I must decide whether the book is 'right for our list'. Each publishing house (or list within it) has a distinct character, more important (and indeed visible) to those within than to those outside, and every editor normally knows instinctively whether or not a book will fit their list. Fifth, I must convince my colleagues of the merits of publishing the book. A publisher can only publish a limited number of first novels each year: they are a very risky publishing proposition. Is this one exceptional enough to claim one of those 'slots'? My paperback colleagues must agree with my judgement, and it's important too that sales and marketing are enthusiastic. Sixth, I must do my financial calculations: if we sell X number of copies at £10.00 per copy how much will the book earn? I have to take into account how many copies might be sold at high discounts, whether the bulk of the sales will be at home or abroad, how many pages the book will make in its final form. I'll get input from sales and production and marketing (if, as is unlikely, there is to *be* a marketing budget), and I'll put it all into a computer and a form known as a 'p&l' (profit and loss) will emerge. Of course everything depends on how big a number X is. And for this judgement editors have, ultimately, only their own instincts to go on.

If the figures on the p&l work (and this means that both the Sales Director and the Business Manager—the famous accountant one reads so much about—will sign it off), the editor will make an offer to the agent. The p&l will indicate the level of advance justified. The editor then attempts to acquire the book for less than that with a first offer, leaving a surplus in case—and it is usually the case—he or she is pushed to a higher figure by the agent.

Perceptions of how much a book is worth can of course change radically during the buying process. Another publisher might have come in with an opening bid vastly higher than one's own, causing everyone to look at the book in a completely different light. It might have just been sold in another territory for a large sum, film rights might have been sold, or the author might have solicited a quotation about the merits of the book from a prominent and influential fellow writer. The final p&l often bears very little resemblance to the first.

All of these processes occur in the same way when one is trying to acquire a second or subsequent novel by a writer already on the list. But there are fundamental differences. With luck (if you've done a good enough job with the last book by that author) there won't be competition from your rivals. You are competing, in effect, with the sum the agent has in his head, his estimation of the book's worth. And you don't have to rely on instinct alone: you will know how many that last book sold. And if, okay, it didn't sell very many, you will have a batch of reviews confirming that your initial judgement was excellent and that this is an author with a glittering career in prospect. You are still gambling, still placing a bet on a horse, but at least this time you'll have the form book to tell you how it ran in its last race.

Novels are very rarely commissioned—unlike non-fiction, most of which is acquired on the basis of an outline or synopsis. In most cases the editor acquiring the novel will have read it in its entirety. The exceptions to this rule are usually either novelists of real stature and large sales, with whom one might enter into a multi-book contract. For the publisher and author it means a long-term commitment and such a relationship has obvious advantages for both parties—as long as things go well. Many agents dislike such contracts on the grounds that they do not allow for the uncertain nature of modern publishing. The editor might leave before the second book is delivered, and be succeeded by someone much less to the author's taste. Or the first book of the deal might win the Booker Prize, going on to sell a million copies in paperback: if he hadn't already committed himself the author could be asking for a million for the next book.

The other category of author from whom a publisher might commission a novel is at the exact opposite end of the scale from the one in the last paragraph: a writer of genuine brilliance who has given up employment in order to write, or whose financial circumstances suddenly become pressing. In these cases publishers will probably pay a slightly lower advance than they would do for a finished book. Their risk, after all, has increased considerably.

There are exceptions. If an agent believes she has something really special, she might try to sell it off a partial, unfinished manuscript, or an editor might read a short story in a small magazine and be so struck by the writer's obvious talent that he takes him or her to lunch and offers a contract for a novel. These days this happens very rarely. Only agents have the incentive—or, indeed, the time—to find writers in this way, and they do not normally have to back their judgement with hard cash until the author has produced a novel.

I have said very little so far about what it is an editor is actually looking for in a manuscript. The reasons are simple. Every editor's taste is unique. He or she can watch what the public seems to be buying, follow trends, pore over statistics. Ultimately, however, everything comes down to that editor's taste, judgement, and, most important of all, instinct. When that book arrives on their desk they will feel a prickle by page 25 and by page 100 they will be designing the jacket in their heads. They know that this book is (*a*) good, possibly very good, and (*b*) saleable.

They are very rarely right on the last point, but when they do get both right the feeling is incomparable.

To write about editing fiction is very much more difficult. All editors are different, their taste is different and their editorial style is different. And what, ultimately, is meant by the term 'editor'? A publishing house might contain many people with that title: assistant editors, copy-editors, desk editors, editors, chief editors, managing editors, editorial directors ...

Our focus so far has been on the role of the acquiring or commissioning editor. These people, the elite of the editorial department in terms of status and salary, are at once only a small part of the editorial process but at the same time its most crucial members. It is their taste and judgement—and negotiating skills—on which the fortunes of the publishing house ultimately depend. Unlike their colleagues, they will be judged by their decisions, and if they keep on getting them wrong, ultimately they will lose their jobs.

Some commissioning editors never 'edit' in the traditional sense. They never engage with an author over their text, never change so much as a semi-colon. They see their skill in finding and buying successful books; the rest of the process—the detailed line-by-line work—is undertaken by their subordinates. Conversely, many of the very best editors have no interest in acquiring. Their expertise is in working with an author on the text. They don't want the stress of being responsible for having bought a book, only to make that book as good as they can. That said, editorial departments today are much smaller than they once were, much of the work being done by outside freelances, and it would be rare to find a commissioning editor who did not also work on the texts he or she had acquired.

Each editor, however, might go about this in an entirely different manner. There are those who are able to look at a novel in draft, see at once what its problems are, and suggest ways of eradicating them. Cut out these two characters, change the narration from third person to first, put the last chapter at the very beginning, and hey presto! Such editors are rare and are rightly very highly valued. They are worth their weight in gold to both authors and publishers. Sometimes, as a result, they are also well paid, but just as often the people with these gifts belong to the category of those who work behind the scenes, known only to a few, and are comparatively badly rewarded compared to their commissioning colleagues.

The majority of commissioning editors do not have this gift. As a result they acquire only books whose problems it is within their competence to solve. A book that everyone agrees is too long by half will only be bought by a publisher who has the time and the skill—or the junior editor—to do the work. Or the desperation. As Diana Athill said of her work as an editor with André Deutsch: 'Not often did one have to do much shaping with fiction. If a fiction writer read so badly that that was necessary, we weren't interested.'[3]

In most cases in my experience the commissioning editor will do the first edit on the manuscript. They will be looking for inaccuracies, obscurities, anachronisms, inconsistencies, points where the pace flags or the plotting is implausible, but chiefly they will be hearing the author's voice. They will be reading the book aloud in their head, listening to the music of each sentence,

---

[3] From Gayle Feldman's interview with Athill, 'An Editor Has her Say', in *Publishers' Weekly*, 2 Feb. 2001, pp. 34–5.

and putting a light pencil line under a passage that doesn't quite ring true. Then they will invite the author in and the real editorial process begins, a conversation that will go on and on and on until the finished copy arrives and it's too late to change anything.

The process of going through a text with an author is very exhilarating and very exhausting. There is that wonderful moment when, together, by talking, you work out the perfect solution to a problem that has been worrying both of you. Or the joy when you at last admit that you can't stand that passage in chapter 12 and the author laughs and says she's always worried about it too and why don't we delete it? But mainly it is just exhausting, a long, slow slog through every line of the manuscript, with frequent disagreements and negotiations as complicated as those before a peace treaty.

At the end of this process the book is better, sometimes much better. Both the editor and the author genuinely believe this. If one or other doesn't, then the process is not over and they must try again. It's very difficult to publish a book successfully if either author or publisher has doubts that it is as good as it could be.

At this point the book goes into copy-editing, undertaken either by a relatively junior editor within the publishing house or by a freelance. The copy-editor's job is to impose the publisher's house style (if there is one), to check spelling, consistency, and accuracy, and to make suggestions of the type already made by the commissioning editor in order to improve the 'music' of each sentence.

If working in-house the copy-editor will go through the manuscript in person with the author, if freelance they'll send a detailed list of queries back with the edited manuscript and the commissioning editor will go through them first, eliminating any that he has tackled already, before consulting with the author once again, either face to face or on the telephone or by email. Some authors, of course, resist any editing and it is their perfect right to do so. They are the ones who will be judged by the critics, not you.

Such people are very rare, though, and normally have another person playing the editor's role—a spouse or agent or friend.

At this point the 'editing' is supposedly done, but the editor's job has barely started. From the moment of acquisition he or she should be working for that book, spreading the word both in and out of house. The destiny of a novel often feels as though it has been ordained at the moment of acquisition. If an editor is perceived to have 'paid too much', it still carries that stigma when it is published. It's in the gossip columns, even in the first paragraph of every review. The editor's job is to make sure that this perception never takes hold, that the 'buzz' in the media, among scouts, in the publishing community, is positive—and, if not positive, at least neutral.

It helps of course if your colleagues are on your side and to that end your very first mention of it at the acquisitions meeting might affect its destiny. You are trying to get everyone else around you to love your baby as if it were their own. If you succeed then everything else becomes very much easier.

Next the editor briefs the designer who will be preparing the jacket. The final say is almost always the author's, but the editor is the person who knows something of his taste, of how he sees his book. The editor must try to represent the author's wishes while at the same time achieving a jacket design that the sales department are enthusiastic about.

Again in tandem with the author, the editor will write the blurb, the advance information sheet that announces the book to the booksellers and the catalogue copy, and liaise with the marketing department about how the book is presented both to the book trade (known as 'selling in') and to the consumer. He will meanwhile have brought the author together with the publicity department and been closely involved in whatever publicity plans are hatched. If the book is a first novel, he will almost certainly solicit pre-publication quotes to adorn the jacket, and he will 'talk the book up' to literary editors and other members of the media who might help to make it a success.

When publication day arrives, he will make the speech at the launch party, get mildly drunk, and then prepare to nurse the author through the next few weeks, when the novel is (or, much worse, is not) being reviewed. This is an anxious time for any author—however distinguished and successful—and the editor, who after all has laid out money on this project, is the person who has the next biggest investment in its success.

One final thought. We are in the electronic age, in the world of ebooks and online publishing. Here the role of the editor is very different indeed. To quote from an article by Mike Petty entitled 'E is also for Editing',[4] the most prominent online publisher, X Libris, 'seems to regard any selection criteria as a restriction of free speech'. Indeed X Libris employs no editors, because 'the whole world exists to act as a quality filter for the author' (i.e. if it's bad it won't sell). The writer goes straight to the consumer with almost no intervention at all by the publisher. Other online publishers operate differently, and edit in the traditional way. Petty quotes Jane Domer, author of *The Internet: A Writer's Guide*. 'I don't think this will drive down standards,' she says. 'It will just drive out the publishers who don't edit, and in the end quality will out.' 'Perhaps,' says Mike Petty. I'm inclined to agree with him.

---

[4] *Bookseller*, 2 Feb. 2001, p. 26.

17

Before it Becomes Literature: How Fiction Reviewers Have Dealt with the English Novel

LINDSAY DUGUID

The English novel has changed a good deal since 1950. It has been transformed from a low-key, realistic, moral story, into a bold, all-embracing, many-voiced text. During this time, the lady novelist turned into the woman writer; the historical novel—previously a branch of romantic fiction—became respectable, even intellectual, and the crime and mystery plot was co-opted by serious novelists; above all, of course, the English novel grew up, forgot its bourgeois origins, took in foreign influences—from Ireland, Scotland, India, the Caribbean—became the British novel. And lived happily ever after.

You can get a good idea of when and how these changes took place by looking at the reception given to the new voices in fiction in the review pages of the British press. Contemporary reviews are immediate. They cannot help but follow fashion and be part of the way in which the novel establishes itself. The newspaper or periodical review has the merit of being just one person's view of the book, his or her answer to the questions: what is it like? Should I read it? Often the reviewer is the first reader of the work who has no vested interest in its success or failure. And the review is the first step in the process by which a work comes into our lives. Before they become literature, before they are tidied up into schools and categories or put in order of the author's development, novels exist for a short time in their own right, of their time, and with their own strengths and weaknesses.

(It is important to state that, although novels do provide opportunities for the reviewer to indulge in low humour, jealousy, revenge, log-rolling, malice, small-mindedness, ignorance of life, and general lack of sensitivity, I am considering here the well-intentioned review.)

Looking back at these first critical responses, you get a kind of relief map of the history of the late-twentieth-century novel— some writers or movements stand out from the rest, peaks among the foothills and the plains. But it is important to know what these authors are standing out from, what sort of novels were appearing alongside them, what reviewers expected from them. This sort of retrospective is well suited to a study of the English novel, traditionally a small-scale work which sticks close to the ground—sometimes the critical terrain seems mainly foothills.

In the early years of the 1950s, reviews of new novels appeared regularly once a week (by tradition on a Thursday) in the serious national newspapers, and in the Sunday papers. They were printed to coincide with the date of publication, and each title was allocated its 700, 500, or 300 words, or put into a 'round up', according to status. There were also the influential weekly or fortnightly publications—the *Listener*, the *Spectator*, the *New Statesman*, *Punch*, *Time and Tide*—which were nonspecialist, popular, confident of their readership, and they all reviewed a novel or two, independent of the publication's editorial policy. The *New Statesman*, in particular, famously had very literary books pages, in contrast to the sternness of the front half of the paper.

The *Times Literary Supplement* has been in existence all this time with an unchanged policy of having regular fiction reviews every week. Its archive of critical opinion, which goes back to 1902, provides a picture of the way literary fashion works, monitoring waves and movements, reputations and genres, and throwing into focus the strange chronicity of themes and subjects. It is easy enough to understand the popularity of the big topics—child abuse, AIDS, the Holocaust—but that of other subjects, taken up at more or less the same time by several different writers, seems simply serendipitous. Why did young authors in their thirties and forties start to become interested in the Second World War in the 1970s? Why should Restoration England all at once have seemed a rich setting for fiction? Or Victorian England a site for eroticism? Why do Indian novelists have a fondness for identical twins? Why are there so many novels these days, from the most literary to the most commercial whodunit, in which women pass as men? In 1999 three British novels and one American novel featured a heroine in a coma. In 2000 two novels (one British, one French) made use of the biblical story of Tobias in a parallel narrative—and that is to ignore the simultaneous popularity of angels in general, along with babies and giants. This evidence of the preoccupations of society is what the literary critics of the future will be able to decode.

The way books are discussed has changed too: this is not just a matter of superficial style. As the novel became more sure of itself and more complex, the critic's stance developed from a straight-faced judgemental assessment to something more tricky and sophisticated, more complicit with the novelists themselves. In the *TLS*, for instance, one of the main changes was that reviewers stopped being anonymous cataloguers of books received. Writing under their own bylines, they were individuals engaging with their equals.

Whichever kind of reviewers they were, they were dealing with a publishing phenomenon. In 1950, there were 3,697 works of fiction published in Britain. In the boom year of 1990 the figure had doubled. In 2000 this figure was over 5,000.

At the beginning, the paid readers who turned this avalanche of books into neat summaries, to a deadline, week after week, were not experts. It is difficult to find out exactly on what basis books were selected—it is still difficult to say exactly how this is done, beyond the fact that generally a single editor has the responsibility and is influenced by personal taste and a sense of duty. Very often, memoirs, biographies, works of politics and sociology (books which have only a limited life and are likely to date quickly) go to the acknowledged experts, celebrities, or highly paid political commentators, but novels (books which are often influential, widely loved, and returned to again and again) are given to more or less anyone. Nowadays, with very few exceptions, the heavyweight *littérateur*—the role played in the past by Cyril Connolly and Peter Quennell—is out of fashion; most novel reviewers are not well-known names. Generally they are taken for granted; often given a low rate of pay for a piece of writing which demands close reading, intelligence, and tact.

Deborah McVeagh and Jeremy Treglown have done some research into the anonymous contributors to the *TLS*—always referred to then as the *Times Lit. Supp.*[1] Many of them were women. From their names and their prose style, which is often all we know about them, they sound middle-aged and genteel. For some reason, it is easy to imagine them leading lives of quiet desperation: Miss C. Jebb (fiction), Sybil Kent (new novels), Miss Alice Sedgwick of Chelsea (American books; children's books; new fiction), and Miss V. Rice, whose address sounds straight out of Evelyn Waugh—the United Services Hotel, Cromwell Road, London W. Today fiction reviewers tend to

---

[1] For information about *The TLS Subscriber Archive* and *The TLS Centenary Archive*, edited by Jeremy Treglown and Deborah McVeagh, published by Primary Source Media (part of the Gale Group: www.tls.psmedia.com) see the TLS Website (www.tls.co.uk). The Centenary Archive identifies the author of almost every anonymous review in the paper and provides biographical information when known. Many big libraries keep bound copies of the *TLS* going back to 1902.

be published authors or to be securely anchored in employment as university teachers; only a few can still claim the romantic-sounding description 'freelance writer'. Poets make good novel reviewers, because they are poor and they pay attention to the writing. Aspiring young writers are always useful; fiction reviewing is something many British novelists have done at one stage before they became successful; at the *TLS*, staff writers have included Anthony Powell, Martin Amis, Alan Hollinghurst, and non-staff reviewers have included Graham Swift, Hilary Mantel, and Penelope Fitzgerald. I am always rather sad to hear that one of my reviewers is writing a novel—it may mean the parting of our ways.

Compared with the present-day reviewer, who is faced with multivoiced narratives, unreliable narrators, allegories, genre dodging, satire, and allusiveness, those gentlefolk of the 1950s seem to have had an easy time. There were novels by the elegant pre-war stylists such as Elizabeth Bowen, Elizabeth Taylor, and Ivy Compton-Burnett, and, as a development from those, the solidly crafted stories of self-improvement with plots based on social and material aspiration. From the way they are reviewed you can see how deeply embedded in social detail these works were. Spotting the status indicators in 1957, our reviewer recognized the hero of John Braine's *Room at the Top*: 'a young man from a mining village', he wrote, 'who has decided that he wants what power can bring, whether it be a real bath room, with tiles and mirrors and scented soap, or a real upper-class girl with pearls and a cashmere sweater. Mr Braine's apprehension of his hero's passion for these things is marvellously acute and exact—his eye both for the girl and the bath room could not be more clear.' This is a good example of the reviewer seeing eye to eye with the novelist. The review of Alan Sillitoe's *Saturday Night and Sunday Morning*, published the following year, was similarly sociological, describing accurately (but somehow disdainfully) the premiss of the novel: 'The hero...works in a Nottinghamshire bicycle factory, earning fourteen pounds a week of which he gives his mother three and spends the rest on ... booze and teddy boy clothes. His ambition is to obtain as much sexual satisfaction as possible.'

Into this class-divided, post-war society came three new writers—Kingsley Amis, William Golding, and Iris Murdoch—all of whom published their first novels in 1954 and all of whom, unwilling to follow established fictional patterns when writing about England, showed what could be done in the way of overt allegory and informal narrative. The newspaper critics could be said to have made the reputation of these novelists in a way which no longer happens (Kingsley Amis's *Lucky Jim* in particular was greeted with joy by V. S. Pritchett in the *New Statesman* and Anthony Powell in *Punch* and even had the distinction of being admired by Edith Sitwell). The critics recognized that something new was happening, but they approached it in a traditional way. The anonymous reviewer in the *TLS* placed Kingsley Amis's Jim Dixon in a social sphere and a literary tradition as 'a day-dreamer with a robust sense of farce whose positive gifts are satiric invention, social blundering of an endearing kind and complete lack of self-importance ... an anti-hero or rather sub-hero ... an intelligent provincial who finds his social position both precarious and at odds with his training. Unlike the heroes of earlier novels of this kind such characters do not aspire to more assured social standing, nor do they become envious or earnest about their predicament.'

The freewheeling qualities of *Under the Net* inspired a critique which—as often happens—tried in some way to imitate the style of the book: 'Miss Iris Murdoch's first novel reveals a brilliant talent. She has a remarkable sense of timing ... Her metaphors and similes are striking and vivid and her English is always fresh and agreeable. Set against this dazzling array of virtues the weaknesses ... pale into their proper insignificance. They are faults of construction and design.... The book slows down and the reader puts his head out of the window only to find that he is a long way from the station.' William Golding's

Lord of the Flies (which has since become *the* modern novel that all English schoolchildren study, along with Harper Lee's *To Kill a Mockingbird*) was assessed as an example of science fiction: 'The story is fantastic in conception and setting; but . . . like all successful fantasies, [it] enlightens and horrifies by its nearness to, rather than its distance from reality.' The positive reception given to these three books not only influenced what the novelists went on to write but it also had some bearing on what type of novel became influential—part of the way in which they became literature. After the mid-1950s, both the realist novel of society and the comedy of manners began to look old-fashioned. Murdoch herself, in her much-reprinted *Encounter* essay 'Against Dryness' (1961), made a distinction between 'journalistic' and 'crystalline' novels, those which reported on the contemporary world and those which created a fictional allegory of it. Writers such as Bowen, Taylor, and, to a certain extent, Angus Wilson, whose effects depended on being firmly rooted in a recognizable setting, and who, in the reviewer's cliché, 'took a look at society', became less visible. It was the unnostalgic writers, Amis, Golding, and Murdoch, all of them offering a new way of looking at Britain, who went on to win awards and titles.

A look at what was being published alongside these new types of novel shows how they stood out from the rest—they were new voices with new views. But new things were also happening down among the genres. The reviewer of Ian Fleming's *Live and Let Die*, in 1954, clearly had a good time: 'Bond's battle with a gangster in a warehouse filled with tanks containing poison fish . . . contains passages which for sheer excitement have not been surpassed by any modern writer of this kind.' But he did not forget his responsibilities: 'With so much to praise, there is also something to regret . . . Mr Fleming writes so very well that it would be a pity if he spoiled his effects through a feeling of superiority to his chosen medium.' In 1954, *The Fellowship of the Ring* by J. R. R. Tolkien was taken very seriously by the schoolmaster-novelist Alfred Duggan: 'the plot lacks balance. All right-thinking hobbits, dwarfs, elves and men can combine against Sauron, Lord of Evil; but their only code is the warrior's code of courage and the author never explains what it is they consider the Good.'

What is noticeable is the strongly moralistic approach which often overrides interest in plot and the quality of the writing. In the pages of the *TLS*, as elsewhere in the 1950s, reviewers employed words like *sordid*, *unwholesome*, *unnecessary*. And writers were expected to know their place. Phyllis Bottome, the little-known author of a popular novel, *Fortune's Finger* (1951), was treated with typical condescension, described as 'a practised novelist of considerable skill at her own level'; this sort of *de haut en bas* tone has almost entirely vanished, at least on the fiction pages. Authors were often blamed for the behaviour of their fictional characters. In 1951, a Miss Folliot, reviewing Graham Greene's *The End of the Affair*, engaged with the notion of saintliness: 'The common-sense point of view is surely that, whatever the inward marks of sanctity, the overruling outward one is that in some way the candidate's life should be more than ordinarily edifying. Is a married woman who gives up her lover for the love of God a saint?' The reviewer of Doris Lessing's *A Proper Marriage* (1954) remarked: 'This patent gift for satiric observation makes it all the more regrettable that Miss Lessing has chosen to present her subject through the eyes of an egotistical, self-righteous and frankly disagreeable girl. It is impossible not to sympathize with the pedestrian husband who has to come home to the prickly Martha every night.' (We must be a bit careful that this was not meant to be somewhat tongue in cheek—one of the many things an anonymous reviewer can be is disingenuous.)

The general pronouncements reviewers were fond of starting their pieces with gives us a clue as to what was popular at the time. In 1957, 'The plots of novels about bullfighting are apt to be rather stereotyped'; in 1959, 'The disillusioned Communist is becoming a familiar figure in modern novels'. And sometimes you can almost see the writer trying to sum up a tendency as it happens. The reviewer of A. L. Barker's *Apology for a Hero* (1950) was explaining something new she had noticed:

Some serious-minded women writers appear to have decided that sensibility by itself is not enough . . . They have been shaken out of their rather self-centred broodings into the intellectual conviction that life is nasty, brutish and short. It is only an intellectual conviction, however, for they are at present content to take over the masculine formulas for the novel and rewrite them in feminine prose. Instead of exploiting their position as onlookers with sympathy or even malice, and doing for men what men have so successfully done for them, women are giving us warmed-up versions of strong meat.

Four years later, commenting on John Mortimer, a new and fashionable novelist, the reviewer made the sort of world-weary lament which still has echoes: 'authors are steadily saying more and more, better and better, about less and less.'

You might expect that the fiction reviewers of the 1960s would be faced with genre-breaking epics, fables of socialism, or manifestos of sexual freedom; in fact, what they seem to have dealt with was young women novelists and plots involving illegitimate children, social deprivation, and working-class characters. And far from abandoning their established critical stance, the critics seem to be even more solid and paternalistic. In the gentlemanly atmosphere of the *Lit. Supp.* you can sense the effort to deal conscientiously with social upheaval, but there is at the same time an absolute refusal to budge. Nell Dunn's *Poor Cow* (1967), which features a husband in prison and a heroine who has what were termed 'lustful urges', was praised for introducing the reader 'to those lower-class citizens whom we so rarely know as neighbours . . . This is a serious and moving little book, but it is scarcely a novel, nor, quite, an original substitute for one.' Margaret Drabble's second novel, *The Millstone*

(1965) ('not just a tale about unmarried pregnancy and the birth of a bastard') is also praised in a manner that would have done justice to *Tess of the D'Urbervilles*: 'Margaret Drabble may still have described only a girl but she is more than worth such exposure.'

Once-notorious books have a way of seeming stale and dull when the fuss is over. Revolutionary titles of the 1960s included *A Clockwork Orange* (given a short notice on the same page with H. E. Bates's *The Golden Oriole*: 'a serious social challenge [used] for frivolous purposes') and Len Deighton's *The Ipcress File*, singled out for its anti-Establishment hero. Both these books caused a stir at the time, but at the end of the decade two novels were published which marked the start of a new kind of English fiction—*The Magic Toyshop* (1967) and *The French Lieutenant's Woman* (1969). Angela Carter's novel, reviewed under a heading which simply read 'Bizarre', seemed to encourage the reviewer to embark on her own flights of fancy: 'It is as if Hayley Mills were starring in a film directed by Iris Murdoch with the screenplay by Ivy Compton-Burnett.' (For those who cannot remember Hayley Mills, this is a lesson in the danger of topical references in reviews.) Angela Carter's work was always well received by the critics, and it is said that more English Literature students are doing postgraduate work on Carter than on any other author. John Fowles has had a much more uneven reception. In its heyday, *The French Lieutenant's Woman* was a popular and a critical success, heralded as innovative, even revolutionary; it seems quite old-fashioned now, placing Karl Marx, whose stock has fallen, firmly on every second page, next to Charles Darwin, whose stock is higher than ever; and its leisurely narrator sounds stiff and pompous, but it was the forerunner both of the idea that Victorian repression was somehow sexy and of the dual time scheme.

The use of a period setting as a self-conscious symbol of an idea or a construct enables the twentieth-century writer to examine the past with the maximum hindsight and irony; as a means of interrogating imperial Britain it was to become more and more popular. Over the next ten years, J. G. Farrell's novels of Empire, Paul Scott's Raj Quartet, M. M. Kaye's romances, and Ruth Prawer Jhabvala's Indian stories all relied on an accepted critique of the British presence in India, while at the same time getting good value out of local colour and imperial adventure. It was against this background, this acceptance of British India, that Salman Rushdie's *Midnight's Children* (1981) leapt into prominence. Reviewers showed remarkably unanimous enthusiasm for this second novel by a more or less unknown writer. But the expected progeny of novels by British Indians has been eclipsed now by novels in English by Indian writers living at least part of the time in India and describing their country before and after Partition. Anita Desai, Vikram Seth, Amit Chaudhuri, Arundhati Roy are, in fact, continuing a tradition begun in India in the 1940s. Followers in Rushdie's footsteps, who include Hanif Kureishi and Zadie Smith, have continued to take on Rushdie's trope of the polyphonic, puzzling text which mirrors post-colonial Britain.

The British Empire was a rich theme for all sorts of novelists. Spotting the allegory in the work of John Le Carré was easy enough in the 1970s. *Tinker, Tailor, Soldier, Spy* could be simply dealt with. Everyone agreed on its virtues: 'The claustrophobic world of espionage and intelligence conceals but does not alter the fact that [Le Carré] is concerned with ambitious themes— betrayal, integrity, the individual against the state treated not only with intelligence and style but with a critical strength amounting to moral fervour.' Le Carré's reviewers over the years, who have included Philip Larkin and Kingsley Amis, have all treated these spy stories to the highest praise granted to a non-literary novel, i.e. that it transcends its genre. This critical manoeuvre has also been applied to the works of certain popular writers, such as Patrick O'Brian, George Macdonald Fraser, and P. D. James. I believe it is reviewer's shorthand for the puzzle that an enjoyable story presents the critic who is more accustomed to difficulty. It is a serious person saying: 'I enjoyed this book, therefore there must be something profound in it.'

For most of the 1970s, English reviewers hesitated between an urge to reprove or moralize and the duty to provide neutral description. On the home front, the fight to comprehend 'Women's Lib', drugs, and general weirdness went on in the pages of the *TLS*. The reviewer of Fay Weldon's *Down among the Women* (1971), an early and, from the current standpoint, rather tame, feminist novel, made an imaginative leap:

Jocelyn, Helen, Sylvia, Audrey, Scarlet, Wanda, Susan: none is happy, none is ordinary, none is even nice .... The interesting thing about this novel is that the blame for empty female lives is not laid at anyone's door. The lives of the men seem almost as fraught and dreary and ridiculous as those of the women who shadow them.

It is easier to make this sort of detached pronouncement when the review is anonymous. Signed reviews were introduced in the *TLS* in 1974—a change which caused some controversy at the time; it was seen as the end of objectivity and the start of the self-indulgent celebrity review. In practice, it meant the end of the use of 'we' and 'one' and the distancing employment of Mr Amis, Miss Mantel. Paradoxically, reviews became less trenchant, more equivocal. From the mid-1970s, reviewers were working out new, slightly defensive critical positions, becoming more involved with what they were reading: for example, those who took on Martin Amis and Ian McEwan often seemed to be trying to be as cool as the novelists; they too had done terrible things: 'Even the accounts of drug taking do not convincingly register a sense of intoxication'; 'though it may sometimes shock [it] could not be accused of doing so gratuitously'—two classic reviewers' moves when faced with disturbing material. Both Amis and McEwan, young writers who were writing against the establishment and might have been expected to be treated with circumspection, were in fact welcomed with great enthusiasm by the newspaper critics.

We now take it for granted that novels contain transgressive material. In the 1970s, however, the reviewers found it difficult to combine an honest personal response with a conventional moral statement. William Trevor's *The Children of Dynmouth* (1976), a sinister account of fiendish children, was reviewed in the *TLS* by the late Anne Duchêne, a long-standing regular reviewer of great intelligence and wit who always thought her way through any problem. She commended Trevor for his 'lack of cosmogony—no useful safety net for him in the Catholic chic of Muriel Spark, the metaphysical casuistries of an Iris Murdoch; he takes the known world, makes his comment, and leaves the mixture just slightly sourer than before.' Since then, bleakness has become a popular trope; writers such as John Lanchester and Jonathan Coe have had their highbrow way with low life. Several of Beryl Bainbridge's novels of the 1970s, including *The Bottle Factory Outing* (1974) and *The Dressmaker* (1973), had scenarios of murder and despair; Penelope Fitzgerald's lighter *Offshore* (1979) was a portrait, as its title suggests, of outsiders. These two novelists, along with other women writers such as Pat Barker, Hilary Mantel, Rose Tremain, and Jeanette Winterson, turned to historical fiction in the 1980s—perhaps as a way of escaping the feminist straitjacket, or just getting out of the kitchen. Barker's First World War *Regeneration* trilogy (1991–5) and Mantel's novel about the French Revolution *A Place of Greater Safety* (1992) used male historical figures to write about women from an adopted male viewpoint.

By this stage, English fiction had accepted the possibilities of magic and fantasy and the self-conscious aknowledgement that this is just a story. The end-of-the-century novel is almost certainly a 1980s development—clever, complicated, full of creative nonsense, a product of prosperity and the large publisher's advance. Written by the graduates of the newly expanded universities, narratives become more complex, made up from conflicting strands, incorporating diaries, letters, newspapers, or relying on pre-existing works.

Challenged by some demanding novels, reviewers became more and more stylish themselves. Kazuo Ishiguro's *A Pale View of the Hills* (1982), with its twin time schemes, was commended in the *TLS* for its 'refusal to show off'. Showing off seemed to become part of the critic's trade. With great elegance, David Coward, Professor of French, described Julian Barnes's elegant *Flaubert's Parrot*: 'if it is non-Baudelairean and unashamedly Flaubertophile, it positively jangles with cross-fertilizing, self-seeding memory-jogging, imagination-releasing resonances. Phrases, images, quotations, incidents recur, and come at you like your own memories.' The novelist Alan Hollinghurst saw *Waterland* (1983) by Graham Swift as 'dense with riverine lore.... The prose itself falls into a recurrent pattern of question and answer which imitates syntactically the historical inquiry it furthers.' Michael Wood commented on Alan Hollinghurst's scandalous first novel of gay promiscuity *The Swimming-Pool Library*: 'It is cruelly, brilliantly specialized, haunted by repetitions, by a relentless sense of what its narrator, William Beckwith, might call *deja eu*' The novelist and Islamicist, Robert Irwin, wrote an all-encompassing review of *The Satanic Verses* (1988) which appeared a few months before the fatwa: 'All this is further enriched by echoes of or references to fictions that parallel Rushdie's own—*The Arabian Nights* obviously, also *Othello, The Island of Dr Moreau, The Golden Ass, Our Mutual Friend* and *The Wizard of Oz*. Doubtless there are others ... In *Satanic Verses* Rushdie has created a fictional universe whose centre is everywhere and whose circumference is nowhere.' We are clearly a long way from Miss V. Rice of the United Services Hotel.

When dealing with the flood of books which are based on other books, critical comment has to perform a balancing act between factual knowledge and novel-reading, information and romance. In the *TLS* at least a good deal of time had to be spent on textual analysis—at its lowest level pointing out mistakes. At their best, though, the reviewers point out why a historical setting can be so rewarding. Reviewing Peter Ackroyd's *The Great Fire of London* in 1982, Galen Strawson criticized Ackroyd's reading of Dickens's *Little Dorrit*, the text on which the novel is based; Ackroyd's novel, he wrote, 'starts inauspiciously with two errors of fictional fact...It is not Arthur Clennam who...discovers that William Dorrit is in fact the heir to a fortune...it is not Little Dorrit's simple protégée Maggy who is "Little Mother".' Rather than reproving Ackroyd, Strawson drew a sophisticated conclusion: 'This second error recurs harmlessly throughout—harmlessly because most fiction is made from altered fact, and can be made from altered fiction too.' A similar point was made by Professor Pat Rogers reviewing Rose Tremain's *Restoration* in 1987. He described the book as an 'anti-historical novel [which] eschews the usual effects and local colouring associated with the genre...the language denies itself any easy evocation of the past. Rose Tremain keeps studiously to modern idiom (blip, picnic, rummy and bezique) as well as to a layer of present-day concepts (simplistic, reciprocity, voyeur). The effect is the opposite of a modern-dress production on the stage: contemporary sensibilities are set off by seventeenth-century costume.' By contrast, A. S. Byatt's *Possession* (1990) was pressed hard by Professor Richard Jenkyns ('*Silas Marner* is mentioned and Tennyson's *Elaine* quoted before they were written, and Christabel should not allude to Traherne's *Centuries*, undiscovered until the twentieth century'). After praising the novel's romantic élan and allusiveness Jenkyns suggested 'there is a defensive note to this talk as though Byatt is thinking of critics rather than readers'.

It was not just in the *TLS* that these sorts of novels were treated in this academic way; the books cried out for serious treatment, and reviewers in the daily and Sunday newspapers raised their game accordingly; clever young critics were drafted in to replace the long-serving hacks who could turn their hands to anything. Reviewing style changed, then changed again, as what is printed on the backs of paperback editions shows. All-purpose enthusiasm—'A gem. Delightful. A tour de force. I doubt there will be a better novel published this year'—appeals to publishers, even if it doesn't really tell you anything about the book. The recent craze for paradoxical comparison—'*Brighton Rock* written by Charlotte Brontë', 'the Camus of the backpacking generation'—may be another by-product of the increased number of literature graduates in publishing and journalism. The current fashion is the adjectival pile-up—'a bold, chilling, profound, alarming story'.

Once the novel enters the area of fact, reviewers feel free to concentrate on anachronistic details and other minor flaws. Sometimes the game of chase-the-mistake takes over, and the reviewer reveals that he has, in one sense, failed to read the book. A well-known example of a textual flaw is the 'mistake' made by William Golding in the first chapter of *Lord of the Flies*, in which the short-sighted Piggy lights a fire using his spectacles. As every ophthalmologist knows, the corrective lens for short sight could not focus the sun's rays to start a fire. Both Christopher Ricks and John Sutherland have drawn attention to this scientific error. It is said that Charles Montieth, Golding's editor at Faber and Faber, had this pointed out to him, and that he replied that it did not matter. And, as it turned out, it didn't. This powerful story, in which small boys also worship a pig's head and kill each other, has gone on to have a long and successful life. Port-lovers who read Kazuo Ishiguro's *The Remains of the Day* (1989) may wince at the way Lord Darlington sends his butler to the cellar for a bottle of vintage port after dinner (no time to settle, decant etc.); most readers will not notice. There is probably no way of balancing these two approaches. You are certainly reading the book in one way if you are spotting this sort of mistake, but the point of a novel is that it carries the reader along past any uncertainty. A novel, as Randall Jarrell pointed out, is a piece of writing with something wrong with it.

A brave challenge to the authority of the reviewer was mounted by the novelist Maggie Gee in the Letters columns of the *TLS* in 1981. Having received a very damning review, she responded boldly:

since the only thing Mr Martin seems to have noticed about the book is the plot, it is a shame that he should have got that wrong in every particular. Felicity does not teach retarded children: he has confused her with Clara. Felicity is not fat. Clara is. John does not leave his wife for Moira. Felicity does not drown in the bath: she burns to death. Macbeth had no intimate contact with Moira at all, though Mr Martin imagines that he took her virginity...

Far from being squashed, the reviewer replied:

Maggie Gee complains that I got the plot of her novel wrong in every particular. She should look again at what she wrote.... If Clothilde were not trying to be an artist why would she select her underwear by 'what an artist wore'...if John hasn't left Felicity for Moira...then why on earth does Felicity say he has on page 92?

Etc. A further rebuttal by Gee of these specific misreadings finally led the reviewer to resort to simple insult (which was perhaps what he wanted to wield in the first place): 'a sloppy, recondite book with too many characters and too little wit'. And the correspondence was closed.

Nit-picking is clearly a way of asserting critical authority. Knowingness is another, as exemplified by Anthony Burgess, perhaps the last of the professional fiction reviewers, who was getting the measure of Martin Amis in the *Observer* in 1984. The author, he wrote, 'eats a yob's breakfast before or after getting on with the unremunerative job of writing'. Every single word there signals fellowship, membership of the same club. (I have recently been told that the Yob's Breakfast was the name given to the fry-ups with red wine which the *New Statesman* journalists used to have in an Italian café near Great Turnstile; this seems to bear out my point.) The Yob's Breakfast school of criticism, which acknowledges the antisocial but is deliberately unfazed by it, has been revived in the 1990s to deal with the challenges coming from Scotland, no longer the romantic realm of John Buchan, Sir Compton Mackenzie, and George Mackay Brown. Like the young Irish writers Roddy Doyle, Patrick McCabe, and Dermot Bolger, the new generation of Scottish writers are turning their backs on the countryside and getting into city life. Coping with Irvine Welsh's novel of Edinburgh drug abuse, the poet Sean O'Brien opted out of any reaction himself: 'When a friend's baby dies in its cot, the immediate issues are shooting up and avoiding the police. The hectic day to day induces amnesia; people disappear and are only noticed when they die. *Trainspotting* seems designed to depress the liberal reader.' The novelist Adam Mars-Jones took a similar tack when considering *How Late It Was How Late*, which he described as James Kelman's 'hefty new instalment of Strathclyde arte povera', categorizing the book as 'hard to enjoy—to be brutally frank, so hard to read—and so much easier to praise instead'. Mars-Jones drew attention to the writer's use of subtler registers within the barrage of banality, but what he deliberately ignored was Kelman's intention to discompose the reader. He was also perhaps unaware that Kelman's novels, like those by Irvine Welsh, Duncan McLean, A. L. Kennedy, Janice Galloway, partly written in transliterated Scottish dialect, are, in fact, eagerly accepted by teenagers from all parts of Britain who do not mind the fact that the books are difficult to read because they promise a glimpse of real life. Alan Warner's *Morvern Callar* (1995) managed to make the local Scottish disco scene sound heroic and even poetic; of Warner's second novel, *These Demented Lands* (1997), Liam McIlvanney wrote: 'The virtues are not those of the conventional novel. There is little in the way of coherent narration or convincing characterization. Instead we can admire Warner's prodigious powers of invention, his marvellously dynamic prose and, above all, his brilliant visual imagination.' This is a successful way of dealing with Warner's deliberately perplexing story of near-drowning, drugs, and derangement. The reviewers of the 1950s and 1960s simply would not recognize either McIlvanney's critical position or his terms of approval.

The presence of these Irish and Scottish novelists, all so young and so full of street cred, could be seen as a threat to the indigenous product. Perhaps it was surprising that there were as many as three English novels on the shortlist for the Booker prize for fiction in 1998. Interestingly, all three employed some kind of distancing device. *England, England*, Julian Barnes's sustained critique of the very idea of Englishness, was contained in a fable-like tale. *Amsterdam*, Ian McEwan's satirical almost-spoof of political and social corruption, made use of a tabloid setting and a thriller format. Beryl Bainbridge's *Master Georgie*, which mounts an attack on English convention and English military history, is set during the Crimean War. All of them contain, actually or by implication, hostile portraits of the British press.

The British press is perhaps not as evil as they describe, but it is as directionless, fragmented, and amazingly irresponsible. The non-specialist weeklies have nearly all disappeared, and newspapers no longer devote the same number of column inches to serious reviews every week. Yet, strangely, the profile of the novel is higher than it used to be, with front-page reporting of prizes, rows, and personalities, and features on the private lives of novelists. The number of words allocated to books is getting smaller and smaller—some newspapers print 80-word summaries next to a picture of the dust-jacket, and often short reviews are buried under everything the sub-editor can throw at them—two-deck heading, photograph, pull quote, and stand-first. Interviews and extracts often replace the review. But it is still true that where books are reviewed at all, a number of them will be novels—even if these seem chosen to promote a writer people have heard of, rather than introduce one they haven't.

And the British novel wanders on its eccentric way. On my desk the week I flew to Los Angeles to deliver the talk from which this chapter derives, there were a sexy novel based on *Jane Eyre*, a fictional exposé of corruption in Charles Haughey's Irish government, a ghost story about a Scottish Covenanter burnt at the stake in 1670, Stanley Middleton's thirty-ninth novel, and a clutch of thrillers, including one with the title *Don't Mess with Mrs In-Between*. How could you *not* be interested?

Notes on Contributors

MARTIN AMIS is the author of nine novels, two collections of short stories and five works of non-fiction. He lives in London.

KATHERINE BUCKNELL has edited W. H. Auden's *Juvenilia: Poems 1922–1928*, three volumes of *Auden Studies* (with Nicholas Jenkins), and Christopher Isherwood's *Diaries: Volume One, 1939–1960* and *Lost Years: A Memoir, 1945–1951*. She is preparing a third and final volume of Isherwood's diaries.

VALENTINE CUNNINGHAM is Professor of English Language and Literature, and Senior English Tutor, Corpus Christi College, Oxford. He writes, lectures, and broadcasts widely on fiction and has twice been a Booker Prize judge. Publications include *In the Reading Gaol: Postmodernity, Texts, and History* (1994), *The Victorians: An Anthology of Poetry and Poetics* (2000), and *Reading After Theory* (2002).

LINDSAY DUGUID has been Fiction Editor at the *Times Literary Supplement* since 1990. She has reviewed fiction for the *TLS*, *The Times*, the *Sunday Times*, the *Guardian*, the *Observer*, the *Independent on Sunday*, the *Washington Post* and the *New York Times*. She has never written a novel.

DAN FRANKLIN is currently the Publishing Director of Jonathan Cape and the Managing Director of Cape, Chatto & Windus, Secker & Warburg, Vintage, and Pimlico. He has worked in publishing since 1970.

P. N. FURBANK is Professor Emeritus of the Open University. He is the author of biographies of E. M. Forster and Denis Diderot, and of *Unholy Pleasure: The Idea of Social Class*. With W. R. Owens he is also general editor of a new large-scale edition of the works of Defoe.

CHRISTOPHER HITCHENS is a columnist for *Vanity Fair* and the *Nation*, and an adjunct Professor of Liberal Studies at the New School for Social Research in New York. His most recent books are *Unacknowledged Legislation: Writers in the Public Sphere*, *The Trial of Henry*

Kissinger, and *Orwell's Victory*. He was born in 1949 and educated at the Leys School, Cambridge and Balliol College, Oxford.

ELIZABETH JANE HOWARD has written twelve novels, a book of short stories, fourteen television plays, and two film scripts. She has also compiled two anthologies, one on gardening and one on love. She has recently completed a memoir entitled *Slipstream*.

ZACHARY LEADER is Professor of English Literature at the University of Surrey Roehampton. He is the author of *Reading Blake's Songs* (1981), *Writer's Block* (1991), *and Revision and Romantic Authorship* (1996), and the editor of *The Letters of Kingsley Amis* (2000). *Percy Bysshe Shelley: The Major Works*, co-edited with Michael O'Neill, will be published by Oxford in 2003. He is writing a biography of Kingsley Amis and is a contributor to the *Guardian*, the *Times Literary Supplement* and *London Review of Books*.

WENDY LESSER is the author of six books of nonfiction, including *Pictures at an Execution*, *The Amateur*, and *Nothing Remains the Same*. She was educated at Harvard, Cambridge, and UC Berkeley, and has received fellowships from the Guggenheim Foundation, the National Endowment for the Humanities, the National Arts Journalism Program, and elsewhere. She is the editor of *The Threepenny Review*, which she founded in 1980, and she lives in Berkeley, California.

IAN MCEWAN has written two collections of stories, *First Love, Last Rites*, and *In Between the Sheets*, and nine novels, *The Cement Garden*, *The Comfort of Strangers*, *The Child in Time*, *The Innocent*, *Black Dogs*, *The Daydreamer*, *Enduring Love*, *Amsterdam*, and *Atonement*. He has also written several film scripts, including *The Imitation Game*, *The Ploughman's Lunch*, *Sour Sweet*, *The Good Son*, and *The Innocent*. He won the Booker Prize for *Amsterdam* in 1998.

LIAM MCILVANNEY teaches in the School of English at the University of Aberdeen and reviews for the *Times Literary Supplement*. His book on Robert Burns, *Burns the Radical: Poetry and Politics in Late Eighteenth-Century Scotland*, is published this year. He is General Editor of the Association for Scottish Literary Studies.

HILARY MANTEL grew up in the north of England, studied at London University, and subsequently spent nine years living in Africa and the Middle East. Her novels include *A Place of Greater Safety*, set in revolutionary Paris, and *The Giant, O'Brien,* which is about an Irishman of amazing stature who exhibited himself in London at the end of the eighteenth century. She hopes to write a novel about the European revolutionary Jean-Paul Marat, polyglot and nomad.

PATRICK PARRINDER's books include critical studies of H. G. Wells, James Joyce, and science fiction. He is author of *Shadows of the Future* (1995) and editor of *Learning from Other Worlds* (2000). He is currently writing on national identity in English fiction from the eighteenth century to the present day, and is a Professor of English at the University of Reading.

MARTIN PRIESTMAN is a Professor of English at the University of Surrey Roehampton, where he lectures on Crime Fiction and Romanticism. He is currently editing *The Cambridge Companion to Crime Fiction,* and has written *Detective Fiction and Literature: The Figure on the Carpet* (1990) and *Crime Fiction from Poe to the Present* (1998). Other books include *Cowper's* Task: *Structure and Influence* (1983) and *Romantic Atheism: Poetry and Freethought, 1780–1830* (2000).

ELAINE SHOWALTER is the Avalon Foundation Professor of the Humanities at Princeton University, where she teaches a course on contemporary fiction. She is also a frequent reviewer of fiction in the United States and England, in such newspapers and periodicals as *The Times, Times Literary Supplement,* the *London Review of Books,* the *Guardian, New Statesman, Washington Post Book World, New York Times Book Review,* and *Los Angeles Times.* Her latest book is *Teaching Literature* (Blackwells).

JAMES WOOD is a senior editor at the *New Republic,* and the author of *The Broken Estate: Essays on Literature and Belief* (1999). His reviews appear regularly in the *London Review of Books,* the *Guardian,* and the *New Yorker.*

MICHAEL WOOD is the author of books on Stendhal, Garcia Marquez, and Nabokov, and of *Children of Silence: On Contemporary Fiction.* His most recent work is a monograph on Luis Buñuel's film *Belle de Jour.* He writes frequently about literature and cinema for the *New York Review of Books,* the *London Review of Books,* and a number of other journals. He is Professor of English and Comparative Literature at Princeton, and a Fellow of the Royal Society of Literature.

Index